DEVELOPING LITERACY IN PRESCHOOL

TOOLS FOR TEACHING LITERACY

Donna Ogle and Camille Blachowicz, *Series Editors*

This highly practical series includes two kinds of books: (1) grade-specific titles for first-time teachers or those teaching a particular grade for the first time; (2) books on key literacy topics that cut across all grades, such as integrating literacy with technology and science, teaching literacy through the arts, and fluency. Written by outstanding educators who know what works based on extensive classroom experience, each research-based volume features hands-on activities, reproducibles, and best practices for promoting student achievement. These books are suitable as texts for undergraduate- or graduate-level courses; preservice teachers will find them informative and accessible.

DEVELOPING LITERACY
in Preschool

Lesley Mandel Morrow

Series Editors' Note by Donna Ogle and Camille Blachowicz

𝔤𝔭

THE GUILFORD PRESS
New York   London

© 2007 The Guilford Press
A Division of Guilford Publications, Inc.
72 Spring Street, New York, NY 10012
www.guilford.com

Printed in the United States of America

This book is printed on acid-free paper.

Last digit is print number: 9 8 7 6 5 4 3 2 1

Library of Congress Cataloging-in-Publication Data

Morrow, Lesley Mandel.
    Developing literacy in preschool / by Lesley Mandel Morrow.
        p. cm. — (Tools for teaching literacy)
    Includes bibliographical references and index.
    ISBN-13: 978-1-59385-462-1 (pbk.: alk. paper)
    ISBN-10: 1-59385-462-5 (pbk.: alk. paper)
    ISBN-13: 978-1-59385-463-8 (hardcover: alk. paper)
    ISBN-10: 1-59385-463-3 (hardcover: alk. paper)
    1. Language arts (Preschool)   2. Children—Language.   I. Title.
LB1140.5.L3M64 2007
372.6—dc22
                                                    2007006564

I dedicate this book to my daughter and son-in-law,
Stephanie and Doug Bushell,
and their preschool children, James Ethan and Natalie Kate,
my grandson and granddaughter. James was 2 to 4 years of age
while I was writing this book, and Natalie, birth to 2.
They added a special dimension to my writing
because I could live their literacy development as I wrote.
As you will notice, many of the photos in the book are of James
and Natalie because I had wonderful access to them
and because I adore them.
I could not have written this book without their help.

ABOUT THE AUTHOR

Lesley Mandel Morrow, PhD, is Professor of Literacy at Rutgers University's Graduate School of Education, where she is Chair of the Department of Learning and Teaching. She began her career as a classroom teacher, became a reading specialist, and received her PhD from Fordham University. She has done extensive research in the areas of early literacy development and the organization and management of language arts programs, which involves working with children and families from diverse backgrounds. Dr. Morrow has authored or edited more than 250 publications that include journal articles, book chapters, monographs, and textbooks. She received the Excellence in Research, Teaching, and Service Awards from Rutgers University, the International Reading Association's Outstanding Teacher Educator of Reading Award, and Fordham University's Alumni Award for Outstanding Achievement. In addition, Dr. Morrow has received numerous grants for research from the federal government and has served as a principal research investigator for the Center for English Language Arts, the National Reading Research Center, the Center for Early Reading Achievement, and the Mid-Atlantic Regional Lab. She was an elected member of the Board of Directors of the International Reading Association, an organization of 90,000 educators in 100 countries, and served as President of the organization from 2003 to 2004. Dr. Morrow was elected to the Reading Hall of Fame in 2006.

SERIES EDITORS' NOTE

As teacher educators and staff developers, we have become aware of the need for a series of books for thoughtful practitioners who want a practical, research-based introduction to teaching literacy at specific grade levels. Preservice and beginning teachers want to know how to be as effective as possible; they also know there are great differences in what students need across grade levels. We have met teacher after teacher who, when starting to teach or moving to a new grade, asked for a guide targeted at their specific grade level. Until now we have not had a resource to share with them.

We also collaborate with staff developers and study group directors who want effective inservice materials that they can use with teachers at many different levels yet that still provide specific insights for individual grade levels. Thus the Tools for Teaching Literacy series was created.

This series is distinguished by two innovative characteristics designed to make it useful to individual teachers, staff developers, and study groups alike. Each Tools for Teaching Literacy volume:

> ➤ Is written by outstanding educators who are noted for their knowledge of research, theory, and best practices; who spend time in real classrooms working with teachers; and who are experienced staff developers who work alongside teachers applying these insights in classrooms. We think the series authors are unparalleled in these qualifications.

> ➤ Is organized according to a structure shared by all the grade-level books, which include chapters on:

>> ▪ the nature of the learner at the particular grade level

>> ▪ appropriate goals for literacy

- setting up the physical environment for literacy
- getting to know students with appropriate assessments and planning for differentiation
- a week in the grade-level classroom—what this looks like in practice with important instructional strategies and routines
- resources for learning

With this common organization across the grade-level books, a staff developer can use several different volumes in the series for teacher study groups, new teacher seminars, and other induction activities, choosing particular discussion and learning topics, such as classroom organization, that cross grade-level concerns. Teachers can also easily access information on topics of most importance to them and make comparisons across the grade levels.

In this volume, Lesley Mandel Morrow writes from her experience as a preschool teacher, a reading specialist, a college professor and researcher, and a mother who is now a grandmother. While the book emphasizes high expectations for children and teachers, it is sensitive to the need to be age appropriate when building the foundations of literacy. She reminds us that "preschoolers are passionate about learning," and we need to capitalize on this passion by immersing them in literacy. We know you will be excited by this volume, which is not only research based but also chock full of teacher-friendly, classroom-tested, accessible, doable ideas to give our youngest students the start they need.

DONNA OGLE
CAMILLE BLACHOWICZ

PREFACE

A great deal has changed concerning literacy development in preschool over the past few years. As a result of current research, we have come to realize not only that preschoolers can learn a lot about literacy but also that they can be taught about it in an appropriate manner. This book deals with methods of teaching literacy to preschoolers from 2 to 5 years old. The book is meant to be a friendly professional development volume with theory, research, policy, and practice included. The practice emphasized includes strategies for intentional teaching of skills in a way that is appropriate for preschoolers.

Chapter 1 visits a literacy-rich preschool classroom. The design of the physical environment, a schedule for the daily routine, and a description of the activities throughout the day are provided to give a total look at what can be done to develop literacy in preschool.

Chapter 2 takes a look at the history, theory, research, and policy that have influenced preschool programs from the 1800s to the present. We learn that practices from the past, such as play, spontaneous learning, exploration, and experimentation, are still valuable today but that the systematic teaching of literacy skills in the areas of emergent reading, writing, listening, speaking, and viewing is equally important.

Chapter 3 helps to create an organizational framework for this literacy-rich preschool and addresses design factors of the physical environment of the classroom that specifically affect literacy development, such as the creation of a literacy center with books, manipulative materials for retelling stories, and technology that motivates early literacy. Parent involvement is another important element in organizing the literacy program.

Chapter 4 discusses organization and management for literacy instruction in preschool. It emphasizes the importance of a curriculum based on themes in promoting discussion, interest, and a purpose for learning. It discusses the way assessment drives instruction and how important it is in the preschool literacy program. Assessment of children should be frequent and should include many different types of measures. Most important, the chapter focuses on the need to differentiate instruction to match children's individual abilities and interests by teaching preschoolers in small groups or in one-to-one settings.

Chapter 5 discusses oral language development in preschool. I discuss development of language from birth and what parents can do at home to enhance language development, and then I move into the school and examine strategies, materials, and assessments to enhance language. The English language learner is considered in this chapter.

Chapter 6 deals with knowledge about print. Many strategies are discussed, such as the reading readiness approach, development of sight words, the language experience approach, context clues, knowledge about books and print, phonological awareness, learning about the alphabet, and some strategies for teaching phonics.

Chapter 7 emphasizes the importance of dealing with strategies for comprehension development. We often overlook children's ability to think critically in the preschool years and hold only literal discussions. This chapter suggests a variety of appropriate activities to enhance children's sophisticated understanding of stories read to them.

Chapter 8 talks about writing in preschool. Preschoolers are anxious to write and make their marks on paper. Stages of writing development are presented, and strategies and materials, as well as means of assessing writing behaviors, are provided.

The book ends with an afterword that suggests the importance of ongoing professional development for teachers. Appendices are included as a resource section, with lists of children's literature, magazines for preschoolers, and professional associations and professional journals. A glossary of words from the book also appears. These words are extremely important for the teacher to learn, to discuss, and to put into practice.

I have not written separate chapters that deal exclusively with family involvement or English language learners. Instead, information about these topics is interspersed throughout each chapter of the book. A graphic icon is placed in the left-hand margin of the page each time such information appears. Samples of each icon are shown here:

ELL

English language learners

Family

It is imperative that young children have public access to preschool. We can no longer afford to wait until a child is 5 years old before he or she can go to public school. Although we can never give up on children and need to keep working at bringing them to grade level in literacy development, the one place that the most progress can be made for those "at risk" is in preschool. The older the child, the more difficult it is to close the gap.

ACKNOWLEDGMENTS

Many people helped to write this book even though only one name appears on the cover as the author. I thank Chris Jennison, Publisher, Education, at The Guilford Press, for his encouragement and continued trust in my work, and Fred Bernardi, Assistant Managing Editor, for his meticulous handling of the volume's production. Thanks also to Lisa Fassi, Paula Aguruso, Kelli Dunston, and Paula Batsiyan, students from Rutgers Graduate School of Education, for their help with appendices, editing, securing permissions, and taking photographs, and to Douglas Bushell and Frank Morrow for photographs they took. Finally, I am extremely grateful to Harriet Worobey, Director of Rutgers University's Cook College Nutritional Sciences Preschool, for her advice and guidance.

CONTENTS

DEVELOPING LITERACY IN PRESCHOOL

CHAPTER 1

A LITERACY-RICH
PRESCHOOL CLASSROOM

We begin our journey into the preschool world with a look into a preschool classroom. We see how the teacher teaches and how her children learn. We talk about preschoolers reading and writing. This is, of course, emerging, unconventional reading and writing, for the most part. Because the children are, however, engaging in reading and writing behaviors, such as pretend reading of a book or scribble writing, we speak of them as readers and writers.

We start with comments from a teacher, whom we will call Paula. Paula is not one teacher but a composite of many excellent preschool teachers I observed and interviewed. The following are her comments, which echo the philosophy for teaching preschool children presented in this book.

"From the first day of school, I try to create a supportive and accepting environment in my classroom. I do this with the help of the children, other teachers, administrators, and the parents. The resulting classroom community allows all of the children to feel secure as they develop socially, emotionally, physically, and intellectually. I want my room to be a happy place, a playful place, and a place that is interesting, with things to explore. I teach using thematic instruction that integrates reading and writing and other content-area skills in a meaningful context. I also teach skills explicitly and systematically. It is important for me to attend to the children's individual needs and interests. It is through small-group and one-to-one lessons that I am able to address those individual needs through differentiated instruction. Along with skill development, I hope to foster a positive attitude toward reading and writing and to help children understand their importance. I want my children to become collaborative problem solvers. I want my children to maintain an enthusiasm for learning throughout preschool. As a teacher, I believe that it is important for me to grow as a professional, just as my students grow to be independent learners. Therefore, I always look for research-based practices that will help my students attain their greatest potential. In addition, I go to conferences and take courses so that I remain current."

Paula teaches preschool in the public sector. She has a bachelor's degree in early childhood education, and her classroom consists of 16 children with one aide. Her classroom contains children from varied backgrounds; there are four Caucasians, three Asian Americans, five African Americans, and four Hispanic Americans. There are seven girls and nine boys. In her school, a collaborative atmosphere is apparent among teachers, administrators, and parents. The preschool classes in her building are included with other grades in all events for teachers, parents, and children. The teachers consider themselves a community of learners and readily share ideas with each other. At various times during her day, parent volunteers assist with classroom routines. The town in which Paula teaches is made up of middle to lower-middle socioeconomic working-class families.

PHYSICAL ENVIRONMENT IN THE CLASSROOM

In the morning, when you enter Paula's classroom, you hear the sounds of children's voices and varied types of music. As the children engage in their different activities, the value placed on literacy is very apparent. The literacy-rich environment is adorned with children's work and a host of environmental print. An interactive word wall serves as a student reference for words the preschoolers can read. The first words, written on yellow cards, are the names of the children in the class. New words from themes they have studied are on pink cards. Pictures on the cards help the children identify them.

In the literacy center are pillows, stuffed animals, a large wicker chair, a child's rocking chair, and child-size tables and chairs. The wicker chair serves as the "special chair," in which Paula or a parent sits to read stories to the class and in which children sit to share their writing and read stories. One wall of the literacy center contains a large bulletin board with materials for various components of the morning meeting, such as a calendar, weather, a daily schedule, daily news, and a monthly countdown. The literacy center includes a reader's corner, taped stories with headsets for listening, computers, word-study manipulatives, writing materials, and storytelling materials, such as a felt board with story characters, puppets, and a roll movie box. There are shelves containing baskets of books separated into themes, such as "animals," "weather," "my family and me," "friends," "school," "famous people," "the farm," "ABC's," and "123's." Some of the books are also grouped by authors' names, such as Eric Carle and Ezra Jack Keats, and there is a basket of books labeled "Old Favorite Books" and a basket labeled "Books by Us." The basket contains books written and illustrated by the children, either independently or with a small group of peers. An area of the literacy center designated the "author's spot" contains various kinds of paper, premade miniature blank books, various kinds of writing implements, envelopes, sight-word lists from the word wall, and stickers.

Four round tables toward the front of the room are labeled with the children's names. Every week Paula tapes a different upper- and lowercase letter to the center of each table. When she calls groups together, the children are called by the letter name on their table. The letters change, until all 26 letters in the alphabet have been used during the year, and then she starts over again. A U-shaped table is used for small-group instruction to meet the individual needs of children. This is located in a position that allows Paula to see all areas of the classroom. By this table is a cart that contains materials for small-group literacy lessons. The cart's drawers contain white slates, magnetic boards, magnetic letters, and sentence strips. There are materials for writing—such as different types of paper, Magic Markers, colored pencils, pens, scissors, highlighting tape, and index cards—and leveled books for reading.

Paula's literacy center is clearly visible and child-accessible. She also has centers for art, math, science, and social studies. Charts, posters, poems, book displays, and children's work around the room conveys the current theme of study, which happens to be animals.

CLASSROOM MANAGEMENT

"Good classroom organization is the foundation of effective instruction. An organized, well-managed classroom will have established clear expectations," Paula says. "If you want children to behave in a certain manner, you must teach them how." She explains that she uses the first month of school to focus on themes such as "manners," "school routines," and "cooperation." A bulletin board called "A Bunch of Manners" highlights positive statements about manners that should occur in the room. Throughout the year, Paula continually reinforces the positive behaviors she wants the children to use. By the second week of school, she finds that the children begin to become familiar with these expectations and are able to express them in their words and actions. Transitions are a major component of the instructional day. When done efficiently, transitions can take only a few moments and help to set the stage for the next activity. Paula uses a variety of strategies to get the children's attention, all of which are effective. In one strategy, she claps out a pattern and has the children clap it back, saying, "1, 2, 3, eyes on me," or "Clean up, clean up, everybody clean up." In another strategy, she sings a series of directions to a familiar tune, such as "Twinkle, Twinkle, Little Star."

Paula has prepared the environment to support her instruction. All materials that students need are accessible. Furthermore, all materials have their own special spots. Various containers with labels are used to organize materials the children use. In addition, Paula arranges her room in a way that enables her to see all areas clearly, no matter where she is.

Paula's careful planning of lessons and the placement of furniture and materials contributes to the success of this classroom. A small shelf by Paula's desk contains all materials that will be needed for the week's lessons. In her plan book, Paula jots down notes concerning what works and what needs to be changed.

TYPES OF READING EXPERIENCES AND SKILLS DEVELOPMENT

Paula uses multiple strategies to teach reading and writing to her preschool children. She uses shared reading experiences that reflect her current theme. A shared reading involves children's participation while the story is being read by chanting a repetitive phrase or a rhyme. When I visited, Paula read the Big Book *Mrs. Wishy-Washy* (Cowley, 1999) while they were studying farm animals. It was obvious from the start of the reading that the children had enjoyed this story in the past. The reading was filled with the excitement of the children's voices and actions to match some of the words; Paula tracked the print from left to right with a pointer as the children read. After reading, Paula carried out a new mini-lesson and had the children discuss what came first in the story, what happened in the middle, and what happened at the end. That week, Paula's shared reading experiences focused on vocabulary development, comprehension through retelling of the story using a felt board and story characters from the book, and echo reading.

During the course of each day, Paula gives her students independent reading time. She says, "This independent reading time is extremely valuable for the children. It is a time for them to pretend read and practice some of the strategies they have learned. They often buddy-read together, taking turns telling the story through the use of pictures on the page. More important, it is a time that fosters a love of books."

Another form of reading in which the class engages is a directed listening and thinking activity. In this type of read-aloud, before reading the book *Piggie Pie* (Palatini, 1997), Paula allows the class a few moments to look at the cover, which is illustrated with drawings of a variety of pigs. She asks the children to turn to a buddy and talk about what they think the story will be about. After 1 minute of talk, Paula asks a few children to share with the class their predictions.

> Student 1: "We think the story is going to be about piggies who want to go out for pizza. But the witch is going to try to eat their pizza."
>
> Student 2: "I think it's going to be about a witch who wants to make a pie, but none of the piggies will help."
>
> Student 3: "I think it is going to be about a witch who wants to eat all the pies the piggies make."

The children are visibly more excited about hearing the story once they have shared their predictions. Paula reads the story and uses a number of character voices. At the end of the reading, Paula asks the children whether their predictions were right. Explicit teaching happens during small-group and whole-group literacy instruction. In one small-group lesson, Paula creates background knowledge and connects the story's theme to the lives of the children. The following excerpt is from the discussion that occurred before reading *Johnny Lion's Rubber Boots* (Hurd, 2001).

> PAULA: What do you do when there's thunder and lightning?
>
> STUDENT 1: I go to my mommy or daddy.
>
> PAULA: What do you and your mommy or daddy do while it's storming out?
>
> STUDENT 1: We read stories and play games.
>
> STUDENT 2: Me and my mommy sing songs.
>
> PAULA: What kinds of things do you do after a rainstorm?
>
> STUDENT 3: Go out and play!
>
> STUDENT 4: I make mud pies!
>
> STUDENT 5: I jump in puddles!
>
> PAULA: Wow! You do keep busy during and after rainstorms, and believe it or not, the lion in this story does some of the same things you do during and after a rainstorm. Let's take a picture walk through this book called *Johnny Lion's Rubber Boots* [Hurd, 2001] to find out what it is about.

After the picture walk, which is guided by picture cues, Paula reads the story to the class. They continue their discussion about what they do and what Johnny Lion did in the rain. Whenever there is an opportunity, Paula has the children break out in chanting a poem that works with the theme. In this case, because it has to do with farm animals, they sing and clap the sounds in the words to the poem "Six Little Ducks." Of course, she is purposefully working on phonological awareness.

The writing experiences in Paula's classroom are as varied as the reading. The children begin each day with independent literacy activities, and they can choose writing as one. Paula uses interactive dictated writing many times throughout the day. As part of the morning meeting, the children create their own news report. Children report news about themselves; for example, Akiem said, "I got new sneakers yesterday." Paula wrote it down on the chart and drew sneakers next to Akiem's news.

Paula also has a writing workshop. She does many mini-lessons about using journals when the students begin to learn to work with them. The first thing they have to learn is to use only one page at a time when they write in a journal. The first time they write in journals, Paula asks them to draw a picture of themselves and write any letter of their names that they can. They are allowed to "scribble write" if they can. She doesn't start journals with a 3-year-old group until January. When she teaches in a 4-year-old group, she starts journals at the beginning of the year. Paula walks around the room as the children work to see that they understand what to do.

CROSS-CURRICULAR CONNECTIONS

All curriculum areas are tied together through thematic instruction in Paula's classroom. She begins her unit about the farm animals with a book called *Mrs. Wishy-Washy* (Cowley, 1999). With 15 different picture storybooks about the farm and farm animals, Paula creates a reading and math activity. After looking through books about farm animals, children count the number of times animals appear in the book. Children record the number of animals on a chart using stickers. If they can, they write the number on a line provided. The activity can be repeated by switching books.

Social studies is brought into the theme with the use of a nonfiction book titled *The Milk Makers* (Gibbons, 1987). After the read-aloud, the class engages in interactive writing and generates a chart that highlights the sequence of the farm-to-table milk-producing process. The book also engages the class in discussions that focus on other items that come from the farm.

TEACHABLE MOMENTS

One of Paula's favorite teachable moments was as follows:

During a thematic unit on snakes, the class enjoyed a read-aloud about different snakes. In the book, the author stated that some snakes are 20 feet long. Michael wanted to know how long 20 feet would be. Some children thought it would be the size of the classroom; others thought it would be as tall as the school. Paula recalls:

> "It was the perfect cross-curricular, teachable moment. We gathered up all of our rulers and yardsticks, and we went outside to the blacktop. We reviewed how a ruler is 1 foot long and that it would take 20 rulers to show us 20 feet. Then, we discovered that a yardstick is three rulers. One ruler and yardstick at a time, we laid them out on the blacktop. When we ran out of measuring tools, we decided that we could mark the beginning of the line with chalk and begin placing the rulers at the other end. When we finally reached 20 feet, the children began to cheer."

THE DAILY SCHEDULE IN PAULA'S ALL-DAY PRESCHOOL CLASSROOM

When Paula plans her day, she is always concerned that the content, materials, and time allowed for activities are all age-appropriate. The following is a schedule of her day:

➢ 8:45–9:05: Children arrive at school. Children enter school and engage in independent work until the day formally begins. These activities include hanging up coats, checking themselves in at the attendance station, returning take-home books to the library center, and completing activites designated at the helper chart, such as watering plants or feeding classroom pets. In addition, children can do independent book reading or write in their journals.

➢ 9:05–9:25: Morning meeting. The whole-group morning meeting begins with a morning message that includes a weather report, daily news about the children, and a shared read-aloud with a literacy skill emphasized.

➢ 9:25–9:50: Center time and small-group instruction.

1. *Center time.* Centers such as the literacy center, with reading and writing activities, math, science, and social studies, are open for children's use during this center time. The teacher introduces the centers that have been used in the past (either as a review or to introduce a new skill). The teacher describes independent and cooperative activities at centers and provides

time for children to get organized so that they are working productively. The teacher assigns children to centers. She rings a bell when children can change centers. The center activities involve the children in practicing skills they have learned. The aide in the room helps the children to work on tasks in the centers.

2. *Small-group instruction.* When the children are settled into center activities, the teacher meets with small groups of children, with no more than four in a group. The groups are organized based on similar needs for literacy instruction. Groups could meet for 5, 10, or 15 minutes, depending on their attention span and what they are learning. They work on reading, writing, and math.

➢ 9:50–10:30: Outdoor play, if weather permits, or play in the gym.

➢ 10:30–10:45: Snack.

➢ 10:45–11:15: Circle time: discussion about the theme being studied. Addition and work with the word wall. Songs and poems related to the theme.

➢ 11:15–12:00: Open center time—dramatic play, art, blocks, workbench, sand, social studies, science, math, literacy center. Some of the centers feature special thematic activities. Teachers use this as a time when children can ask for their Very Own Words.

➢ 12:00–12:45: Lunch, clean up, use bathroom.

➢ 12:45–1:15: Rest on mats with classical music and books to look at if children wish.

➢ 1:15–1:45: Open center time or outdoor play; children may continue napping.

➢ 1:45–2:30: Art activity, music, and movement.

➢ 2:30–2:45: Mini-lesson in math or literacy or writing workshop can occur here.

➢ 2:45–3:00: Clean up; pack up to go home, discussion about most important activities of the day.

If Paula had a half-day program, it might look like this.

➢ 8:45–9:05: Children arrive at school. Children enter school and engage in independent work until the day formally begins. These activities include putting belongings away, checking in at the attendance and lunch station, returning take-home books, helper chart activities, and quiet reading, writing, and math activities.

➢ 9:05–9:25: Morning meeting. The whole-group morning meeting begins with a morning message that includes a weather report, daily news about the children, and a shared read-aloud with a literacy skill emphasized.

➤ 9:25–9:50: Center time and small-group instruction.

   1. *Center time.* Centers such as the literacy center, with reading and writing activities, math, science, and social studies, are open for children's use during this center time. The teacher introduces the centers that have been used in the past. The teacher describes independent and cooperative activities at centers and provides time for children to get organized so that they are working productively. The teacher assigns children to centers. She rings a bell when children can change centers. The center activities involve the children in practicing skills they have learned. The aide in the room helps the children to work on tasks in the centers.

   2. *Small-group instruction.* When the children are settled into center activities, the teacher meets with small groups of children, with no more than four in a group. The groups are organized based on similar needs for literacy instruction. Groups could meet for 5, 10, or 15 minutes, depending on their attention span and what they are learning. They work on reading, writing, and math.

➤ 9:50–10:20: Outdoor play, if weather permits, or play in the gym.

➤ 10:20–10:35: Snack.

➤ 10:35–11:15: Art activity, music and movement, or math lesson.

➤ 11:15–11:35: Open center time—dramatic play, art, blocks, workbench, sand, social studies, science, math, literacy center. Some of the centers feature special thematic activities. Teachers use this as a time when children can ask for their Very Own Words.

➤ (Teacher works with one or two small groups for writing workshop.)

➤ 11:35–11:50: Circle time: discussion about the theme being studied. Addition and work with the word wall. Review important work of the day.

➤ 11:55–12:00: Clean up, pack up to go home.

Because there is so much less time in the half day, not everything gets done every day. The teacher needs to alternate lessons.

A DESCRIPTION OF PAULA'S DAY

The children arrive at school. As they enter, they check themselves in at the attendance/lunch station, proceed to their cubbies, and unpack. They return borrowed books. Following these routines, the children then complete any "class helper" jobs that they have been assigned. The children then work on designated quiet literacy activities in reading, writing, and math.

The children gather on the rug in the literacy center for their morning meeting. On the message board Paula has written, "Today is Thursday, February 16. It is windy and cold today." Then she asks who has some news for the message. Tressa raises her hand and says, "I got a new hat for the winter." Paula asks what color it is. Tressa says, "It is red and blue with a pom-pom on top." Paula writes, and says at the same time, "Tressa got a new red and blue hat with a pom-pom on the top." At the end of the sentence she draws a red and blue hat with a pom-pom on it. She takes her pointer and has the children read it together.

For their shared reading experience, Paula has chosen to tell the story *The Mitten* (Brett, 1989) to match their winter theme. She emphasizes the following concepts about books: the title, the author's name, and the illustrator's name. She asks the children to predict what might occur in the story related to the mitten, based on the picture on the cover of the book. On the cover is a mitten with many animals stuffed into it and more trying to get in. Josh says, "Some animals will go 'cause they can't get in." Elena says, "I think the mitten will get torn." Before beginning to read, Paula says, "As I tell the story, see if what you thought about actually does happen." Paula tells the story using a felt board with felt figures. There is a big mitten on the felt board, and as she mentions different animals, she places them on top of the mitten.

As Paula nears the end of the book, she says, "I'm wondering what you think will happen." Some children say that everyone who wants to get into the mitten will. Some say that some animals will leave because it is too crowded. At the end of the story, the mitten explodes, and all the animals come flying out. Paula finishes the story to find out what happened. She then invites children to tell the class what part of the story they like best.

At this time Paula asks the children to review what they said in their morning message and some ideas about the story she read. She reminds the children that the mitten story with the felt figures will be in the literacy center for them to use to retell the story.

Center time comes next, with activities in the various centers that Paula reviews. The children have participated in these types of activities before. There is partner reading, writing, a listening activity, and work with the alphabet. Paula has prepared the following activities for the children to participate in:

ELL

➢ *Partner reading.* Children pair off and read the same book together. They may also read separate books and then tell each other about their stories. The selection of books includes those they have heard before. Because they are studying winter, they can only select books from the baskets that include stories and informational books about this season. Children are to draw or write something about the book they looked at. The mitten story with the felt figures can be used, as well as a puppet story they have heard and seen before.

> *Writing activity.* Children are to rewrite the story read to them earlier in the day. In their rewritings, the children can write just one word, can copy words, or can do whatever they are capable of doing. There are multiple copies of the book for the children to consult. Each day there is a writing activity related to the story read earlier; the children are familiar with how to do this. They can also copy winter words from the word wall.

> *Working with the alphabet.* The center has envelopes, each of which contains two copies of eight diferent magnetic letters. Children spill them out and put the magnetic letters that are identical next to each other on their magnetic boards.

> *Listening center.* The children listen to taped stories. They draw something about each story on a sheet of paper. The story on the tape for the unit about winter is *The Snowy Day* (Keats, 1962).

Once all children are in their centers and actively engaged, and the aide is circulating to help them stay on task, Paula calls her first small group for their special instructions. When the group assembles, Paula puts on a colorful beaded necklace with 18 beads—one bead to represent each person in the class, including the teacher and the aide. Paula refers to this as her "cooperation necklace." When she is wearing it, the children are not to disturb her or the group or individuals she is working with unless it is an emergency. The necklace is a constant reminder to the children that they need to work together and independent of the teacher.

The four children in the first group are working with phonological awareness activities. First they sing a song and clap the sounds of the song. The song is "Bingo," but instead of "Bingo" Paula uses the children's names. "There was a teacher who had a child and Avonna was her name, A-v-o-n-n-a, A-v-o-n-n-a, A-v-o-n-n-a and Avonna was her name." Paula asks how many claps are in "Avonna." Jason says two, and Avonna says three. Paula says, "Let's do it together." When they do it together, Jason agrees that there are three. Then Jason says, "How many claps in my name?" Paula says, "Say it and clap it." He claps "J-a-s-on" and calls out "five." "That's right," says Paula.

The children recite "Humpty Dumpty," and Paula writes down and says the words that rhyme. She explains that rhyming words sound the same, such as *wall* and *fall, men* and *again.* "James, what would your name sound like if we put a "Puh" sound in instead of "Juh" so it rhymes with James? Kim yells out "Pames, that sounds funny." They continue rhyming their names. Paula puts the poem "Humpty Dumpty" in an envelope with the rhyming words underlined for the children to take home. She suggests that they say the poem with their parents, review the rhyming words, and make up more rhyming words with their names and their family's names.

Paula meets with two other groups of children who need help with a similar skill. One group is working on colors; the other group is working on letters of the alphabet. Before each group she rings a bell for the children at centers to change activities. The aide helps them move from one place to the next. Each group meeting lasts no longer than 10 minutes and, in one case, only 5.

To signal that center time is over, Paula sings a clean-up song. The children return to their tables after cleaning up. As part of their routine, Paula and the children then proceed to share compliments with one another, focusing on behaviors observed during center time. Student compliments include "I like how Ivory helped me retell *The Mitten* (Brett, 1989). Jennifer says, "Whitney, Josh, and me did a good job putting the same alphabet letters together." Brandon says, "I like how I worked with somebody new in the writing center. We did good jobs writing." These brief exchanges bring about a positive closure to this important instructional time.

Next, children go outdoors to play. It is cold outside, but they are working on a theme about winter, and it is a good opportunity to play in the snow on the playground. A few children build a little snowman, some make snowballs, and some write their names in the snow. A few children make snow angels. Paula asks some children to collect some snow in a pail to bring inside and watch how it melts in the warm classroom.

When they come indoors, the aide has some hot chocolate ready for the children. She has cookies and white icing for children to put on them to make them look as though they are topped with snow.

After cleaning up, it is circle time. Paula gets the pail of snow to look at. It has already melted a lot. The class observes that snow filled the pail more and that when it melts the pail looks less full of water. Paula directs the children to the word wall. Each one has to read another child's name from the word wall and point to it. Then they look at the winter words they have added, *snow* and *snowman*. Jovanna suggests they add the words *sled* and *snow angels*. Paula takes two cards and writes the words, with pictures next to them. "What letter of the alphabet should I put these words under?" Everyone says *S* at the same time. "Can you point to any other words on the big word wall that have *S*'s in them?" James raises his hand and points to the *S* in his name. Sarah raises her hand and points to the *S* in her name.

The class sings the song "I'm a little snowman short and fat, / Here are my buttons, / Here is my hat, / When the sun comes out during the day, / I can't play since I melt away."

Open center time is next. In the clay area, children make snowmen with white play dough. They have Ivory Snow flakes and water to use like finger paint on the tables to make snow-white pictures and collage materials, such as white cotton, white wool, white doilies, white chalk, silver foil, and dark blue paper, to make winter collages.

Of course there are winter books in the literacy center, blank books cut like snowmen in the writing center, and the book *The Big Snow* (Hader, 1967) on a CD with headsets. In the sand table, which was filled with white rice, were snowplow trucks to clean up the snow around the town built on the table. All the centers

Children can choose blocks and other building materials to make their own creations. They are encouraged to label what they create.

have paper and pencils for children to write notes to each other and about their work.

Children can choose blocks and other building materials such as Legos to make their own creations or build items to match the theme. They are encouraged to label their structures.

A pretend soup-and-sandwich shop in the dramatic-play area is equipped with menus, pads for taking orders, bills for paying with play money, and a cash register. This restaurant changes frequently to reflect the topic of study.

In Paula's classroom, children have their Very Own Word boxes. During open center time she will fill out a card for any child who wants a word for his or her box. Today there are many requests for *melt, mitten,* and *snow angel.* She always draws a picture to represent the word.

The children then eat lunch, which includes mashed potatoes. They talk about the potatoes as if they were snow. They also comment that their milk is white as snow. Lunch is a time to socialize and talk.

Although most of the children no longer nap, many can use a rest after lunch. Some winter music is put on a CD player. Children can take books if they like, write in their journals, or just rest. If they fall asleep, they are allowed to stay asleep until they wake on their own; but after 45 minutes, most are ready to get up.

Another session of open center time follows for children who didn't get to do some of the special themed activities. The teacher may use this time to work with different children in the centers, to start conversation, or to take one child at a time for additional help he or she may need on a skill.

The next activity varies among art, music, and movement. Today the children decorate paper cutout mittens with all sorts of designs. When they are done, there is time to do some movement activities, such as rolling like a snowball down a hill on the floor of the classroom, pretending to be making angels, or having a pretend snowball fight with tissue paper snowballs and music playing in the background.

Writing workshop includes many types of writing experiences, such as stories dictated by children that the teacher writes down, interactive writing with the class during which the children and teacher write together, and journal writing. Young children need a lot of supervision with journals. During writing workshop today, children will be writing in their journals. Today's journal entry will be about winter and snow. First they discuss or brainstorm ideas about snow that happened at school. For example, the class sings a snow song, heard *The Mitten* (Brett, 1989), played in the snow and made angels, snowmen, and snowballs, made snow collages, finger-painted snow pictures, and decorated mittens. Each child is asked what he or she will write and draw about so the children have a purpose for their writing. They know from practice that they are to use only one page and to fill the page. They draw the picture first, and then the aide or teacher writes a word or sentence that the child would like to say about his or her picture. Some children then copy the word or words, and some write a word or just one letter on their own. Some children scribble write. Their "Very Own Word Box" contains words that children have requested, and they can copy these words for their journal entries. They are encouraged to use the morning message and the word wall to find words they need. The entry is dated.

As the children are writing in their journals, Paula and the aide walk around the room, talk with individuals, and answer questions. As the children finish their journal entries, they share them with Paula and the aide, who provide every child with specific, positive feedback. For example, when looking at Jill's work, Paula says, "I like how you wrote the beginning letter and the ending letter in these two words."

Now that it is February of their preschool year, the children are able to handle journal writing quite well and understand the rules. When the writing time is up, some children talk about or read what they wrote. Paula mentions that she likes Damien's ideas and how he spoke about them, and then the children chime in that they like one child's work or another and the reason why.

With 5 minutes left in the school day, it is time to clean, pack up, and check out a book. Paula calls everyone to the literacy center to review all the activities of the day. She writes them down as the children dictate them. Then they count how many they remember. They have a list of nine activities. Paula asks everyone to pick the three they liked the most and tell their parents about them. Some mentioned *The Mitten* (Brett, 1989), the new word wall words, journal writing, and their play in the hot-soup restaurant. Paula reminds the children to check their books out on the way home and bring them back the next day. Each child has some work to do at home, such as rhyming words from their small-group instruction.

As the children line up to go home, they sing to the tune of "Here We Go 'Round the Mulberry Bush": "This is the way we go on home, we go on home, we go on home. This is the way we go on home, in the afternoon."

SUMMARY AND IMPLICATIONS

The children in this early childhood classroom experience literacy in many different forms. The children are involved in an environment that incorporates literacy into the entire day. The literacy experiences are planned appropriately to accommodate individual needs and learning styles. Paula is enthusiastic about her teaching, and excitement is contagious. As a result, her students assume a positive attitude toward literacy learning, one another, and themselves.

The children have extensive exposure to children's literature through the use of shared readings, independent reading, buddy reading with a peer, and small-group reading instruction for skill development. Writing experiences include journal writing in the writing workshop and language experience activities. Both reading and writing include systematic skill development, and skill development is done with an authentic purpose.

Paula's room is rich with materials so that children experience choice, challenging activities, social interaction, and success. The school day is structured to include varied experiences appropriate to the developmental level of the children. Children are taught rules, routines, and procedures for using the classroom materials when they are in self-directed roles. Paula is consistent in her management techniques. Therefore, the children know what is expected of them and, consequently, they carry out the work that needs to be done. Consistent routine allows the day to flow smoothly from one activity to another.

The affective quality in the room is exemplary. Paula speaks to the children with respect and in an adult manner. She does not raise her voice, nor does she use punitive remarks, facial expressions, or intonations. In this atmosphere, children learn to understand appropriate classroom behavior.

Paula allows time for children to grow at their natural pace, with concern for social, emotional, and intellectual development. She also is aware of the need to foster development with appropriate materials for exploration and specific skills instruction for individual needs. She integrates the language arts curriculum and content-area teaching by building one on the other to develop listening, speaking, reading, writing, and viewing skills. In addition, she utilizes information from content areas to teach literacy skills. She intentionally aims to build skills and develop the joy of learning.

CHILDREN'S LITERATURE

Brett, J. (1989). *The mitten: A Ukranian folk tale.* New York: Putnam.

Cowley, J. (1999). *Mrs. Wishy-Washy.* New York: Putnam.

Gibbons, G. (1987). *The milk makers.* New York: Macmillan.

Hader, B. H. (1967). *The big snow.* New York: Simon & Schuster.

Hurd, E. T. (2001). *Johnny Lion's rubber boots.* New York: HarperCollins.

Keats, E. J. (1962). *The snowy day.* New York: Viking.

Palatini, M. (1997). *Piggy pie.* Boston: Houghton Mifflin.

CHAPTER 2

RESEARCH ABOUT PRESCHOOL THAT INFORMS GOOD PRACTICE

Now that we have visited an excellent preschool program, it is important that we understand the research that has informed the practice. I also discuss the history, theory, research, and policy that have shaped our present programs.

HISTORY, THEORY, RESEARCH, AND PRACTICE THAT HAVE INFLUENCED PRESCHOOL PROGRAMS

Philosophers have influenced early literacy instruction, and theorists have focused on child development, early childhood education, and literacy development. Philosophers such as Johann Heinrich Pestalozzi and Friedrich Froebel (Rusk & Scotland, 1979) talked about natural environments in which children would develop through sensory experiences, involving learning through touch, smell, taste, size, and shape. Play was crucial, as was the social, emotional, and physical development of the child. Intellectual development was important; however, it was no more a priority than were social, emotional, and physical development. John Dewey's (1916/1966) progressive education philosophy had a strong influence on preschool and kindergarten practices from the 1920s throughout the rest of the 20th century. Dewey led us to themed units of study that connect learning to meaning and purpose. He influenced the environments in preschool and kindergarten, in which classrooms are set up with different content-area activity centers. The block corner, music and art centers, dramatic-play area, science and social studies displays, and the library corner were the result of Dewey's ideas. A typical day included the following:

➤ Circle time to talk about the weather and the calendar and to focus discussion on a science or social studies theme. If the theme were "good health," for example, the class would listen to a story and sing a song in keeping with this theme.

➤ Free play, in which children could paint at easels, build with blocks, and engage in dramatic play with dress-up clothing and a pretend kitchen. Children explored and experimented with the materials in social settings, with little direction other than safety precautions.

➤ Snack and rest time, included because of the emphasis on good health and learning about good nutrition.

➤ Outdoor play for large motor development.

➤ A storybook reading at the end of the day.

➤ No attempt at formal lessons; in fact, they were frowned on as inappropriate for the developmental stage of the child. However, teachable moments were used to advantage. There was no place in this program for formal reading instruction.

Montessori (1965) had a strong effect on early childhood and literacy instruction, believing that materials for children needed to serve a purpose for learning. She created manipulative activities to develop skills that focused on getting the right answer. Very few group lessons occur in this program, except to introduce new materials into the classroom. Children work independently and at their own pace and level. According to Montessori, young children need to use their senses to learn; therefore, she created many materials that involved the senses, such as tactile letters and wooden letters with different colors for long and short vowels.

Learning theorists Piaget (Piaget & Inhelder, 1969) and Vygotsky (1978) also had a strong impact on early childhood and literacy instruction. Both suggested social settings for learning. Those who interpret Piaget's theory of cognitive development for instruction describe a curriculum that encourages exploration of natural environments and learning rather than direct or explicit teaching. Vygotsky described learning in a similar manner to that of Piaget; however, he proposed that adults should "scaffold" and model behaviors they wanted children to learn. These theories and philosophies that influenced early childhood education were concerned with the following:

> Prepared and natural environments for learning.

> Equal emphasis on social, emotional, physical, and intellectual development.

> Support from adults who encourage social interaction for learning.

> A focus on learning rather than teaching.

> Awareness that children must be actively involved to learn.

READING READINESS AND EARLY LITERACY

Morphett and Washburne (1931) believed in postponing formal reading instruction until the child was developmentally "old

Early childhood theorists have always promoted play as an important early childhood activity.

enough." Their research concluded that children with a mental age of 6 years and 6 months made better progress on a test of reading achievement than younger children. Although many educators believed that natural maturation was the precursor to literacy, others grew uncomfortable with simply waiting for children to become ready to read. They did not advocate formal reading instruction in early childhood but did begin to provide experiences that they believed would help children become ready for reading. Instead of waiting for a child's natural maturation to unfold, educators focused on nurturing that maturation by teaching children what they believed to be a set of prerequisite skills for reading, which include: focusing on auditory discrimination of familiar sounds, similar sounds, rhyming words, and sounds of letters; visual discrimination, including color recognition, shape, and letter identification; left-to-right eye progression; visual motor skills, such as cutting on a line with scissors, and coloring within the lines; and large motor abilities, such as skipping, hopping, and walking a straight line. Although the practice of many of these skills can still be seen in today's classrooms, new research has extended our understanding of the ways in which young children's literacy abilities develop and subsequently have influenced our classroom practices.

EARLY LITERACY RESEARCH IN THE PAST 35 YEARS

Research from the 1960s through the 1990s brought to light new information about the importance of children's oral language development, early writing development, emergent reading behaviors, and family literacy experiences. With this new information and the whole-language movement, educators moved away from the abstract reading readiness activities thought to be the precursors to reading toward more natural ways of developing reading, as in the past. Although the explicit teaching of skills was seen as not appropriate for young children, "emergent literacy behaviors" were being recognized and encouraged. Marie Clay (1966) promoted use of the term *emergent literacy* and the reading of good literature to children. The concept of emergent literacy recognized scribble writing and invented spelling as the beginning of conventional writing and encouraged these behaviors.

Children who engage in pretend reading often use pictures or props to help them read the story. Emergent literacy saw a dynamic relationship between the communication skills (reading, writing, oral language, and listening) because each influences the others in the course of development. Development occurs in everyday contexts of the home, community, and school through meaningful and functional experiences that require the use of literacy in natural settings. For example, when studying a theme such as dinosaurs from whole-language and emergent literacy perspectives, the teacher may focus on some of the letters and sounds from the initial consonants found in the dinosaurs' names. Family involvement in a child's development of emergent literacy skills is also encouraged.

COMPREHENSIVE AND BALANCED LITERACY INSTRUCTION

A position statement by the International Reading Association, titled *Using Multiple Methods of Beginning Reading Instruction* (1999), suggests that there is no one single method or single combination of methods that can successfully teach all children to read. "The position paper recommends that teachers need to know varied strategies when teaching reading and spend time learning about student individual needs to design a balanced program." A comprehensive balanced perspective in reading instruction means the careful selection of the best theories available and the use of learning strategies to match the learning styles of individual children. This might mean the use of more skill-based explicit instruction for some or of holistic problem-solving strategies for others (Morrow & Tracey, 1997). According to Pressley (2006), explicit teaching of skills is a good start for constructivist problem-solving activities, and constructivist activities permit consolidation and elaboration of skills. One method does not preclude or exclude the other. A balanced perspective is not simply a combination of random strategies. A teacher may select strategies from different learning theories to provide balance. One child, for example, may be a visual learner and benefit from sight-word instruction. Another child's strength may be auditory learning, and he or she will learn best from phonics instruction. The balanced approach focuses more on what is important for each individual child than on the latest fad in literacy instruction.

Balanced instruction is grounded in a rich model of literacy learning that encompasses both the elegance and the complexity of the reading and language arts processes. Such a model acknowledges the importance of both form (phonics, mechanics, etc.) and function (comprehension, purpose, and meaning) of the literacy processes and recognizes that learning occurs most effectively in a whole–part–whole context.

The preschool years, ages 3 and 4, are extremely important for social, emotional, physical, and cognitive development. High-quality preschool experiences can translate into academic and social competence (Barnett, 1995; Neuman & Dickinson, 2001). Research studies and syntheses conducted over the past decade have helped us understand the importance of young children's experiences with oral and written language. The preschool years are especially important for oral language development and for initial experiences with reading and writing that link to later school achievement (Snow, Burns, & Griffin, 1998).

CURRENT EVIDENCE FOR LANGUAGE AND LITERACY DEVELOPMENT IN PRESCHOOL PROGRAMS

All preschool-age children need rich language and literacy experiences to prepare them to benefit from reading and writing instruction in school. Currently, only some 3- and 4-year-olds benefit from literacy experiences as a result of family involvement and/or access to quality preschool programs (International Reading Association & National Association for the Education of Young Children [IRA/ NAEYC], 1998).

Children who have high-quality preschool experiences with an emphasis on language and literacy are more likely to acquire strong language and literacy skills that translate into achievement in the early grades and throughout their schooling. Children who attend high-quality preschools are less likely to be retained in grades from kindergarten through grade 3; they have higher graduation rates from high school and fewer behavior problems (Barnett, 1995; Campbell & Raney, 1995; Cunningham & Stanovich, 1997; Peisner-Feinberg & Burchinal, 1997; Reynolds, Temple, Robertson, & Mann, 2001). If a child does not have the appropriate language development by age 3, he or she is not likely to succeed in school. With quality preschool, a child can catch up and go on to be successful. The benefits of having a preschool education are found across economic backgrounds, although children from families with the least formal education and the lowest incomes appear to benefit the most (Barnett, 2001; Barnett, 1995; Fuerst & Fuerst, 1993; Schweinhart, Barnes, Weikart, Barnett, & Epstein, 1993).

Publications from the federal government and professional associations, such as *Preventing Reading Difficulties in Young Children* (Snow et al., 1998), *Learning to Read and Write: Developmentally Appropriate Practices* (IRA/NAEYC, 1998), and *Teaching Children to Read* (National Reading Panel, 2000), all deal with concerns about early literacy instruction and how to improve it. In the spring of 2002, the Elementary and Secondary Education Act, which includes the No Child Left Behind legislation, was passed. Although early literacy development has been a focus throughout the years, it is presently in the spotlight more than ever because of these documents. The National Reading Panel (NRP) report (2000) suggests that instruction in early literacy needs to be organized and systematic. It also identifies areas addressed in kindergarten through grade 3 that predict literacy success: (1) phonemic awareness, (2) phonics, (3) comprehension, (4) vocabulary, and (5) fluency. It is important to know that the panel did not study all areas in literacy development. The NRP did not study writing and its connections to reading success, nor did it study motivation. According to the NRP, some areas were omitted because not enough scientific research was available to determine their importance. The panel reviewed only studies considered to be scientifically based research with quantitative experimental designs.

The National Early Literacy Panel (2004) studied research that identifies abilities of children from birth through 5 that predict later achievement in literacy. The abilities identified were oral language development, phonological/phonemic awareness, alphabetic knowledge, print knowledge, and invented spelling. Researchers have also found that experiences with storybook reading, discussions about books, listening comprehension, and writing are crucial in early literacy development (Bus, van IJzendoorn, & Pellegrini, 1995; Wells, 1985).

Based on the evidence provided, access to many language and literacy experiences will enhance young children's development. Thus preschools need to focus on a wide range of language and literacy experiences organized into the curriculum.

LANGUAGE AND LITERACY EXPERIENCES PROVIDED BY HIGH-QUALITY PRESCHOOL PROGRAMS

High-quality preschool programs are concerned with the social, emotional, physical, and cognitive development of children. Quality preschool programs provide literacy instruction that is integrated throughout the curriculum. Classroom themes allow teachers to design meaningful activities for literacy development that incorporate experiences in science, social studies, math, art, music, and play (Dewey, 1916/1966). Quality programs focus on language and literacy development and include standards for learning, with outcomes described. These preschool programs have teaching plans that are intentional and developmentally appropriate for young children. This means that instruction is organized so that it happens in small groups, in one-to-one teacher–child interactions, and in child-initiated experiences. Providing language and literacy experiences in preschool does not mean moving reading and writing instruction from kindergarten and the primary grades into preschool; rather, it means integrating appropriate literacy activities throughout the traditional preschool curriculum in a thoughtful way (Dickinson, 2002). Teachers design their classroom environment to be rich with literacy materials, including books, magazines, paper, and writing supplies (Hendrick, 2004). Teachers integrate literacy into play by setting up areas that represent real-life situations, such as a restaurant or a veterinarian's office. In these settings, children learn about behavior that is appropriate to particular social situations, and they learn how to interact with others (Whitehurst & Lonigan, 1998). Adults provide models for reading and writing when literacy materials are included, such as reading the menu and taking orders for food in the "restaurant." In the "veterinarian's office," the nurse takes appointments, the doctor writes up reports on patients, and those in the waiting room read while they wait (Morrow & Gambrell, 2004; Vukelich & Christie, 2004).

Quality preschools include oral language experiences that focus on gestural expression, verbal expression, vocabulary development, building background knowledge, and listening to others to understand and comprehend what they say (Dickinson, Cote, & Smith, 1993). Children learn phonological awareness, that is, that words are made up of individual sounds. They learn this in oral language experiences such as chanting poems, singing songs, and clapping the sounds they hear in words they sing and chant (Adams, 1990, 2001; Carroll, Snowling, Hulme, & Stevenson, 2003; Strickland & Schickedanz, 2004).

Quality preschools include experiences for literacy development, as they expose children to print conventions and book handling. This means that children learn that there is a front, back, top, and bottom to books. They learn that there is a left-to-right sequence in books and that there is a difference between the print and the pictures. They learn letter names and sounds and to identify letters visually. It is a meaningful experience when children's names are used to teach them that words contain different sounds and to identify letters and letter sounds. However, preschoolers are not expected to learn all of these things (Strickland & Schickedanz, 2004).

Good preschools help children learn about different types of text, such as stories, informational books, menus, signs, and newspapers, as well as to be aware of and read print in the environment. Quality literacy development in preschools helps children learn to comprehend stories and develop an interest in books. Research demonstrates that one of the most important activities for building success in literacy is reading aloud to children. The experience is most valuable when accompanied by interactive discussions with adults and children to introduce new vocabulary and language structures. This conversation leads to understanding or comprehension of the story read (Morrow & Gambrell, 2004; Storch & Whitehurst, 2002; Bus et al., 1995; Wells, 1985). Finally, experiences with beginning writing are important to literacy development as children make their first writing attempts by scribbling, making letter-like forms, using invented spelling, and writing in a conventional manner. Writing teaches children about letters, sounds, and the meaning of text (Schickedanz & Casbergue, 2004).

Daily routines in a quality preschool program include whole-group morning meetings in which children gather on a rug and discuss and write a morning message about the theme being studied. Children work individually and in small groups at centers, where they engage in reading and writing. For example, they read with partners in the literacy center, write in their journals at the writing center, or work in the literacy-enriched themed-play setting. While children are engaged independently, the teacher meets with small groups and works on literacy activities suited to their needs. During the day the teacher reads a story related to the theme, and discussion before and after reading helps to develop comprehension. Mini-lessons deal with developing phonological awareness as songs and poems are sung and chanted. Other mini-lessons deal with letter identification in meaningful contexts. Children explore in playful content-area centers during a time set aside. The whole group meets again for a conversation that summarizes the activities of the day and predicts what might happen tomorrow (Roskos, Tabors, & Lenuart, 2004; Dickinson, McCabe, Anastasopoulos, Peisner-Feinberg, & Poe, 2003). Throughout the day literacy instruction is integrated into other content areas, and the teacher makes the children aware of the literacy skills they are learning (Morrow, 2005).

TEACHER PREPARATION AND PROFESSIONAL DEVELOPMENT

Teachers in early childhood programs are better able to provide quality programs in language and literacy when they understand the continuum of reading and writing development and its integration in the preschool curriculum. In the past, many preschool teachers have been criticized for not being well prepared. Preschool teachers need to know about the individual needs of children, taking into consideration social, emotional, physical, and cognitive abilities. Teachers must be sensitive to children from different cultural backgrounds. Quality preschools have teachers with college degrees and early childhood teaching certification. In their preparation they have a strong background in language and literacy development. To be on the cutting edge of language and literacy instruction, preschool teachers and directors need to engage in continuous professional development (Anders, Hoffman, & Duffy, 2000; Showers & Joyce, 1996; Shulman, 1998; Sparks & Loucks-Horsley, 1990; Taylor, Pearson, Clark, & Walpole, 2000). Research shows that excellent teachers are not only well-prepared teachers but also those who continue to participate in professional development during their careers. In addition, children at risk, those from diverse socioeconomic backgrounds and marginalized populations who often fail, do better in schools that have the greatest number of well-trained teachers. The Afterword at the end of this book contains more specific discussion about quality professional development programs.

THE BASIS FOR THE PHILOSOPHY PRESENTED IN THIS BOOK

Quality preschool is based on history, theory, research, and policy. The contents of this book are influenced by the joint position statement of the International Reading Association and the National Association for the Education of Young Children titled *Learning to Read and Write: Developmentally Appropriate Practices for Young Children* (1998). It also takes into account the National Reading Panel report (2000); *Put Reading First* (2001), developed by the Center for the Improvement of Early Reading Achievement; the National Early Literacy Panel report (2004); and the International Reading Association position paper, *Reading in Preschool* (2006). Other pertinent research dealing with this topic is documented throughout. This book is based on the following rationale:

1. Literacy learning begins in infancy.
2. Families need to provide a literacy-rich environment and literacy experi-

ences at home to help children acquire skills. Families need to be actively involved in their children's literacy learning when they enter school.

3. Teachers need to be aware that children come to school with prior knowledge about reading and writing and that this knowledge is different from one child to the next.

4. Literacy learning requires a supportive environment that builds positive feelings about self and literacy activities.

5. Learning requires a rich literacy environment with accessible materials and varied experiences.

6. Teachers and parents must serve as models for literacy by scaffolding and demonstrating strategies that need to be learned.

7. During literacy experiences children should interact within a social context to share information, which motivates them to learn from one another.

8. Early reading and writing experiences should be meaningful and concrete and actively engage children.

9. Early reading and writing experiences need to provide systematic, intentional, and explicit instruction in skills.

10. A literacy development program should focus on experiences that include reading, writing, listening, speaking, and viewing.

11. Diversity in cultural and language backgrounds must be acknowledged and addressed in early literacy development.

12. Differences in literacy achievement from one child to the next in the same grade will vary and must be addressed with small-group instruction, early intervention, or inclusion classroom programs.

13. Assessment of achievement should be frequent, should match instructional strategies, and should use multiple formats for evaluating student behavior.

14. Standards for early literacy grade-level benchmarks should be tied to instruction and assessment and used as a means of reaching the goal of having all children read fluently by third grade.

15. We must work toward having universal preschool in the public sector for 3- and 4-year-olds and all-day kindergarten.

16. Programs should be research based. For example, we know from the results of the National Reading Panel (2000) report that there are necessary components in reading instruction to ensure student success.

LITERACY DEVELOPMENT EXPECTATIONS FOR PRESCHOOLERS

Babies begin to acquire information about literacy from the moment they are born. They continue to build on their knowledge of oral language, reading, and writing as they go through early childhood and beyond based on the experiences they have at home and in school. A great deal of attention is now being focused on literacy development in early childhood and especially preschool, an area somewhat neglected in the past. Teachers, parents, and administrators have not perceived preschoolers as readers or writers. As the result of increased research, very young children are now viewed as individuals with literacy skills. Although the literacy activities that preschool, kindergarten, and some first-grade children demonstrate and participate in are not conventional, they must be acknowledged and encouraged because they have implications for future success in reading. Like a child's first words and first steps, learning to read and write should be an exciting, fulfilling, and rewarding experience. Table 2.1 presents goals for preschool literacy development.

SOCIAL, EMOTIONAL, PHYSICAL, AND INTELLECTUAL DEVELOPMENT OF THE CHILD

Early childhood education has always been concerned about the physical, social, emotional, and cognitive development of the child. The curriculum, therefore, should emphasize all four areas. One cannot discuss early literacy without being concerned with the total child. This information is needed when preparing instructional environments and activities. This knowledge will also help determine whether children have special needs related to learning disabilities, giftedness, or communication disorders, for example. Considering the total, not just the cognitive, development of the child has been and always should be a hallmark in early childhood education and must influence early literacy development, as well. Table 2.2 describes the developmental characteristics of children from birth through 6 years. It can be used as a reference throughout this volume in teaching and assessing child development and as a checklist for evaluating child development.

TABLE 2.1. Goals for Preschool Literacy Development

Phase 1: Awareness and exploration (goals for 3-year-old preschoolers)

Children can:

- Enjoy listening to and discussing storybooks.
- Understand that print carries a message.
- Engage in reading and writing attempts.
- Identify labels and signs in their environment.
- Participate in rhyming games.
- Identify some letters and make some letter–sound matches.
- Use known letters or approximations of letters to represent written language (especially with such meaningful words as their names and such phrases as "I love you").

What teachers do:

- Share books with children, including big books, and model reading behaviors.
- Talk about letters by name and sound.
- Establish a literacy-rich environment.
- Reread favorite stories.
- Engage children in language games.
- Promote literacy-related play activities.
- Encourage children to experiment with writing.

What parents and family members can do:

- Talk with children, engage them in conversation, tell them names of things, show interest in what a child says.
- Read and reread stories with predictable texts to children.
- Have children recount experiences and describe ideas that are important to them.
- Visit the library regularly.
- Allow children to draw and print, using markers, crayons, and pencils.

Phase 2: Experimental reading and writing (goals for 4- and 5-year-old preschoolers)

Children can:

- Use descriptive language to explain and explore.
- Recognize letters and letter–sound matches.
- Show familiarity with rhyming and beginning sounds.
- Understand left-to-right and top-to-bottom orientation and concepts about print.
- Match spoken words with written ones.
- Begin to write letters of the alphabet and some high-frequency words.

What teachers do:

- Encourage children to talk about reading and writing experiences.
- Provide many opportunities for children to explore and identify sound–symbol relationships in meaningful contexts.
- Help children to segment spoken words into individual sounds and blend the sounds into whole words (e.g., by slowly writing a word and saying its sound).

(continued)

TABLE 2.1. *(continued)*

- Frequently read interesting and conceptually rich stories to children.
- Provide daily opportunities for children to write.
- Help children build a sight vocabulary.
- Create literacy-rich environments for children to engage in reading and writing.

What parents and family members can do:
- Read daily and reread narrative and informational stories to children.
- Encourage children's attempts at reading and writing.
- Allow children to participate in activities that involve writing and reading (e.g., cooking, making grocery lists).
- Play games that involve specific directions (such as Simon Says).
- Have conversations with children during mealtimes and throughout the day.

Note. Data from International Reading Association and National Association for the Education of Young Children (1998).

TABLE 2.2. Children's Stages of Development from 1 to 6 Years of Age

Ages 1 to 2 years

Physical
- Begins to develop many motor skills.
- Continues teething till about 18 months; develops all 20 teeth by age 2.
- Develops large muscles. Crawls well, stands alone (at about a year), and pushes chair around.
- Places ball in and out of box.
- Releases ball with thrust.
- Creeps down stairs backward.
- Develops fine motor skills. Stacks two blocks, picks up a bean, and puts objects into a container. Starts to use a spoon. Puts on simple things—for instance, an apron over the head.
- By end of 18 months, scribbles with a crayon in vertical or horizontal lines.
- Turns pages of book.
- During second year, walks without assistance.
- Runs but often bumps into things.
- Jumps up and down.
- Walks up and down stairs with one foot forward.
- Holds glass with one hand.
- Stacks at least six blocks and strings beads.
- Opens doors and cupboards.
- Scribbles spirals, loops, and rough circles.
- Starts to prefer one hand to the other.
- Starts day control of elimination.

(continued)

TABLE 2.2. *(continued)*

Social
- At age 1, differentiates meagerly between self and other.
- Approaches mirror image socially.
- By 18 months, distinguishes between terms *you* and *me.*
- Plays spontaneously; is self-absorbed but notices newcomers.
- Imitates behavior more elaborately.
- Identifies body parts.
- Responds to music.
- Develops socialization by age 2. Is less interested in playing with parent and more interested in playing with a peer.
- Begins parallel play, playing side by side, but without interaction.
- By age 2 learns to distinguish strongly between self and others.
- Is ambivalent about moving out and exploring.
- Becomes aware of owning things and may become very possessive.

Emotional
- At age 1 is amiable.
- At 18 months is resistant to change. Often suddenly—won't let mother out of sight.
- Tends to rebel, resist, fight, run, hide.
- Perceives emotions of others.
- At age 1, shows no sense of guilt. By age 2, begins to experience guilt and shows beginnings of conscience.
- Says "no" emphatically. Shows willfulness and negativism.
- Laughs and jumps exuberantly.

Cognitive
- Shows mental imagery: looks for things that are hidden, recalls and anticipates events, moves beyond here and now, begins temporal and spatial orientation.
- Develops deductive reasoning; searches for things in more than one place.
- Reveals memory; shows deferred imitation by seeing an event and imitating it later. Remembers names of objects.
- Completes awareness of object permanence.
- Distinguishes between black and white and may use names of colors.
- Distinguishes one from many.
- Says "one, two, three" in rote counting, but not often in rational counting.
- Acts out utterances and talks about actions while carrying them out.
- Takes things apart and tries to put them back together.
- Shows sense of time by remembering events. Knows terms *today* and *tomorrow,* but confuses them.

Ages 3 to 4 years
Physical
- Expands physical skills.
- Rides a tricycle.
- Pushes a wagon.

(continued)

TABLE 2.2. *(continued)*

- Runs smoothly and stops easily.
- Climbs jungle-gym ladder.
- Walks stairs with alternating feet forward.
- Jumps with two feet.
- Shows high energy level.
- By 4, can do a running broad jump.
- Begins to skip, pushing one foot ahead of the other.
- Can balance on one foot.
- Keeps relatively good time in response to music.
- Expands fine motor skills, can work zippers and dress self.
- Controls elimination at night.

Social

- Becomes more social.
- Moves from parallel play to early associative play. Joins others in activities.
- Becomes aware of racial and sexual differences.
- Begins independence.
- By 4, shows growing sense of initiative and self-reliance.
- Becomes aware of basic sex identity.
- Not uncommonly develops imaginary playmates (a trait that may appear as early as age 2½).

Emotional

- Begins enjoying humor. Laughs when adults laugh.
- Develops inner control over behavior
- Shows less negativism.
- Develops phobias and fears, which may continue until age 5.
- At 4, may begin intentional lying but is outraged by parents' white lies.

Cognitive

- Begins to develop problem-solving skills. Stacks blocks and may kick them down to see what happens.
- Learns to use listening skills as a means of learning about the world.
- Still draws in scribbles at age 3, but in one direction and less repetitively.
- At age 4, drawings represent what child knows and thinks is important.
- Is perceptually bound to one attribute and characteristic. "Why" questions abound.
- Believes everything in the world has a reason, but the reason must accord with the child's own knowledge.
- Persists in egocentric thinking.
- Begins to sort out fantasy from reality.

Ages 5 and 6 Years Old

Physical

- Well controlled and constantly in motion.
- Often rides a bicycle, as well as a tricycle.
- Can skip with alternating feet and hop.

(continued)

TABLE 2.2. *(continued)*

- Can control fine motor skills. Begins to use tools such as toothbrush, saw, scissors, pencil, hammer, needle for sewing.
- Has established handedness well. Identifies hand used for writing or drawing.
- Can dress self but may still have trouble tying shoelaces.
- At age 6, begins to lose teeth.

Social
- Becomes very social. Visits with friends independently.
- Becomes very self-sufficient.
- Persists longer at a task. Can plan and carry out activities and return to projects next day.
- Plays with two or three friends, often for just a short time only, then switches play groups.
- Begins to conform. Is very helpful.
- By age 6, becomes very assertive, often bossy, dominating situations and ready with advice.
- Needs to be first. Has difficulty listening.
- Is possessive and boastful.
- Craves affection. Often has a love–hate relationship with parents.
- Refines sex roles. Has tendency to type by sex.
- Becomes clothes-conscious.

Emotional
- Continues to develop sense of humor.
- Learns right from wrong.
- At age 5, begins to control emotions and is able to express them in socially approved ways.
- Quarrels frequently, but quarrels are of short duration.
- At age 6, shifts emotions often and seems to be in emotional ferment.
- New tensions appear as a result of attendance at school all day. Temper tantrums appear.
- Giggles over bathroom words.
- At age 5, develops a conscience, but sees actions as all good or all bad.
- Accepts rules and often develops rigid insistence that they be obeyed.
- May become a tattletale.

Cognitive
- Begins to recognize conservation of amount and length.
- Becomes interested in letters and numbers. May begin printing or copying letters and numbers. Counts.
- Knows most colors. Recognizes that one can get meaning from printed words. Has a sense of time, but mainly personal time. Knows when events take place in his or her day or week.
- Recognizes own space and can move about independently in familiar territory.

Note. Adapted from Seefeldt and Barbour (1998). Copyright 1998 by Pearson Education, Inc. Adapted by permission.

REFERENCES

Adams, M. J. (1990). *Beginning to read: Thinking and learning about print*. Urbana: University of Illinois Center for the Study of Reading.

Adams, M. J. (2001). Alphabetic anxiety and explicit systematic phonics instruction: A cognitive science perspective. In S. B. Neuman & D. K. Dickinson (Eds.), *Handbook of early literacy research* (pp. 66–80). New York: Guilford Press.

Anders, P. A., Hoffman, J. V., & Duffy, G. G. (2000). Teaching teachers to teach reading: Paradigm shifts, persistent problems, and challenges. In M. Kamil, P. Mosenthal, P. D. Pearson, & R. Barr (Eds.), *Handbook of reading research* (Vol. 3, pp. 721–744). Mahwah, NJ: Erlbaum.

Barnett, W. S. (1995). Long-term effects of early childhood programs on cognitive and school outcomes. *Future of Children, 5*(3), 25–50.

Barnett, W. S. (2001). Preschool education for economically disadvantaged children: Effects on reading achievement and related outcomes. In S. Neuman & D. Dickinson (Eds.), *Handbook of early literacy research* (pp. 421–443). New York: Guilford Press.

Bus, A., van IJzendoorn, M., & Pellegrini, A. (1995). Joint book reading makes for success in learning to read: A meta-analysis on intergenerational transmission of literacy. *Review of Educational Research, 65*, 1–21.

Campbell, F. A., & Raney, T. L. (1995). Cognitive and school outcomes for high-risk African-American students in middle adolescence: Positive effects of early intervention. *American Educational Research Journal, 32*(4), 743–772.

Carroll, J. M., Snowling, M. J., Hulme, C., & Stevenson, J. (2003). The development of phonological awareness in preschool children. *Developmental Psychology, 39*(5), 913–923.

Center for the Improvement of Early Reading Achievement. (2001). *Put reading first: The research building blocks for teaching children to read*. Washington, DC: U.S. Department of Education.

Clay, M. M. (1966). *Emergent reading behavior*. Unpublished doctoral dissertation, University of Auckland, New Zealand.

Cunningham, A. E., & Stanovich, K. E. (1997). Early reading acquisition and its relation to reading experience and ability 10 years later. *Developmental Psychology, 33*(6), 934–945.

Dewey, J. (1966). *Democracy and education*. New York: Free Press. (Original work published 1916).

Dickinson, D. K. (2002). Shifting images of developmentally appropriate practice as seen through different lenses. *Educational Researcher, 31*(1), 26–32.

Dickinson, D. K., Cote, L., & Smith, M. W. (1993). Learning vocabulary in preschool: Social and discourse contexts affecting vocabulary growth. In C. Daiute (Ed.), *The development of literacy through social interaction: New directions in child development* (pp. 67–78). San Francisco: Jossey-Bass.

Dickinson, D. K., McCabe, A., Anastasopoulos, L., Peisner-Feinberg, E., & Poe, M. (2003). The comprehensive language approach to early literacy: The interrelationships among vocabulary, phonological sensitivity, and print knowledge among preschool-aged children. *Journal of Educational Psychology, 95*(3), 465–481.

Fuerst, J., & Fuerst, D. (1993). Chicago experience with an early childhood program: The special case of the child–parent program. *Urban Education, 28*(1), 69–96.

Hart, B., & Risley, T. (1995). *Meaningful differences in the everyday experiences of young American children.* Baltimore: Brookes.

Hendrick, J. (Ed.). (2004). *Next steps toward teaching the Reggio way: Accepting the challenge to change.* Upper Saddle River, NJ: Pearson Education.

International Reading Association. (1999). *Using multiple methods of beginning reading instruction.* Newark, DE: Author.

International Reading Association. (2006). *Reading in preschool.* Newark, DE: Author.

International Reading Association & National Association for the Education of Young Children. (1998). *Learning to read and write: Developmentally appropriate practices for young children.* Newark, DE: International Reading Association.

Montessori, M. (1965). *Spontaneous activity in education.* New York: Schocken.

Morphett, M. V., & Washburne, C. (1931). When should children begin to read? *Elementary School Journal, 31,* 496–508.

Morrow, L. M. (2005). *Literacy development in the early years: Helping children read and write* (5th ed.). Boston: Allyn & Bacon.

Morrow, L. M., & Gambrell, L. B. (2004). *Using children's literature in preschool: Comprehending and enjoying books.* Newark, DE: International Reading Association.

Morrow, L. M., & Tracey, D. H. (1997). Strategies used for phonics instruction in early childhood classrooms. *Reading Teacher, 50*(8), 664–651.

National Early Literacy Panel Report. (2004). Washington, DC: National Institute for Literacy, National Family Literacy Association.

National Reading Panel. (2000). *Teaching children to read.* Washington, DC: National Institute of Child Health and Human Development.

Neuman, S. B., & Dickinson, D. K. (Eds.) (2001). *Handbook of early literacy research.* New York: Guilford Press.

Peisner-Feinberg, E. S., & Burchinal, M. R. (1997). Relations between preschool children's child-care experiences and concurrent development: The cost, quality, and outcomes study. *Merrill-Palmer Quarterly, 43,* 451–477.

Piaget, J., & Inhelder, B. (1969). *The psychology of the child.* New York: Basic Books.

Pressley, M. (2006). *Reading instruction that works: The case for balanced teaching* (3rd ed.) New York: Guilford Press.

Reynolds, A. J., Temple, J. A., Robertson, D. L., & Mann, E. A. (2001). Long-term effects of an early childhood intervention on educational achievement and juvenile arrest: A 15-year follow-up of low-income children in public schools. *Journal of the American Medical Association, 285,* 2339–2346.

Roskos, C., Tabors, P. O., & Lenuart, L. A. (2004). *Oral language and early literacy in preschool: Talking, reading, and writing.* Newark, DE: International Reading Association.

Rusk, R., & Scotland, J. (1979). *Doctrines of the great educators.* New York: St. Martin's Press.

Schickedanz, J., & Casbergue, R. (2004). *Writing in preschool: Learning to orchestrate meaning and marks.* Newark, DE: International Reading Association.

Schweinhart, L. J., Barnes, H. V., Weikart, D. P., Barnett, W. S., & Epstein, A. S. (1993). *Significant benefits: The High/Scope Perry Preschool study through age 27* (Monographs of the High/Scope Educational Research Foundation No. 10). Ypsilanti, MI: High/Scope Press.

Seefeldt, C., & Barbour, N. (1998). *Early childhood education: An introduction* (4th ed.). Upper Saddle River, NJ: Pearson.

Showers, B., & Joyce, B. (1996, March). The evolution of peer coaching. *Educational Leadership,* 12–16.

Shulman, L. S. (1998). Theory, practice, and the evolution of professionals. *Elementary School Journal, 9,* 511–526.

Snow, C. E., Burns, M. S., & Griffin, P. (1998). *Preventing reading difficulties in young children.* Washington, DC: National Academies Press.

Sparks, D., & Loucks-Horsley, S. (1990). Models of staff development. In R. Houston (Ed.), *Handbook of research on teacher education* (3rd ed., pp. 234–250). New York: Macmillan.

Storch, S. A., & Whitehurst, G. J. (2002). Oral language and code-related precursors to reading: Evidence from a longitudinal structural model. *Developmental Psychology, 38,* 934–947.

Strickland, D., & Schickedanz, J. (2004). *Learning about print in preschool. Working with letters, words, and beginning links with phonemic awareness.* Newark, DE: International Reading Association.

Taylor, B. M., Pearson, P. D., Clark, K. M., & Walpole, S. (2000). Effective schools and accomplished teachers: Lessons about primary-grade reading instruction in low-income schools. *Elementary School Journal, 101,* 121–165.

Vukelich, C., & Christie, J. (2004). *Building a foundation for preschool literacy: Effective instruction for children's reading and writing development.* Newark, DE: International Reading Association.

Vygotsky, L. S. (1978). *Mind in society: The development of psychological processes.* Cambridge, MA: Harvard University Press.

Wells, G. (1985). *The meaning makers.* Portsmouth, NH: Heinemann.

Whitehurst, G. J., & Lonigan, C.J. (1998). Child development and emergent literacy. *Child Development, 69*(3), 848–872.

CHAPTER 3

ORGANIZING AND MANAGING A LITERACY-RICH PRESCHOOL ENVIRONMENT

We as teachers live in our classrooms. They are our second homes and the second homes of the children who attend. The classroom environment needs to be thought about as a part of the curriculum. When speaking about the literacy-rich preschool, I discuss the physical environment of the classroom and include the creation of play settings to promote literacy and the use of materials that motivate children to want to read, such as storytelling props, varied genres of children's literature, and quality technology programs. I discuss the importance of providing an environment that is rich in literacy for all children, recognizing the different backgrounds they come from. I acknowledge their families and discuss their importance as an integral part of the preschool program. This is the only way to create a literacy-rich environment.

THE PHYSICAL ENVIRONMENT
IN EXEMPLARY PRESCHOOL CLASSROOMS

The physical environment of a classroom, including the arrangement of space, choice of materials, and the aesthetic quality created in the room, are essential ingredients for successful learning in preschool. The literacy-rich classroom is filled with meaningful language experiences and materials that encourage exploration (Morrow, 2005). The preparation of a classroom's physical environment is often overlooked in instructional planning. We concentrate on lesson planning and forget to give similar consideration to spatial arrangements in which teaching and learning occur. It is crucial that the curriculum and the environment are coordinated so that effective literacy instruction can take place.

PREPARING THE ENVIRONMENT
FOR ENGLISH LANGUAGE LEARNERS

Our schools include children from varied backgrounds. It is part of the organization and management of our programs to provide for the differences. Teachers need to be aware of cultural differences so that they can understand their effects on a child's lifestyle, values, and worldview. Teachers need to make English language learners feel comfortable learning to function in the new culture and to speak English and also to feel good about retaining their culture and first language. Good instructional strategies work for all children; however, there are many things that can be done to help English language learners. English language learners benefit from solid routines that are used daily. Teachers need to speak slowly but not in a loud voice. An English language learner can be paired with a buddy who can speak in both their native language and English. Words can be posted in English and in the home languages of the children in the class. Different colors can be used for the different language labels. A teacher can give children jobs to do, such as feeding the fish, passing out papers, and so forth, to get them immediately involved in the class routines. Pictures and props can be used in teaching. Books in the child's home language can be provided, as well as books about their culture that are written in English. The goal is to develop the child's ability to speak, read, and write English while respecting their home language (Barone, 1998; Tabors, 1998). One of our greatest challenges in schools today is the large population of English language learners who come from many different cultures and speak many different languages. When activities discussed in this book are particularly appropriate for English language learners, the icon pictured here is used. The discussion of rich literacy environments is particularly pertinent to helping English language learners.

LITERACY-RICH ENVIRONMENTS

ELL   The preschool classrooms that are exemplary are arranged so that they are "child friendly." Materials are stored for easy access, both visually and physically. The teachers find that having a variety of materials enables them to meet the different abilities and interests of their children. One classroom I observed was in the basement of an old inner-city school and was by no means picturesque. The ingenuity of the teacher, however, made the environment literacy rich, warm, and inviting. The space was adequate for the 16 children in the room, there was good lighting, and it was kept clean. A rug, rocking chair, colorful curtains on the windows, stuffed animals, a literacy center with lots of books, an author's spots with lots of writing materials, and bulletin boards featuring children's work all contributed to making it attractive and a place that was filled with literacy materials.

Literacy-rich classrooms have children's tables arranged close together so that four or five youngsters can socially interact. The rooms provide for whole-group instruction, with students sitting at their tables or on a rug in the literacy center. The area for whole-group meetings contains a chalkboard or white board, a pocket chart, and an easel with experience-chart paper. Teachers have rocking chairs that they use when doing whole-class mini-lessons or reading stories to the children.

The classrooms all have morning-meeting areas that include functional print, such as a a calendar, a weather chart, a helper chart, and rules for the classroom. Signs communicate information, such as "Quiet Please" and "Please Put Materials Away after Using Them."

Print materials from the real world, such as traffic signs and familiar food and department store names and logos, are displayed as well. All print material has some type of picture or logo to help children understand what is written. The rooms have notice boards used to talk with the children through writing. In addition, there are word walls. The children's names are the most prominent words on the walls, and there are words dealing with current themes being discussed, for example, animals in the forest or plants. The word wall is described more thoroughly in Chapter 6. Other materials in the room represent the units being studied, such as children's fictional and informational literature, books made by the class, artwork, and so forth. An alphabet chart is on the wall at eye level for children to see.

In addition to whole-class instruction, the teachers I observed have all arranged their rooms for small-group and one-on-one teaching. A table in the shape of a half moon is situated on one side of the room. At this table, the teacher

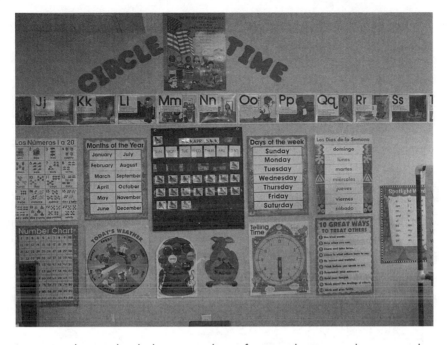

Literacy-rich preschool classrooms have functional print, such as a pocket calendar chart, weather charts, helper charts, and rules for the classroom.

meets with small groups and individual children for lessons that are based on the children's needs and that include explicit instruction in literacy. The teacher has all the materials she or he uses for skill instruction in this area. These include a pocket chart, an experience chart, individual writing slates, and magnetic boards with magnetic letters for dealing with knowledge about print and writing. In addition, there are theme related books and folders for assessing and recording student accomplishments and needs. There are corrugated cardboard bins labeled with children's names, where they store individual work. These materials are packaged in zip lock plastic bags.

The entire classroom is student friendly, with quiet areas such as the literacy center next to the math area and blocks next to the dramatic-play area (see Figure 3.1). To accommodate small-group, independent work, there are *learning centers,* each labeled according to content areas. The centers integrate literacy learning into content areas by featuring reading and writing activities. The teachers believe that literacy activities have more meaning when integrated into content areas. Therefore, it is common to find paper and pencils in the block and dramatic-play areas, and books in the art and music centers. The teachers use themes such as the family, the community, or the seasons to develop new vocabulary, new ideas, and purposes for reading and writing. Each of the centers has general materials that are typical of the content they represent but also special materials that are linked to the current thematic topics of study and literacy materials, as well.

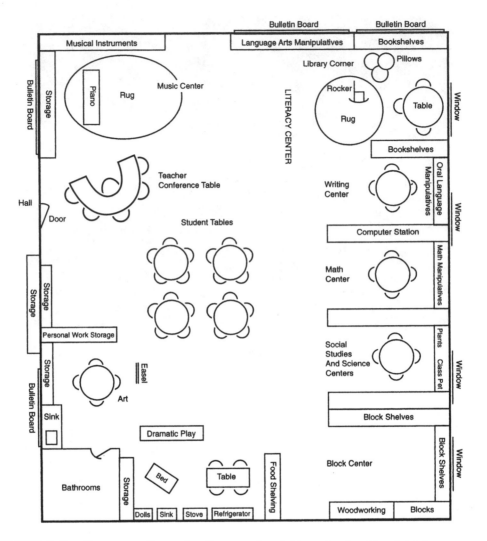

FIGURE 3.1. Classroom floor plan for preschool. From Lesley Mandel Morrow, *Literacy Development in the Early Years: Helping Children Read and Write,* 5th ed. Published by Allyn and Bacon, Boston, MA. Copyright © 2005 by Pearson Education. Reprinted by permission of the publisher.

The Music Center

This area includes a piano, guitar, or other real instruments. There are also rhythm instruments, such as bells, triangles, rhythm sticks, or cymbals, with an effort to feature some from different countries, such as maracas from Mexico and a Caribbean steel drum. CDs feature music that connects to themes, such as songs about the different seasons. One teacher selected "Rain Rain Go Away" and "If All of the Raindrops Were Lemon Drops and Gumdrops" when studying spring; it was the rainy season in the area where these children lived. The children learned new vocabulary words from these songs and selected some words for their word wall. Another activity included drawing rain pictures and dictating to the teacher something they wanted written on them. Some children could write a word or two on their pictures themselves. The rain pictures became a class book.

The Art Center

This center includes easels and multiple types of paper in different sizes. There are colored pencils, markers, watercolors, and collage materials such as pipe cleaners, foil paper, wool, string, and fabrics for all types of creative artwork. Depending on the theme, different materials are added. Play dough was put into the center when the class was studying zoo animals so children could create models of animals. Books that illustrate animals are available for children to look at to help with their designs. Labels are provided so the children can write down the type of animal they made and their animal's name.

The Social Studies Center

This center is particularly important for themes such as the study of different cultures, the family, friends, and the community. These themes focus on getting along with others, on recognizing and appreciating differences and likenesses in people, on learning to respect oneself and others, on developing values, and on a sense of community in the classroom. Appropriate books accompany these ideas. In addition, some general social studies materials include maps, a globe, flags from various countries, pictures of community figures, traffic signs, current events, and artifacts from other countries. When the class was studying Mexico, Jose's father came to read *The Three Pigs* (Brenner, 1972), in Spanish, and then

ELL the teacher read it in English. The children talked about some words that sounded the same in both languages. Juan's mom made tortillas for the class to eat for their snack.

The Science Center

This center is always popular, with interesting objects to explore and experiment with, such as magnets, simple machines, and plants. Other equipment includes an aquarium, terrarium, thermometer, compass, prism, shells, rock collections, a stethoscope, a kaleidoscope, and a microscope. When the class studies the five senses or good nutrition and good health habits, materials are added.

The Math Center

Children will find an abacus, varied types of currency, scales, rulers, measuring cups, clocks with movable parts, a stopwatch, a calendar, a cash register, a calculator, a number line, a height chart, an hourglass, different types of manipulative numbers (felt, wood, magnetic), fraction puzzles, and geometric shapes in the math center. The units that will be studied in this preschool program include activities that emphasize measuring, in "Growing Like Me," and recording numbers of members in "My Family and My Community." There are, of course, books and paper to add to this area to enrich the ideas discussed. Content areas interrelate, as in this example social studies and math are being used in the same unit.

Block Area

In the block center are found many different sizes, shapes, and textures of blocks, figures of people, animals, toy cars, trucks, and items related to themes being studied, such as tractors for the building unit. Books about the themes are useful for constructing theme-related structures. There need to be paper and pencils to make labels for constructions created by the children.

The Dramatic-Play Center

This center includes dolls, dress-up clothing, a telephone, stuffed animals, a mirror, food cartons, plates, silverware, newspapers, magazines, books, a telephone book, cookbooks, notepads, and a kitchen setting with a table and chairs. The area has a broom, a dustpan, a refrigerator, storage shelves, and a theme that coordinates with the theme studied. For example, there may be restaurants from different cultural backgrounds in the dramatic-play area, such as a Chinese or Italian restaurant with menus, recipes, a cash register, play money, and checks. One day I recorded the following conversation between two children, Darlene and Jamal, as they were pretending to be a mom and dad going to the supermarket. "Now let's make a list for the supermarket. I have the pencil and paper. What do we need?" said Darlene. "We need more Sugar Pops cereal. We are all out of it." Jamal said, "That's not so good for your teeth, and we will get fat from all of that sugar. We have to find another cereal. Just write down cereal. Here, it says it on this box. You can copy it." "I know," said Darlene. "We can get some cereal bars. They taste good and my mommy said they are good for you. They have protein and other good stuff."

This conversation went on for quite a while, with discussions about calories, fat content, protein, carbohydrates, sugar, and so forth. The children were studying good nutrition, and what they were learning was being assimilated into their play. The materials in the environment and some modeling and scaffolding by teachers encouraged this productive activity.

In Chapter 5, I elaborate on the importance of play to stimulate language and to enhance social interaction, as well as problem solving. Several play settings that enhance language and literacy are mentioned there. In play settings, children interact and collaborate in small groups. When it is designed to promote literacy learning, the dramatic-play area is coordinated with a social studies or science theme that is being studied to bring meaning to the experience. Materials for reading and writing are provided to support the play theme, and during play children read, write, speak, and listen to one another, using literacy in functional ways.

Although early childhood educators have realized the value of play for social, emotional, and physical development, in the past it has not been viewed as a way to develop literacy. Play has gained greater importance as a medium for literacy development because it provides motivating, meaningful, and functional social settings. Literacy development involves a child's active engagement in cooperation and collaboration with peers, builds on what the child already knows, and thrives on the support and guidance of others. Play provides this setting. During observations of children at play, one can see the functional uses of literacy that children incorporate into their play themes. Children have been observed engaging in attempted and conventional reading and writing in collaboration with other youngsters (Morrow, 1990, Neuman & Roskos, 1992).

The Literacy Center

The literacy center (see Figure 3.2) should be one of the focal points in a preschool classroom. It should give the message that literacy is so important that a special spot is made to provide space for writing, reading, oral language, listening, comprehension, and word-study materials and that time is provided to use this space.

This area contains a rocking chair and rug, as many of the activities in this center take place on the floor. It is here that the teacher has group meetings, lessons, and story time. Pillows and stuffed animals add an element of softness.

Books are stored in open-faced shelving for displaying titles about themes being studied. These books are changed with the themes and to feature special selections. Books are also stored in plastic baskets that are labeled by genre, such as books about animals, seasons, poetry, families, and so forth. Pictures accompany the labels.

Well-stocked preschool classroom libraries have five to eight book selections per child at about three to four different levels of difficulty. Ways to enhance the number of books in your collection inexpensively include visiting flea markets, redeeming points from book clubs, getting donations from parents, and using allotted classroom budgets. The teachers rotate their books regularly to maintain children's interest in them, and children can check books out of the classroom to read at home.

To ensure continued interest, the teacher must introduce new books and materials and recirculate others in the library corner. Approximately 25 new books should be introduced every 2 weeks, replacing 25 that have been there for a while. In this way, "old" books will be greeted as new friends a few months later.

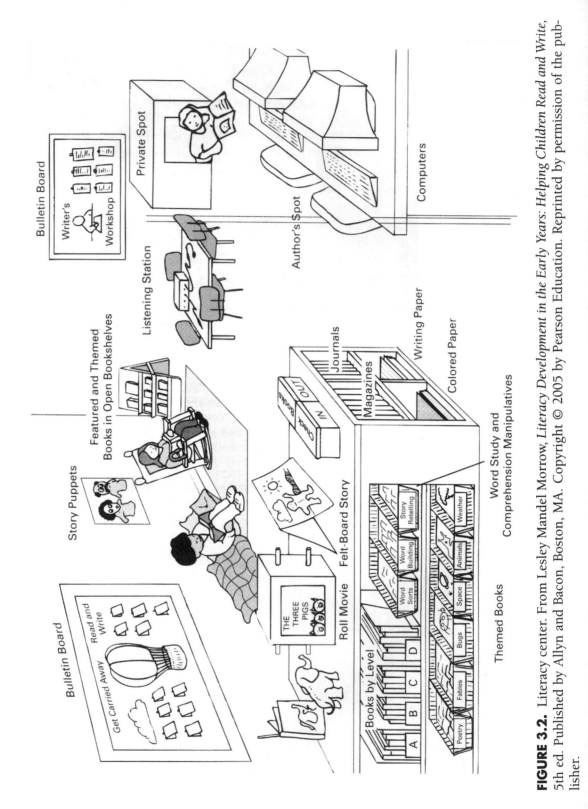

FIGURE 3.2. Literacy center. From Lesley Mandel Morrow, *Literacy Development in the Early Years: Helping Children Read and Write*, 5th ed. Published by Allyn and Bacon, Boston, MA. Copyright © 2005 by Pearson Education. Reprinted by permission of the publisher.

BOOKS IN THE LIBRARY CORNER

Books and other materials selected for the library corner should appeal to a variety of interests and span a range of grade levels. It is advisable to stock multiple copies of popular books. Children sometimes enjoy reading a book because a friend is reading it (Morrow, 1985). Several types of children's literature should be represented.

➤ *Picture storybooks* are most familiar to us as children's literature. Their texts are closely associated with their illustrations. Picture storybooks are available on a wide range of topics, and many are known for their excellence. The Caldecott Medal is awarded annually to the illustrator of an outstanding picture storybook. Many of these books have become classics and their authors renowned—Dr. Seuss, Ezra Jack Keats, Tomie dePaola, Maurice Sendak, and Charlotte Zolotow, to name just a few. Every child should have the benefit of hearing some of these books read. However, emergent readers will often find the vocabulary and syntax too sophisticated to read on their own. Quality picture storybooks will include a setting, a well-defined theme, episodes closely tied to the theme, and a resolution to the story.

➤ *Informational books* offer nonfiction for children. For a while we didn't include much expository text in our libraries, thinking that young children liked narratives more. As adults we read material that is mostly nonfiction; therefore, we need a lot of experience with this type of text. Informational text can be about foreign countries, communities, dinosaurs, famous people, and so forth. These texts broaden children's background information, help them to explore new ideas, and often stimulate a deep interest in a particular topic. Quality expository texts will have a definitive structure. Good structures found in expository texts include description, sequence, compare and contrast, cause and effect, problem and solution, and exemplification.

➤ *Picture concept books* are appropriate for the very young child. Most picture concept books do not have story lines, though they often have themes, such as animals or toys. Each page usually carries a picture identified by a printed word. Many picture books are made of cardboard, cloth, or vinyl to withstand rigorous handling. Alphabet and number books are also considered picture concept books.

➤ *Traditional literature* includes nursery rhymes and fairy tales, familiar stories that are part of our heritage and that originated in the oral tradition of storytelling. We assume that children are familiar with *Goldilocks and the Three Bears* (Izawa, 1968a) and *The Three Little Pigs* (Brenner, 1972), yet many youngsters have not been exposed to these traditional stories. Children who do know the stories welcome them as old friends.

➤ *Realistic literature* is a category within picture storybooks that deals with real-life problems. *Tight Times* (1983) by Barbara Hazen, for example, describes how a family handles the problems that arise when the father loses his job. He tries to explain the situation to his son so that he will understand when he calls it "tight times." Books in this category deal with issues that many children face, such as bedtime fears or problems that arise when a new baby comes into the family. These books touch on very sensitive issues, such as divorce, drugs, alcohol, and death. Many can be read to the entire class if they address issues that all share. Teachers should use discretion in determining what to read to the whole class. They can recommend specific titles to families of children who face difficult issues.

➤ *Easy-to-read books* are designed to be read by emergent readers themselves. They have limited and repeated vocabularies, and many of them rhyme, making them predictable and easy to read independently. Because of their limited vocabularies, few easy-to-read books rate as quality literature, but many preschool and kindergarten children begin to read independently with them.

➤ *Fables and folktales* retell many of the myths and traditional stories that are available in picture-book style for the younger child. Many of these stories originate in other countries and cultures and therefore broaden a child's experience and knowledge base.

➤ *Wordless books* carry definite story lines within pictures but use no words. They are often thought appropriate for very young children and are confused with picture books. They are designed not for babies but for children 3 years and older. The child creates the story by reading the pictures, some of which are intricate.

➤ *Poetry* is too often forgotten in collections of children's literature at home and in school. Many themed anthologies have been compiled for young children, and they are an important part of the literacy center. These add to the study of specific topics. There are multiple types of poetry to which children should also be exposed.

➤ *Biography* is another genre appropriate for young children. Simple biographies of historical figures and popular figures in sports and on television are available.

➤ *Big Books* are usually large versions of smaller picture storybooks or original picture storybooks in this large format. They are oversized books that rest on an easel in order to be read. The purpose of the Big Book is to allow children to see the print as it is being read, to make the association between oral and written language, and to see how the print is read from left to right across the page.

In addition to these categories of books, young children enjoy joke and riddle books; craft books; cookbooks; participation books, which involve them in touching, smelling, and manipulating; books in a series built around a single character; and books related to television programs appropriate for their age. As mentioned, magazines and newspapers should also be choices for reading in the library corner.

They provide a nonthreatening format, different topics, and reading matter for diverse ability levels, and they include multicultural material. Newspapers and magazines appeal to parents, as well.

Children particularly enjoy literature that is predictable because it helps them understand the story line more easily and enables them to read along with the individual reading to them. Predictable literature contains rhyme; repetition; catch phrases; conversation; familiar sequences, such as days of the week or numbers; cumulative patterns, in which events are repeated or added on as the story continues; stories about familiar topics; familiar or popular stories; uncluttered illustrations that match the text; and stories that have well-developed story structures (setting, theme, plot episodes, and resolution).

Literacy manipulatives, such as puppets, stories on tape with headsets, felt boards with story characters, and electronic stories, are included in the literacy center to engage children with books through different modalities. The story manipulatives help children learn to retell stories, an excellent comprehension strategy and assessment tool. The literacy center also has a shelf of manipulative materials that offer practice in concepts concerning print. These materials, which include matching games, rhyming games, and magnetic, wood, and felt letters, help children learn the alphabet, phonemic awareness, and some sound–symbol relationships.

CREATIVE STORYTELLING MATERIALS TO ENRICH THE ENVIRONMENT

Reading stories to children is crucial and is discussed in Chapter 7. Storytelling is another means of attracting children to books (Ritchie, James-Szanton & Howes, 2003). Storytelling frees the storyteller to use his or her hands for gestures and to use creative techniques. It also has the advantage of keeping the storyteller close to the audience. Telling a story produces an immediate response from the audience and is one of the surest ways to establish a rapport between the listeners and the storyteller. Long pieces of literature can be trimmed so that even very young children can hear whole stories in one sitting. Considered an art, storytelling can be mastered by most people.

It is not necessary to memorize a story, but be sure that you know it well. Use all the catch phrases and quotes that are important to the story. Use expression in your presentation, but do not let your dramatic techniques overshadow the story itself. Look directly at your audience and take their attention into consideration. Storytelling allows you to shorten stories if the attention spans of your listeners are short. Always have the original book at hand when you have finished telling a story so that the children can see it and enjoy it again through its pictures and printed text. Storytelling can be done without props, and it is important to do. Storytelling with creative techniques adds another dimension to the art.

Creative techniques help storytelling come alive. They excite the imagination, involve the listeners, and motivate children to try storytelling themselves and eventually to create their own techniques. Take clues for creative techniques from the story. Some stories lend themselves to the use of puppets, others are perfect for the felt board, and still others can be worked up as chalk talks.

➤ *Felt boards with story characters* are a popular and important tool in a classroom. You can make characters or purchase them. Prepare your own with construction paper covered with clear contact paper or laminate. Attach strips of felt or sandpaper to the backs of the cutouts so they cling to the felt board. Narrative and expository texts that lend themselves to felt-board retelling are those with a limited number of characters who appear throughout the story or with a limited number of ideas.

➤ *Puppets* are used with stories rich in dialogue. There are many kinds of puppets, including finger, hand, stick, and face puppets. Shy children often feel secure telling stories with puppets. Such stories as *The Gingerbread Boy*

Story retelling with props such as a felt board helps language development and comprehension development with English language learners and English-speaking children as well.

(Holdsworth, 1968) and *The Little Red Hen* (Izawa, 1968b) are appropriately told with puppets because they are short, have few characters, and repeat dialogue. An informational book can be retold by a puppet as well.

➤ *Sound–story techniques* allow both audience and storyteller to provide sound effects when called for in a book. The sounds can be made with voices, rhythm instruments, or music. When preparing to tell a sound story, select those parts of the story for which sound effects will be used. Then decide on each sound to be made and who will make it. As the story is told, children and the story-teller chime in with their assigned sounds. Record the presentation, and then leave the recording in the literacy center with the original book for the children to listen to. Among books that adapt easily to sound–story techniques are *Too Much Noise* (McGovern, 1967) and *Mr. Brown Can Moo! Can You?* (Dr. Seuss, 1970).

➤ *Prop stories* are easy to develop. Simply collect stuffed animals, toys, and other articles that represent characters and objects in a story. Display the props at appropriate times during the storytelling. Three stuffed bears and a yellow-haired doll aid in telling *Goldilocks and the Three Bears* (Izawa, 1968a). Several toy trains aid in *The Little Engine That Could* (Piper, 1954) and could be used with an infor-mational book about trains, as well.

➤ *Chalk talks* are another technique that attract listeners. The storyteller draws the story while telling it. Chalk talks are most effective when done with a large chalkboard or white board and markers so that the story can keep going in sequence from beginning to end. The same technique can be carried out on mural paper hung across a wall. With mural paper, the storyteller simply uses crayons or markers. The chalk talk technique can also be adapted to chart paper on an easel or on an overhead projector. Choose a story with simple illustrations. Draw only a select few pictures as you tell the story. Don't worry about how your illustrations look. There are stories that have been written as chalk talks, including an entire series, *Harold and the Purple Crayon* (Johnson, 1955).

➤ *Headsets with stories on CDs* are also popular materials in the literacy cen-ter. This is not a substitute for reading and telling stories but another source for hearing them. When children listen to a CD of a story, they can follow along in the text. They are helpful with English language learners because they provide a model for correct English. They are also good for preschoolers, who can follow along in the text while listening to a fluent reader. Have parents, the principal, teachers, the nurse, the superintendent, and others known to the children record stories on CDs. Eventually children can make their own CDs by pretend reading or retelling a story they know well. Numerous techniques for storytelling that are not mentioned can be added to the list. All techniques and materials need to be mod-eled for children so they can become storytellers themselves.

ELL

CHILDREN'S CREATION
OF STORYTELLING TECHNIQUES

Children can create their own storytelling techniques themselves. The teacher should help them select a piece of children's literature they know well, such as *The Little Red Hen* (Izawa, 1968b) or *Goldilocks and the Three Bears* (Izawa, 1968a). They may tell the story of *Goldilocks* using three stuffed bears and a doll. When it is complete, the children who worked on the project can present it to the class and leave it in the center for others to use.

Storytelling activities involve children in literal comprehension because they must know the sequence, details, and elements of the story. They must problem solve as they create the materials, deciding what parts of the story to include or delete. They interpret voices of characters as they present their finished projects to the class.

INDEPENDENT READING AND WRITING

Research has shown that the amount of free reading done by children, both in and out of school, correlates with reading achievement. In a large-scale investigation of elementary school children, it was found that students who reported reading 2 minutes a day outside of school scored at the 30th percentile on standardized reading tests. Children who read 5 minutes a day scored at the 50th percentile. Those who read 10 minutes a day scored at the 70th percentile, and children who read 20 minutes a day scored at the 90th percentile (Anderson, Fielding, & Wilson, 1988; Taylor, Frye, & Maruyama, 1990). Children who read voluntarily develop lifelong positive attitudes toward reading.

Reading and looking at books in preschool is important. The habit of voluntary independent reading can begin here. With preschool children we need to structure quiet book time a bit. The book selection should consist of books children have heard read to them. The selection should be limited to a small number of books so children don't find it difficult to select one. Children can read alone or with a partner. Before they begin quiet book time, teachers should discuss the rules, such as staying with one or two books during the reading time, talking softly if they talk, or that they will be asked to talk about their books after the period is done. After quiet book time, we can ask some children to report on something about their book, such as which picture they like best and why, the part of the story they liked best, and so forth. Independent reading should take place on the rug in the literacy center (Ritchie, James-Szanton, & Howes, 2003).

The Author's Spot

A portion of the literacy center called the "author's spot" is set aside and includes a table, chairs, and writing materials such as colored markers, crayons, pencils, chalk, a stapler, a hole punch, a chalkboard, and a white board. There are various types and sizes of paper, such as newsprint, mural paper, lined paper, and colored paper. Classrooms should have bookbinding machines for making class books. Children are provided with journals, and their use is supervised. There are index cards used for recording children's Very Own Words, which are stored in index boxes. Folders, one for each child, are used to collect picture and writing samples. Classrooms should have about two computers in each room that are in good working order with excellent software for writing and reading activities.

Teachers prepare blank books for children to write in that relate to themes being studied, for example, different animal-shaped books when studying animals or books shaped like snowmen, flowers, and so forth, to represent different seasons. There is a place for children to display their written work, and a mailbox, stationery, envelopes, and stamps for children to write to each other and to pen pals.

Observations in preschools of children in literacy centers during center time revealed the following discussions and activities.

Natalie, James, and Jovanna snuggled together in a large refrigerator box that had been painted to make it more attractive. Furnished with stuffed animals, it created a "private spot" for reading.

Jamal and Veronica were using the felt board and story characters for *Mr. Rabbit and the Lovely Present* (Zolotow, 1962), taking turns retelling the story while looking at the pages of the book and putting the figures up on the felt board at the appropriate times. When they came to repetitive phrases in the story *Goldilocks and the Three Bears* (Izawa, 1968a), such as "Who's been sleeping in my bed?," they chanted the words together.

Four children were listening to a CD on headsets to the story *The Very Busy Spider* (Carle, 1985). Each child had a copy of the book. When they came to the phrase that is repeated often, "The spider didn't answer, he was very busy spinning his web," the children chanted along. Daniel and Damien were at the author's table looking at informational books about frogs. They drew pictures and copied words from the books while discussing the characteristics of the frogs, such as, "This one is green and has a pointy tongue." "This one is eating a fly."

Keisha had multiple copies of a story the teacher had read to the class several times. She handed out the copies to the other children and kept one for herself. She made a circle of chairs in which the group then sat as she pretended to be the teacher. She pretend read to the others. She asked the children questions about the story when she was done reading.

TECHNOLOGY MATERIALS IN THE PRESCHOOL

James knew how to turn on the computer and had used it, with the help of one of his parents, before he was 2. By the time he was 2½ he could find the CD he wanted, put it in the right drive in the computer, and use the mouse. By age 3 he was totally adept at manipulating the mouse on a PC or a touch pad on a laptop. He could adjust the sound volume as well. The computer is part of his life. He is familiar with the keyboard and is beginning to type words with assistance, to copy words, and to write some alone. Of course, he can type his name.

Technology is crucial in preschool, especially for children who do not have access to computers at home. Everyone will have to be computer literate in order to obtain any kind of job. Technology offers young children opportunities to develop literacy skills. Computers allow children to construct knowledge in social or independent literacy settings. For example, electronic books provide a wonderful model of reading for preschool children. Computers are a source of motivation for literacy development.

Computer Software

Teachers most commonly use software programs when using computers with children. Computers need CD-ROM and DVD drives to run software programs.

The following features should be looked for when selecting software (Wepner & Ray, 2000):

> The activity should be concise, clear, and easy to use.

> The activities should be engaging, should promote active participation, and should hold the attention and interest of young children.

> The content should match and expand on what children are learning in the school curriculum.

> The program should provide practice with concepts being learned.

> The text should be narrated for children to enable them to do the activities independently.

> There should be a guide to introduce teachers to the software and help them use it.

> Assessment should be provided.

> Skills are introduced in a predictable sequence.

> Feedback should be focused and immediate.

> The software program should provide repetition and feedback.

> Children should be engaged in an active manner with the software.

Quality software is available for every type of literacy skill, such as the development of phonemic awareness, listening comprehension, vocabulary, writing, and so forth.

The Internet

ELL   The Internet has endless possibilities in the classroom. Instead of corresponding with pen pals through regular mail, children now e-mail other children instantly all over the world. The World Wide Web is an unlimited resource for information related to whatever children are studying. For example, for a unit about bugs, the teacher can collect books about bugs for the room and locate an appropriate website for children to use as a source for more information. In addition, schools and classrooms can create their own websites to post children's work and let parents know what they are studying.

Evaluating Literacy-Rich Environments

Based on the evidence it is clear that the environment is an important part of literacy instruction. Teachers can evaluate the richness of their literacy environment with a measure called the Classroom Literacy Environmental Profile (CLEP; Wolfersberger, Reutzel, Sudweeks, & Fawson, 2004). This instrument was tested in a systematic manner and examines the "print richness" of early childhood classrooms. Rooms are rated with a point scale containing descriptors that evaluate the quantity, utility, and appropriateness of literacy-related objects or tools and the quantity of genres, levels, formats, and content of books. It measures the classroom organization of print and student literacy product displays, forms of written communications, writing utensils, writing surfaces, publishing supplies, and technology available.

FAMILY INVOLVEMENT ENRICHES THE LITERACY ENVIRONMENT

Family members are children's first teachers. They are the teachers that children have for the longest period of time. Quality early childhood programs in literacy-rich environments engage family members as an integral part of the language and literacy programs in school and at home. All children are likely to become more successful readers and writers when teachers include a strong family involvement component in their literacy programs (Wasik, 2004). In addition to participating in such activities as back-to-school nights, coming to watch their children perform in school programs, bringing cupcakes for birthday parties, helping on class trips, and running off black-line masters, parents must be informed about the literacy program and how they can help at home and in school. Equally important, teachers need to learn about children's home lives and literacy experiences from their parents. Parents should come to school during the day to observe the program, to read to children, to share their cultural backgrounds and special skills, to help make center materials, and to supervise during center time. Working parents should be able to spend an hour twice a year if they are given a variety of times during which they can come to school. A newsletter should go to families once a month to keep them informed about what is happening in school, what they can to at home to help, what they can send to school to help, and what they can do in school to help. Families must feel welcome in school and as partners in the education of their children. Following are some activities teachers can provide to help parents help their children develop literacy.

1. Provide a monthly newsletter about literacy-related activities in school.

2. Ask parents to participate in literacy-related activities in school, such as reading to children; sharing hobbies, jobs, and their cultural traditions; and coming to school to help at center time so teachers can work with individual children.

3. Have a workshop for parents to discuss activities in the school literacy program and what they can do at home to help.

4. Provide a list for parents with suggestions of books to buy for their home libraries or to borrow from the public library.

Family involvement is crucial to the success of a literacy program in preschool.

Family involvement is crucial to the success of a literacy program in preschool. Information about family activities is embedded throughout the book, marked by the family icon shown at the left.

FINAL COMMENTS ABOUT THE ENVIRONMENT

Everything in classrooms should have a purpose, a function, and a place to be stored. The teacher models new materials and discusses what the materials teach, how they are used, and where they belong. Early in the school year, only a few items are in the centers, so the children can learn to use them properly. The teacher adds items slowly as different themes and skills are studied.

Teachers establish clear rules, routines, and expectations for behavior. These rules and routines are consistent on a day-to-day basis (Weinstein & Mignano, 1996). The teacher communicates the rules and expectations in a supportive manner, showing respect for students at all times.

Historically, theorists and philosophers emphasized the importance of the environment in early learning and literacy development. Montessori (1965), for example, advocated carefully prepared classrooms to promote independent learning and recommended that each kind of material be easily accessible and have a specific learning objective.

Children like cozy private corners with pillows and rugs to retreat to. Privacy is important for those who are distractible and have difficulty relating to peers (Weinstein & Mignano, 1996). Young children work best in rooms with variation; that is, that have warm and cool colors, some open areas and cozy spots, and both hard and soft surfaces (Morrow, 2005; Neuman & Roskos, 1992; Olds, 1987).

The preschool classroom environment described contains the characteristics proven to be important for effective organization and management of instruction. With the support of appropriate materials for lessons planned by teachers, well-designed classrooms, concern for diverse backgrounds, and parent involvement, children's literacy development should flourish.

REFERENCES

Anderson, R. C., Fielding, L. G., & Wilson, P. T. (1988). Growth in reading and how children spend their time outside of school. *Reading Research Quarterly, 23,* 285–303.

Barker, R. G. (1978). Stream of individual behavior. In R. Barker & Associates (Eds.), *Habitats, environments, and human behavior* (pp. 3–16). San Francisco: Jossey-Bass.

Barone, D. (1998). How do we teach literacy to children who are learning English as a second language? In S. Neuman & K. Roskos (Eds.), *Children achieving: Best practices in early literacy* (pp. 56–76). Newark, DE: International Reading Association.

Cambourne, B. (2001). What do I do with the rest of the class? The nature of teaching-learning activities. *Language Arts, 79*(2), 124–135.

Chall, J. S., Jacobs, V. A., & Baldwin, L. W. (1990). *The reading crisis: Why poor children fall behind.* Cambridge, MA: Harvard University Press.

Clark, C. M., & Peterson, P. L. (1986). Teachers' thought processes. In M. C. Wittrock (Ed.), *Handbook of reading research on teaching* (pp. 255–296). New York: Macmillan.

Froebel, F. (1974). *The education of man.* Clifton, NJ: Kelly.

Gump, P. V. (1989). Ecological psychology and issues of play. In M. N. Bloch & D. Pellegrini (Eds.), *The ecological context of children's play* (pp. 35–56). Norwood, NJ: Ablex.

Holmes, R., & Cunningham, B. (1995). Young children's knowledge of their classrooms: Names, activities, and purposes of learning centers. *Education and Treatment of Children, 18*(4), 433–443.

Kershner, R., & Pointon, P. (2000). Children's views of the primary classroom as an environment for working and learning. *Research in Education, 64,* 64–78.

Labba, L. D., & Ash, G. E. (1998). What is the role of computer-related technology in early literacy? In S. B. Neuman & K. A. Roskos (Eds.), *Children achieving: Best practices in early literacy* (pp. 180–197). Newark, DE: International Reading Association.

Loughlin, C. E., & Martin, M. D. (1987). *Supporting literacy: Developing effective learning environments.* New York: Teachers College Press.

Montessori, M. (1965). *Spontaneous activity in education.* New York: Schocken Books.

Moore, G. (1986). Effects of the spatial definition of behavior settings on children's behavior: A quasi-experimental field study. *Journal of Environmental Psychology, 6,* 205–231.

Morrow, L. M. (1985). Retelling stories: A strategy for improving children's comprehension, concept of story structure, and oral language complexity. *Elementary School Journal, 85,* 647–661.

Morrow, L. M. (1990). Preparing the classroom environment to promote literacy during play. *Early Childhood Research Quarterly, 5,* 537–554.

Morrow, L. M. (2002). *The literacy center: Contexts for reading and writing* (2nd ed.). York, ME: Stenhouse.

Morrow, L. M. (2005). *Literacy development in the early years: Helping children read and write* (5th ed.). Boston: Allyn & Bacon.

Neuman, S., & Roskos, K. (1997). Literacy knowledge in practice: Contexts of participation for young writers and readers. *Reading Research Quarterly, 32*(1), 10–33.

Neuman, S. B., & Roskos, K. (1992). Literacy objects as cultural tools: Effects on children's literacy behaviors in play. *Reading Research Quarterly, 27*(3), 203–225.

Olds, A. R. (1987). Designing settings for infants and toddlers. In C. S. Weinstein & T. G. David (Eds.), *Spaces for children: The built environment and child development* (pp. 117–138). New York: Plenum Press.

Pressley, M., Rankin, J., & Yokoi, L. (1996). A survey of the instructional practices of outstanding primary-level literacy teachers. *Elementary School Journal, 96,* 363–384.

Ritchie, S., James-Szanton, J., & Howes, C. (2003). Emergent literacy practices in early childhood classrooms. In C. Howes (Ed.), *Teaching 4- to 8-year-olds: Literacy, math, multiculturalism, and classroom community* (pp. 71–92). Baltimore: Brookes.

Rivlin, L., & Weinstein, C. S. (1984). Educational issues, school settings, and environmental psychology. *Journal of Environmental Psychology, 4*, 347–364.

Rusk, R., & Scotland, J. (1979). *Doctrines of the great educators.* New York: St. Martin's Press.

Tabors, P. (1998). What early childhood educators need to know: Developing effective programs for linguistically and culturally diverse children and families. *Young Children, 53*(6), 20–26.

Taylor, B. M., Frye, B. J., & Maruyama, M. (1990). Time spent reading and reading growth. *American Educational Research Journal, 27*, 351–362.

Taylor, N. E., Blum, I. H., & Logsdon, D. M. (1986). The development of written language awareness: Environmental aspects and program characteristics. *Reading Research Quarterly, 21*(2), 132–149.

Vygotsky, L. S. (1978). *Mind in society.* Cambridge, MA: Harvard University Press.

Wasik, B. H. (Ed.). (2004). *Handbook of family literacy.* Mahwah, NJ: Erlbaum.

Weinstein, C. S. (1981). Classroom design as an external condition for learning. *Educational Technology, 21*, 12–19.

Weinstein, C. S., & Mignano, A. J., Jr. (1996). *Elementary classroom management.* New York: McGraw-Hill.

Wepner, S. B., & Ray, L. C. (2000). Sign of the times: Technology and early literacy learning. In D. S. Strickland & L. M. Morrow (Eds.), *Beginning reading and writing* (pp. 168–182). New York: Teachers College Press.

Wolfersberger, M., Reutzel, D. R., Sudweeks, R., & Fawson, P. F. (2004). Developing and validating the Classroom Literacy Environmental Profile (CLEP). A tool for examining the "print richness" of elementary classrooms. *Journal of Literacy Research, 36*(2), 211–272.

CHILDREN'S LITERATURE

Brenner, B. (1972). *The three little pigs.* New York: Random House.

Carle, E. (1985). *The very busy spider.* New York: Philomel.

Dr. Seuss (1940). *Horton hatches the egg.* New York: Random House.

Dr. Seuss (1970). *Mr. Brown can moo! Can you?* New York: Random House.

Eastman, P. D. (1960). *Are you my mother?* New York: Random House.

Galdone, P. (1975). *The three bears.* Boston: Houghton Mifflin.

Hazen, B. (1983). *Tight times.* New York: Picture Puffin.

Holdsworth, W. (1968). *The gingerbread boy.* New York: Farrar, Straus & Giroux.

Izawa, T. (1968a). *Goldilocks and the three bears.* New York: Grosset & Dunlap.

Izawa, T. (1968b). *The little red hen.* New York: Grosset & Dunlap.

Johnson, C. (1955). *Harold and the purple crayon.* New York: Harper & Row.

McGovern, A. (1967). *Too much noise.* Boston: Houghton Mifflin.

Piper, W. (1954). *The little engine that could.* New York: Platt and Munk.

Zolotow, C. (1962). *Mr. Rabbit and the lovely present.* New York: Harper & Row.

CHAPTER 4

ORGANIZING AND MANAGING INSTRUCTION IN PRESCHOOL

Small-group instruction with the teacher.

One of the advantages of preschool is that teachers work with the same group of children in a half- or whole-day setting. As a result, teachers can really get to know their students and design instruction based on student interests and needs. In addition, preschool teachers are responsible for creating the classroom environment, teaching all of the content areas, administering assessment measures, putting instruction together in a meaningful way, and working with parents. In this chapter I discuss three important issues related to classroom organization and management when teaching literacy skills: (1) thematic instruction; (2) assessment to guide instruction; and (3) instruction in whole-class, small-group, and one-to-one settings to ensure that individual needs are met.

THEMATIC INSTRUCTION: INTEGRATION OF LITERACY AND CONTENT

As mentioned in Chapter 2, John Dewey (1916/1966) was largely responsible for bringing the concept of an interdisciplinary approach to teaching. This interdisciplinary approach, or the integrated school day, teaches skills from all content areas within the context of a topic or theme being studied. The themes that are studied at school come from children's real-life experiences and topics of interest. Learning experiences are socially interactive and process-oriented, giving children time to explore and experiment with varied materials. If, for example, a class is studying dinosaurs, the students talk about them, read about them, write about them, do art projects related to dinosaurs, and sing songs related to the theme. In doing so, they learn about dinosaurs and develop skills in all of the content areas. Literacy activities are purposefully integrated into the study of themes and in all content areas throughout the school day (Pappas, Kiefer, & Levstik, 1995).

Preparing a Thematic Unit

Themes that are used to integrate the curriculum can be selected by the teacher and the children. Giving students a choice between two or three themes to learn about is important. It gives the students a sense of empowerment. When the topic is selected, allow the children to brainstorm about what they would like to learn (Rand, 1993). For example, in preparation for a unit on the four seasons, I asked a class of preschool children to help with the unit by deciding what they wanted to learn. I used a web to chart their ideas. I started it for them by writing the words "The Four Seasons" inside a circle at the center of the paper. Next I drew spider-like lines projecting from the "Four Seasons" circle. I then drew a circle at the end of each line. Each circle on the web was filled with one of the following questions that children posed:

"What are the four seasons?"

"What is it like in the winter and what do we do?"

"What is it like in the summer and what do we do?"

"What is it like in the spring and what do we do?"

"What is it like in the fall and what do we do?"

When planning a unit, such as the four seasons, the teacher needs to include theme-related literacy activities in all of the content areas scheduled throughout the school day.

Figure 4.1 presents a mini-unit written by Ms. Nagy. As you will see, she integrates content-area activities throughout the day that focus on the theme being studied and on literacy development. If a class is studying the four seasons, the teacher creates activities to enhance language and literacy within different content areas.

Parents can be helpful in supplying materials for different units or sharing expertise related to the unit.

Thematic instruction adds interest to the school day and gives a purpose for learning reading, writing, listening, speaking, and viewing skills.

1. *Literacy and content skills developed:* Vocabulary development, listening comprehension, letter identification, word identification, science information about seasons.
   Activity: The teacher reads an informational book about the four seasons. After the book is read, the children discuss and role-play their favorite seasonal activities. The teacher writes and illustrates the activities mentioned, such as planting in spring, swimming in summer, raking leaves in fall, and building a snowman in winter. The teacher identifies the letters *S* for spring and summer, *F* for fall, and *W* for winter. Children identify letters in their names that appear in the season words and read the words together.

2. *Literacy and content skills developed:* Vocabulary development, phonological and phonemic awareness, working with rhymes and syllables, music in the form of singing together.
   Activity: The teacher and children sing a song about spring. As they sing and clap the syllables of the words, the teacher lists and illustrates the words that rhyme. The class reads the words and talks about them.

3. *Literacy and content skills developed:* Reading and understanding photos, identifying details in photos, modeling writing, science information about the season.
   Activity: The teacher encourages discussion about three different photographs that include information about the fall. The photos include people raking leaves, children picking apples and selecting pumpkins at a farm, and so forth. The information children generate is written on a chart. The class reads the chart together.

4. *Literacy and content skills developed:* Vocabulary development, following directions, reading whole words, art experience.
   Activity: The teacher provides the children with dark blue construction paper for a background, along with bits of silver foil, white doilies, cotton balls, white tissue paper, white yarn, and chalk. The children are asked to create a winter collage or picture. The children are encouraged to talk about the materials and their pictures while creating them. The teacher writes down each student's favorite picture-related words on an index card to create a Very Own Word box for each child. The children then read their Very Own Words with the teacher.

5. *Literacy and content skills developed:* Hypothesizing, predicting, vocabulary development, writing, science.
   Activity: The teacher asks the children to observe a pan filled with water and discuss what the water looks like, how it feels, and what it does. She asks the children to predict what the water will look like frozen. The water is put in the freezer or outside, if it is cold enough to freeze. When it is frozen, the discussion focuses on what the water looks like and how it feels. The class then allows the ice to melt and discusses freezing and melting again. The teacher records and illustrates what was found in experiments and reads the written recording together with the class.

FIGURE 4.1. Thematic instruction: Seasons.

GUIDING INSTRUCTIONAL PLANNING THROUGH THE USE OF ASSESSMENT

The purpose of assessment is to find out how well a child is progressing, but more important, to organize an instructional plan to meet the child's needs. It is difficult to talk about assessment and instruction separately. Assessment guides instruction. Some basic principles and procedures for assessment are discussed here. However, practical applications for assessment of children's performance are discussed throughout the book in chapters that deal with the different skills and instructional strategies. Early literacy educators, with their concern for children's interests, learning styles, and individual levels of ability, have made us begin to take a closer look at our methods of assessing performance. It is apparent that standardized group paper-and-pencil tests are not always sensitive to strategies drawn from early literacy constructs. In addition, it has become clear that one measure cannot be the main method of evaluating a child's progress. Rather than testing children, we need to assess their performances for growth in many areas and under many conditions. Assessment should help the teacher, child, and parent determine a child's strengths and weaknesses and plan appropriate instructional strategies. Assessment should match educational goals and practices. To meet the needs of the different populations in our schools, assessment measures need to be diverse, because some children may perform better in some situations than in others.

The joint position statement of the International Reading Association (IRA) and the National Association for the Education of Young Children (NAEYC) on learning to read and write (1998) recommend that evaluation for preschoolers be appropriate for their ability level and cultural backgrounds. When selecting an assessment measure, be sure it matches the objective in the preschool curriculum. Quality assessment should be drawn from real-life writing and reading tasks and should continuously follow a range of literacy activities.

The type of assessment referred to here is often called *authentic assessment.* There are many definitions of the term, but one that seems to capture its essence is that authentic assessment represents and reflects the actual learning and instructional activities of the classroom. Several principles emerge from an authentic assessment perspective. The following is adapted from guidelines set forth by Ruddell and Ruddell (1995).

1. Assessment should be based primarily on observations of children engaged in authentic classroom reading and writing tasks.

2. Assessment should focus on children's learning and the instructional goal of the curriculum.

3. Assessment should be continuous, based on observations over a substantial period and the collection of daily performance samples.

4. Assessment should take into account the diversity of students' cultural, language, and special needs.

5. Assessment should be collaborative and include the active participation of children, parents, and teachers.

6. Assessment should recognize the importance of using a variety of observations rather than relying on one assessment approach.

7. Assessment must be knowledge based and reflect our most current understanding of reading and writing processes for the age and grade of the child being assessed.

To accomplish these goals, assessment must be frequent and include many types of assessment. The main goal is to observe and record actual behavior that provides the broadest possible picture of a particular child. A well-known authentic measure is Clay's (1979) Concepts about Print Test, which evaluates what the child knows about print and how it is used in books. Every chapter in this book that deals with a specific area of literacy development, such as comprehension, contains a section with suggestions for collecting assessment information related to that particular skill. A list of general authentic assessment measures that will help paint a comprehensive picture of a child is provided in the next section.

AUTHENTIC ASSESSMENT: MEASURES AND STRATEGIES

Observations

Prepared forms or teacher-created forms are used to record children's behavior. Observation forms usually have broad categories, with large spaces for notes about children's activities. Goals for observing should be planned, and forms should be designed to meet the goals. Teachers can write down interesting, humorous, and general comments about the child's behavior in the classroom. Observations should focus on one particular aspect of the child's performance, such as oral reading, silent reading, or behavior while listening to stories or writing. Within the descriptions of behavior, dialogue is often recorded.

Daily Performance Samples

These are samples of the child's work in all content areas that are done on a daily basis. Various types of samples should be collected periodically. Samples of writing, artwork, science, and social studies reports can be collected throughout the school year.

Audiotapes

Audiotapes are another form of assessment that can be used for the following purposes: to determine language development, to assess story comprehension through recorded retellings, and to analyze progress in the fluency of oral reading. Audio-tapes can also be used in discussion sessions related to responses to literature as tools to help teachers understand how students function in a group. In addition, the tapes can help teachers identify and understand the types of responses that children offer. Children can listen to their own audiotapes to evaluate their story retellings and their fluency.

Videotapes

Videotapes relate information similar to that in audiotapes, with the additional data that can be gained by seeing the child in action. Videotapes can be used for many different purposes. Therefore, they should be done with a purpose in mind and evaluated with a checklist or observation form. Teachers can also use video-tapes to assess their own performance.

Surveys and Interviews

Surveys can be prepared by teachers to assess children's attitudes about their own learning or student's likes and dislikes about school. Surveys can be in the form of questionnaires or interviews with written or oral answers.

Parent Assessment Forms

Authentic assessment also involves parents as evaluators of their children. Parents may be asked to collect work samples from home and to write anecdotes about behav-ior. They may be provided with forms for observing and recording behavior. Parents need to encourage their children to talk about their schoolwork at home. A survey for parents about their child's reading and writing habits at home is useful. Parents are an important resource for information about the child from the home perspective.

Conferences

Conferences allow the teacher to meet with a child on a one-to-one basis for the following purposes: to assess skills such as reading aloud, to discuss a child's progress, to talk about steps toward improvement, to instruct, and to prescribe activities. Children should take an active role in evaluating their progress and are equal partners in the assessment process. Parents also are involved in conferences with teachers about their child's progress. They meet with teachers alone and with their child. They bring materials they have collected at home to add to the packet of information.

Checklists

Inventories that include lists of developmental behaviors or skills for children to accomplish are a common form of authentic assessment. The list is prepared based on objectives a teacher may have for instruction. Therefore, the inventory is designed to determine whether goals set forth have been accomplished. Checklists for skills are presented throughout this book for your use.

Portfolio Assessment

A portfolio provides a way for teachers, children, and parents to collect representative samples of children's work. The portfolio can include work in progress and completed samples. It tells what children have done and what they are capable of doing now to determine where they should go from this point forth. The teacher's portfolio should include work selected by the child, teacher, and parent. It should represent the best work that a child can produce and should illustrate any difficulties he or she may be experiencing. It should include many different types of work samples and represent what the child has been learning.

The physical portfolio is often an accordion-type folder with several pockets to hold work. The folder can be personalized with a drawing by the child, a picture of the child, and his or her name. Portfolios are often passed on to the next grade; as a result, the pieces collected need to be carefully selected to limit the size of the folder. The portfolio should include different samples to represent different areas of literacy and the best work the child has to offer. Included, for example, should be: daily work performance samples, anecdotes about behavior, audiotapes of oral reading, language samples, story retellings, checklists that record skill development, interviews, standardized test results, a child's self-assessment form, journals, a writing sample, and artwork.

Throughout the chapters of this book, assessment is discussed at the end of sections that deal with specific skill development. Multiple measures are offered to include in a portfolio of assessment materials for children. These materials should help teachers create appropriate instructional strategies, help parents understand their child's development, and make the child aware of his or her strengths and weaknesses and how he or she can improve.

Standardized Tests

Standardized tests are being used in preschools. Therefore, it is important to know what they measure, how they are created, and how they should be used. Standardized tests are supposed to measure what students have learned. These tests are prepared by publishers and are norm-referenced; that is, they are administered to large numbers of students in order to develop norms. Norms represent the average performance of students who are tested at a particular age. When selecting a standardized test, it is important to check its validity for your children. That is, does the test evaluate what it says it tests for? Does it match your goals? The reliability of the test is important, as well. That is, are scores accurate and dependable? Other features of standardized tests are as follows:

1. *Grade-equivalent scores* are raw scores converted into grade-level scores. For example, consider a preschool student who takes a test. Is the student's score equivalent to the scores of students at the same age and grade level? Or is the score considered above or below age or grade level?

2. *Percentile ranks* are raw scores converted into percentiles. They tell where the child ranks compared with all children who took the test at his or her grade and age level. Therefore, if a youngster receives a percentile rank of 80, it would mean that he or she scored better than or equal to 80% of those students who took the test at his or her grade and age level and that 20% of the children who took the test scored better.

Although many criticisms are associated with standardized measures, they do present another source of information about a child's performance. It must be realized, though, that a standardized test is just one type of information, which is no more important than all of the other measures discussed earlier. Many question, however, whether it is necessary to use standardized tests with very young children.

Concerns Associated with Standardized Testing

There are a number of problems associated with standardized tests. We must recognize that they represent only one form of assessment; their use must be coordinated with that of other assessment measures. Some standardized tests do not accord with the instructional practices suggested by the latest research and theory on early literacy. Teachers may feel pressured to teach to the test because schools are sometimes evaluated on how well children perform on standardized tests. Teachers who succumb to this temptation could use inappropriate strategies for teaching young children. In addition, teachers may spend a great deal of time preparing children for standardized tests by drilling them on sample tests similar to the real ones. Administrators and teachers must understand the shortcomings of standardized tests and the importance of using multiple methods of assessment. The use of multiple assessment tools given frequently throughout the school year would tend to prevent undue emphasis on the standardized measure. If standardized tests are used, teachers need to help youngsters learn about them. Children need to learn how to follow the directions and how to fill in the answers.

Another concern with standardized tests is bias. For example, standardized test scores are less reliable with younger children than with older children. Furthermore, some standardized tests are still biased in favor of white, middle-class children despite genuine attempts to alleviate the problem. Their use tends to place rural, African American, and bilingual youngsters at a disadvantage. Prior knowledge plays a large role in how well children do on the test. Children from white, middle-class homes tend to have experiences that lead to better achievement on the tests. In addition, following test directions such as "Put your finger on the star" or "Circle the goat that is behind the tree" is often a problem for the young child. Children who have never seen a goat may not circle anything because the animal on the page might look like a dog to them.

Preschoolers can take standardized tests only on a one-to-one basis. In a group setting, children will not be able to follow directions or stay on task. Finding suitable tests is difficult. Some standardized tests that have been accepted for use in the preschool community are the Peabody Picture Vocabulary Test (Dunn & Dunn, 1997), a test given on a one-to-one basis to assess vocabulary development. A comprehensive measure for preschool is called the Dynamic Indicators of Basic Early Literacy Skills (DIBELS; Good & Kaminski, 2003). DIBELS is a set of short, standardized, individually administered measures of early literacy development designed for regular monitoring of the development of prereading and early reading skills. The Phonological Awareness Literacy Screening for Preschool (PALS; Invernizzi, Sullivan, Meier, & Swank, 2004) is a standardized, individually administered assessment of phonological awareness. Another well-accepted standardized measure for preschool is the Early Language and Literacy Classroom Observation (ELLCO) Toolkit (Smith, Dickinson, Sangeorge, & Anastasopoulos, 2002), which is a three-part test. It is an observation form that (1) evaluates the classroom literacy environment by using a checklist; (2) assesses classroom literacy instruction through an observation rating scale; and (3) uses a structured teacher interview to determine teacher knowledge about literacy development in preschool. The instrument has been shown to be reliable and valid.

According to recommendations by the International Reading Association (1999) concerning high-stakes assessment in reading, it is recommended that teachers:

➤ Construct rigorous classroom assessments to help outside observers gain confidence in teacher techniques.

➤ Educate parents, community members, and policy makers about classroom-based assessment.

Preschool standards are being written for literacy development of 3- and 4-year-olds. We recognize that children this young are capable of learning many literacy skills and enjoy learning them if they are engaged in activities in an appropriate manner. As a result of a study in 15 states, Schickedanz (2004) created a list that was representative of preschool literacy objectives (see Table 4.1).

TABLE 4.1. Preschool Literacy Objectives

Listening comprehension

- Listens with increased attention.
- Listens for different purposes.
- Understands simple oral directions.
- Listens to and engages in conversation.
- Listens to tapes and responds to directions on the tapes.

Speech production and discrimination

- Identifies differences between similar-sounding words (e.g., *tree* and *three).
- Produces speech sounds with increased ease and accuracy.
- Experiments with language.

Vocabulary

- Shows an increase in listening and speaking vocabulary.
- Uses new vocabulary in daily communication.
- Refines understanding of words.
- Increases listening vocabulary.

Verbal expression

- Uses language for a variety of purposes.
- Uses sentences of increasing length and grammatical complexity.
- Uses language to express routines.
- Tells a simple personal narrative.
- Asks questions.
- Begins to retell stories in sequence, that are narrative and informational texts.

Phonological awareness

- Begins to identify rhymes.
- Begins to attend to beginning sounds.
- Begins to break words into syllables or claps along with each syllable.
- Begins to create words by substituting one sound for another.
- Begins to segment and blend words.

Print and book awareness

- Understands that reading and writing are ways to obtain information and knowledge and to communicate thoughts and ideas.
- Understands that illustrations carry meaning but cannot be read.
- Understands that letters are different from numbers.
- Understands that a book has a title and an author.
- Understands that print runs from left to right and top to bottom.
- Begins to understand basic print conventions (e.g., letters are grouped to form words, words are separated by spaces).

(continued)

TABLE 4.1. *(continued)*

Letter knowledge and early word recognition

- Begins to associate letter names with their shapes.
- Identifies 10 or more printed letters.
- Begins to notice beginning letters in familiar words.
- Begins to make some letter–sound relationships.
- Begins to identify some high-frequency words.

Motivation to read

- Demonstrates an interest in books and reading.
- Enjoys listening to and discussing books.
- Asks to be read to and to have the same story reread.
- Attempts to read and write.

Comprehension

- Can retell the who, what, when, and where about a story.
- Predicts what will happen next in a story.
- Imitates special language in a book.
- Asks questions about the information or events in a book and answers questions.
- Connects information and events in books to real life.

Written expression

- Attempts to write messages.
- Uses letters to represent written language.
- Attempts to connect the sounds in a word with letter forms.
- Begins to dictate words and phrases to an adult who records them on paper.

Adapted from Schickedanz (2004). Copyright 2004 by the International Reading Association. Adapted by permission.

ORGANIZING INSTRUCTION TO MEET INDIVIDUAL NEEDS

There are many strategies for organizing instruction. Children can be taught as a whole class, in small groups, and individually. Children can be organized in homogeneous groups based on ability or needs or placed in heterogeneous groups based on interests or friends. The use of many organizational strategies is important because some children benefit more in one setting than in another. Having children participate with different children in different groups makes it likely that they will interact with many other children. Preschoolers need to meet in whole-class, small-group, and one-to-one settings for different reasons. Whole-class meetings create a total classroom community, whereas small-group and one-to-one settings provide the teacher with the opportunity to identify their students' individual needs and teach to those needs.

WHOLE-CLASS, SMALL-GROUP, AND ONE-TO-ONE LEARNING SETTINGS

Whole-class instruction is difficult to handle with preschool children because they can listen and concentrate for only a short period of time. Whole-class lessons, sometimes referred to as shared experiences, are appropriate for some situations, such as storybook readings, group singing, and class discussions.

Small groups are effective when close interaction with children is necessary for intentional instruction and assessment of skills. The purpose is to work with children who are at the same level of instruction and who have the same needs. One-to-one instruction provides an opportunity for the teacher to offer personal attention to a child and to learn even more about him or her. When a teacher works with a child alone for instruction and assessment, children can get help with specific skills they are having difficulty with. Children enjoy meeting in small groups and alone with the teacher; they like that private attention. Teachers need several groups so that all children can fit. Teachers select the appropriate instructional skill needs and materials for the small-group instruction. The teacher could be working on letters, colors, sight words, phonological awareness, concepts about books, reading stories to develop listening comprehension, and so forth.

MANAGING DIFFERENT TYPES OF GROUP INSTRUCTION

It is important for teachers to engage children in many group settings for instruction. Whole-class settings are excellent for building a classroom community, brainstorming activities, and having the entire class of children with different backgrounds and abilities working together. Typical activities for whole-class activities in preschool are story time, circle time, music, planning time, writing the morning message, and summarizing the school day.

Small-group instruction and one-to-one interactions between teacher and child are very important in preschool. Small groups are good for projects that require children to work independently of the teacher in centers. Small groups are very important for explicit instruction in skills based on need. There are small friendship groups and groups based on interests. Children also work in pairs or in threes for independent reading and writing.

One important purpose of small-group work is for children to learn to work independently of the teacher and in cooperative social settings with peers. It is a time for children to practice skills already learned. During center time children engage in self-selected reading and writing activities and work with a partner or alone. The teacher acts as a facilitator by answering questions and keeping children on task if necessary.

When children know how to work independently, then the teacher can take a small group for skill instruction. When teachers take small groups for explicit instruction, the other children need to learn that they are not to disturb her. Therefore, the children who are not involved in the lesson need to know exactly what to do, when to do it, and where. A visit to Ms. Shea's preschool classroom provides a look at the organization of independent work.

The activities for independent work that Ms. Shea models for her class are often skill- and theme-related. At the beginning of the school year, she spends time introducing children to the centers in the room and the types of activities they include. She has her class practice working on the different activities. At this time, Ms. Shea does not work with small groups during center time; rather, she helps the children so that they eventually will be able to work independently.

The children are assigned some tasks. The activities they participate in are ones they have done before and involve practicing skills learned. Ms. Shea assigns activities 1, 2, 3, and 4 as follows:

1. For partner reading, children pair off and read the same book together. They also may read separate books and then tell each other about the story they read. The class is studying animals, so the children are to select books from the open-faced bookshelves that include stories and expository texts about animals. Children draw pictures about their books.

2. In the writing center the children look through the book *Rosie's Walk* (Hutchins, 1968), which Ms. Shea read at the morning meeting. They are to copy words that the teacher wrote on the experience chart with icons to help the children remember what they say. Children can look through the book and copy any words they would like and draw pictures to go with their print.

3. The art center has magazines with many photos of animals that children can cut out and use to create animal collages.

4. The computer center has literacy software with activities about animals.

Ms. Shea assigns the children to centers using a chart that indicates who will be going where. The children change from one center to the next when Ms. Shea feels it is time to do so. If she meets with a group for only 5 minutes, she will have the students stay at the same center they just were assigned to; if she meets with a group for 10 minutes, she will have the children change centers at that time and all at the same time. She often coordinates the changing of centers with the changing of small-group meetings. A basket is designated for completed center work.

The management of center time is crucial for its success. Students must know where to go when, they must be familiar with the activities they will use, and they must know where to put completed work. Rules for children to follow when working independently are as follows:

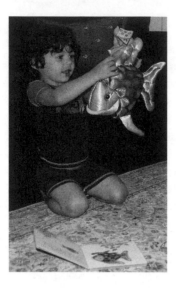

Manipulative materials such as a puppet that represents a story encourage children to work independently and practice skills such as retelling stories.

Rules for Using Materials and Completing Work

➤ Speak in soft voices; people are working.

➤ Put materials back in their place.

➤ Take care of the materials so they are in good condition for others.

➤ Put your completed work in the center basket; accountability for independent work is important.

➤ If you have questions, use the "ask three and then me" rule. Seek help from other students designated as helpers before asking the teacher when she is in a small instructional group.

Rules for Cooperating and Collaborating

➤ Share materials in collaborative activities.

➤ Take turns.

➤ Listen to your friends when they talk.

➤ Offer help to others you are working with if they need it.

Parents can be a wonderful source of help during center time.

LITERACY INSTRUCTION IN SMALL GROUPS IN PRESCHOOL

The objectives for small-group literacy instruction are to focus on a systematic sequence of skills to be developed and to emphasize skills children are experiencing difficulty with. During the lessons many experiences are drawn on to help children with sight words, learning colors, phonological awareness, concepts about books and print, and so forth (Reutzel, 1997; Reutzel & Cooter, 2004).

Typically, there are two to three preschoolers in a group. Materials selected for instruction meet the needs of the students, as well as of the lesson itself. The objectives for the lessons depend on the students' abilities and needs. In these small literacy lessons, children are assessed regularly, and their groups can change as their literacy ability changes. The number of groups formed is not set but is determined by the number of different ability levels represented in a given classroom.

Activities are provided in centers for children who are not in the small literacy-lesson groups. Children are actively engaged in interesting, productive work, practicing the skills they learned during literacy lessons.

In addition to generating a rich literacy atmosphere, an interdisciplinary approach, and assessment, instruction is designed to use different teaching methods, organizational strategies, and grouping procedures so that the differences among children can be accommodated. The centers provide space for independent or social learning, exploration, and self-direction. The classrooms I am describing provide a place for whole-class instruction. The teacher's conference table is a place for individual learning or small-group lessons. All furniture is, of course, movable so that any other needed teaching arrangement can be accommodated. The centers are located to create both quiet, relatively academic areas and places for more active play. The teacher's conference table is situated in a quiet area yet allows the teacher a view of the rest of the classroom. While the teacher is involved in small-group or one-to-one instruction at the conference table, the rest of the class is working independently. The table's location allows the teacher to see all of the children even while working with just a few.

This type of instruction is not an easy task. However, with proper practice that prepares the children to get ready for independent work, and with the help of an aide and parents who volunteer on a regular basis, this small-group instruction is effective and rewarding in terms of student achievement.

Small-group and one-to-one instruction enable the teacher to assess children's achievement and to teach to their specific needs.

REFERENCES

Clay, M. M. (1979). *The early detection of reading difficulties: A diagnostic survey with recovery procedures*. Auckland, New Zealand: Heinemann Educational Books.

Dewey, J. (1966). *Democracy and education*. New York: Free Press. (Original work published 1916).

Dunn, L. M., & Dunn, L. M. (1997). *Peabody Picture Vocabulary Test* (3rd ed.). Circle Pines, MN: American Guidance Service.

Good, R. H., III, & Kaminski, A. R. (2003). *Dynamic Indicators of Basic Early Literacy Skills (DIBELS)*. Longmont, CO: Sopris West Educational Services.

International Reading Association. (1999). *High stakes assessment in reading*. Newark, DE: International Reading Association.

International Reading Association & National Association for the Education of Young Children. (1998). *Learning to read and write: Developmentally appropriate practices for young children*. Newark, DE: International Reading Association.

Invernizzi, M., Sullivan, A., Meier, J., & Swank, L. (2004). *Phonological awareness literacy screening for preschool (PALS-Pre-K)*. Charlottesville, VA: University of Virginia.

Pappas, C., Kiefer, B., & Levstik, L. (1995). *An integrated language perspective in the elementary school: Theory into action*. New York: Longman.

Rand, M. (1993). Using thematic instruction to organize an integrated language arts classroom. In L. M. Morrow, J. K. Smith, & L. C. Wilkinson (Eds.), *Integrated language arts: Controversy to consensus* (pp. 177–192). Boston: Allyn & Bacon.

Reutzel, D. R. (1997, March). Maintaining balance as a teacher of children: Reading instruction for all. Paper presented at the 29th Annual Conference on Reading and Writing, Rutgers University, New Brunswick, NJ.

Reutzel, D. R., & Cooter, R. B. (2004). *Teaching children to read: Putting the pieces all together* (4th ed.). Upper Saddle River, NJ: Pearson/Merrill Prentice Hall.

Ruddell, R., & Ruddell, M. R. (1995). *Teaching children to read and write: Becoming an influential teacher*. Boston: Allyn & Bacon.

Schickedanz, J. (2004). The role of literacy in early childhood education. *Reading Teacher, 58*(1), 86–100.

Smith, M. W., Dickinson, D. K., Sangeorge, A., & Anastasopoulos, L. (2002). *Early Language and Literacy Classroom Observations (ELLCO) toolkit*. Baltimore: Brookes.

CHILDREN'S LITERATURE

Hutchins, P. (1968). *Rosie's walk*. New York: Collier Books.

CHAPTER 5

ORAL LANGUAGE DEVELOPMENT IN PRESCHOOL

I n this chapter, I discuss some theories related to how language is acquired. I focus on language development from birth through age 5 and discuss strategies teachers and parents can carry out to encourage language development for that age group. Another area discussed is how to help English language learners develop English proficiency while at the same time respecting their language and cultural differences. Finally, I talk about techniques for assessing children's oral language.

From the moment of birth, the infant is surrounded by oral language. The development of language is one of the child's first steps toward becoming literate; it helps make reading and writing possible. Among the many things researchers have observed is that children are active participants in their learning of language. To learn, children involve themselves in problem solving and interacting with those individuals around them who are generating language. These strategies have implications for initial instruction in early literacy.

Christopher ran into the classroom all excited and announced, "My dog Fluffy grew puppies last night." From what Christopher observed, it appeared as if the mother dog was "growing" puppies, and it was the only word he could think of to describe the event. He selected a word for the situation that made perfect sense. The teacher explained that babies do grow inside the mother but that when they come out we say, "My dog Fluffy *had* puppies last night." Children think in very literal ways and create language to fit the situation based on their background knowledge. His teacher took the time to enhance his vocabulary in a spontaneous and appropriate manner. Children do not learn language passively; they actually construct—or reconstruct—language as they learn. Although language acquisition is based somewhat on developmental maturity, research has found that children play an active role in their acquisition of language by constructing language. They imitate the language of adults and create their own when they do not have the conventional words they need to communicate their thoughts. Their first words are usually functional words, and they are motivated to continue generating language when their attempts are positively reinforced. Children who are constantly exposed to an environment rich in language and who interact with adults using language in a social context develop more facility with oral language than children who lack these opportunities do (Gaskins, 2003).

HOW DO CHILDREN ACQUIRE LANGUAGE?

 Children learn language in many ways. According to the behaviorist theory, adults provide a language model, and children learn through imitating that model. The child's language acquisition is encouraged by the positive reinforcement of an adult (Cox, 2002; Hart & Risley, 1999). For example, when newborns coo or make other verbal sounds, most parents are delighted and respond with gentle words of encouragement. The infant, in turn, responds to the positive reinforcement by repeating the cooing sounds. As babies become able to formulate consonant and vowel sounds, they try them out. It is not uncommon to hear a 6-month-old playing with sounds such as *ba, ba, ba,* or *ma, ma, ma.* The responsive, interactive parent perceives such sounds as the child's first words and assumes that the child's *ma-ma* means *mommy.* The delighted adult encourages the baby and says, "Come on, now say it again, *ma, ma, ma.*" The baby is pleased with the warm reception and tries to repeat the sounds to receive additional interaction and positive reinforcement. Unfortunately, the converse is also true. If a baby's babbling is considered annoying, if the parent is annoyed by the sound and responds with negative reinforcement by telling the baby in harsh tones, "be quiet and stop making so much noise," the child is not likely to continue to explore language.

The constructivist theory describes children as the creators of language concepts. They describe language as an active and social process. The child constructs language, often making errors. But making errors is a necessary part of learning how language works. We need to accept language errors in a child's first years (Brown, Cazden, & Bellugi-Klima, 1968; Halliday, 1975).

The process of acquiring language is continuous and interactive; it takes place in the social context of the child's interactions with others (Hart & Risley, 1999). Children also learn by playing with language themselves. They imitate adult language, but they also try out new words, involve themselves in monologues, and practice what they have learned (Au, 1998). It is as if children need to express themselves but do not have sufficient conventional language to draw on. Therefore, they create their own language based on their background knowledge and their awareness of semantics and syntax. The following examples demonstrate this theory.

> Natalie's mom and dad were going to a wedding. The 3-year-old girl looked at her mom when she came into Natalie's room dressed in a formal gown. Never having seen her mother dressed like this, Natalie said, "You look pretty, Mommy. What does Daddy's costume look like?"

> A 4-year-old boy described his new jacket as having "French fries hanging from the sleeves." He was referring to the fringe on the suede jacket.

Children's talk is mostly about themselves and what they do. Their early language and their general development relates to actions, objects, and events they have experienced through touching, hearing, seeing, tasting, and smelling (Piaget & Inhelder, 1969).

In early language acquisition, adults provide children with names of things; they direct and make suggestions. As children become more competent, adults gradually withdraw the amount of help they give (Vygotsky, 1978). To promote language development, adults need to interact with children by encouraging, motivating, and supporting them (Morrow & Rand, 1991).

Parents and teachers can help with language development in very spontaneous ways. For example, when a child points to a toy, such as a ball, and names it, the attentive parent and teacher can expand and extend the language (Burns, Snow, & Griffin, 1999). After the child says, "ball," the adult might say, "Yes, that is a nice, big, round, red ball." Through such expansion by the adult, the child acquires new language. The adult can also extend on the baby's words by asking questions, for instance, "Now what can you do with that nice red ball?" Such extension requires the child to think, understand, and act (Dickinson & Tabors, 2001).

According to Halliday (1975), children's initial language development is based on function: What can be said reflects what can be done. Language is learned when it is relevant and functional. Halliday's functions of language are as follows (Halliday, 1975, pp. 19–21):

➤ *Instrumental:* Children use language to satisfy a personal need and to get things done.
  Example: "Cookie Mommy."

➤ *Regulatory:* Children use language to control the behavior of others.
  Example: "No sleep now."

➤ *Interactional:* Children use language to get along with others.
  Example: "You want to play?"

➤ *Personal:* Children use language to tell about themselves.
  Example: "I'm running now."

➤ *Heuristic:* Children use language to find out about things, to learn things.
  Example: "What are cows for?"

➤ *Imaginative:* Children use language to pretend, to make believe.
  Example: "Let's play space."

➤ *Informative:* Children use language to communicate information to others.
  Example: "I'll tell you how this game works."

Children's language grows according to their need to use it, to their interests, and to the meaning it has for them. Children's language is acquired through exploration and invention and is affected by their maturity. Language acquisition is fostered by positive interactions regarding language between the child and an adult.

STAGES IN LANGUAGE DEVELOPMENT

Children acquire language by moving through predictable stages that are based on their maturity. As they develop, they discover the rules that govern the structure of language—specifically, rules of phonology (sound), syntax (grammar), and semantics (meaning). There are 44 separate sounds, or phonemes, in English. Children who grow up in a language-rich environment can learn these sounds quite easily and turn them into language. They learn appropriate articulation, pronunciation, and intonation. Intonation involves pitch, stress, and juncture.

Pitch refers to how high or low a voice is when producing a sound, *stress* to how loud or soft it is, and *juncture* to the pauses or connections between words, phrases, and sentences (Berk, 1997). *Syntax* refers to the rules that govern how words work together in phrases, clauses, and sentences. Internalizing the syntactic rules of language helps children understand what they hear and what they read. Syntax includes rules for forming basic sentence patterns, rules for transforming those patterns in order to generate new sentences, and rules for embedding, expanding, and combining sentences to make them more complex. Brief examples (from Morrow, 1978) follow:

Some Basic Sentence Patterns

➤ *Subject–verb:* "The girl ran."

➤ *Subject–verb–object:* "The girl ran the team."

➤ *Subject–verb–indirect object–direct object:* "Susan gave Lynn a dime."

➤ *Subject–to be–noun or adjective or adverb complement:* "Tom was the captain." "He was happy." "He was there."

➤ *Subject–linking verb–adjective:* "Jane is tall."

Some Basic Sentence Transformations

➤ *Question*
kernel: "Jim went to the store."
transformation: "Did Jim go to the store?"

➤ *Negative*
kernel: "Jane is a cheerleader."
transformation: "Jane is not a cheerleader."

➤ *Passive*
kernel: "Jennifer gave Lisa some bubble gum."
transformation: "Some bubble gum was given to Lisa by Jennifer."

Some Embeddings (Sentence Expansion and Combination)

➤ *Adding modifiers (adjectives, adverbs, adverbial, and adjective phrases)*
kernel: "The boy played with friends."
transformation: "The boy in the red pants played with three friends."

➤ *Compounding (combining words, phrases, or independent clauses to form compound subjects, verbs, etc.)*
kernel: "Jane ran." "Jane played." "Jack ran." "Jack played."
transformation: "Jane and Jack ran and played."

Semantics deals with the meaning that language communicates, both through content words and through function words. Semantics largely governs vocabulary development. Content words carry meaning in themselves. Function words have no easily definable meanings in isolation, but they indicate relationships between other words in a sentence. Function words include prepositions, conjunctions, and determiners (Pflaum, 1986).

Although we have identified stages of language growth, the pace of development may differ from child to child. An individual child's language development also tends to progress and then regress, so that the stages of growth are not always easy to recognize. However, language development has been studied to the extent that it can be described.

From Birth to 1 Year

In the first few months of infancy, oral language consists of a child's experimenting or playing with sounds. Infants cry when they are uncomfortable and babble, gurgle, or coo when they are happy. Parents are able to distinguish cries; one cry is for hunger and another is for pain. Infants learn to communicate specific needs by producing different cries. They communicate nonverbally by moving their arms and legs to express pleasure or pain.

When babies are about 8 months old, their babbling becomes more sophisticated. They are usually capable of combining a variety of consonant sounds with vowel sounds. They tend to repeat these combinations over and over. As mentioned, it is at this stage that parents sometimes think they are hearing their child's first words. The repeated consonant and vowel sounds, such as *da, da, da,* or *ma, ma, ma,* do sound like real words, ones that the parents are delighted to hear. Most parents positively reinforce the child's behavior at this stage. Through repetition of specific sounds and continued reinforcement, the child is led to associate the physical mechanics of making a particular sound with the meaning of the word the sound represents.

From 8 to 12 months, children increase their comprehension of language dramatically; their understanding of language far exceeds their ability to produce it. They do, however, tend to speak their first words, usually those most familiar and meaningful to them in their daily lives, for instance, *Mommy, Daddy, bye-bye, baby, cookie, milk, juice,* and *no.* As they become experienced with their first words, children use holophrases—one-word utterances that express an entire sentence (Hart & Risley, 1999). For example, a baby might say "cookie," but mean "I want a cookie," "My cookie is on the floor," or "I'm done with this cookie."

From 1 to 2 Years

A child's oral language grows a great deal between the ages of 1 and 2. Along with one-word utterances, the child utters many sounds with adult intonation, as though speaking in sentences. These utterances are not understandable to adults, however. Children begin to use telegraphic speech from 12 months on—the first evidence of their knowledge of syntax.

Telegraphic speech uses content words, such as nouns and verbs, but omits function words, such as conjunctions and articles. However, the words are delivered in correct order, or syntax: "Daddy home" for "Daddy is coming home soon," or "Toy fall" for "My toy fell off the table." Language grows tremendously when children begin to combine words. By 18 months, most can pronounce four-fifths of the English phonemes and use 20 to 50 words (Bloom, 1990).

From 2 to 3 Years

The year between ages 2 and 3 is probably the most dramatic in terms of language development. Typically, a child's oral vocabulary grows from 300 words to 1,000.

The child can comprehend, but cannot yet use, 2,000 to 3,000 additional words. Telegraphic sentences of two or three words continue to be most frequent, but syntactic complexity continues to develop and the child occasionally uses functional words such as pronouns, conjunctions, prepositions, articles, and possessives. As their language ability grows, children gain confidence. They actively play with language by repeating new words and phrases and making up nonsense words. They enjoy rhyme, patterns of language, and repetition (Bloom, 1990). Consider the following transcription of Tyler's dialogue with his cat. Tyler was 2 years, 10 months at the time. "Nice kittie, my kittie, white and black kittie, furry, nicey kittie. Good kittie, my kittie, dittie, mittie. Kiss kittie, kiss me, kittie, good kittie." Tyler's language is repetitive, playful, silly, and creative. He demonstrates some of the characteristics of language production for a child his age.

From 3 to 4 Years

A child's vocabulary and knowledge of sentence structure continues to develop rapidly during the 4th year. Syntactic structures added to the child's repertoire include plurals and regular verbs. Indeed, children of this age are prone to overgeneralization in using these two structures, mainly because both plural formation and verb inflection are highly irregular in the English language (Jewell & Zintz, 1986). Four-year-old James illustrated both problems when he had an accident in class and came running over very upset. He said, "Mrs. Morrow, I dropped a block on my foots and hurted myself." James knew how to form a plural by adding an s to *foot* and the past tense of a verb by adding *ed* to *hurt,* but he did not know about irregular plurals such as *feet* and irregular verbs such as *hurt.* Jessica came over to the teacher to tell her. "The mices are fighting in their cage." Jessica knew about adding an s to form a plural, but again was unaware of irregular plural forms, such as *mice* for *mouse.*

As they approach age 4, children seem to have acquired all the elements of adult language. They can generate language and apply the basic rules that govern it. Although their ability with language has grown enormously and they sound as though they are using adult speech, children have acquired only the basic foundations. Language continues to grow throughout our lives as we gain new experiences, acquire new vocabulary, and find new ways of putting words together to form sentences. Between the ages of 3 and 4, children talk about what they do as they are doing it. They often talk to themselves or by themselves as they play, as if they are trying to articulate their actions (Seefeldt & Barbour, 1986). While playing with play dough, Jonah said to himself, "I'm pounding the yellow play dough and making a cake. I'm rolling it and cutting it. I'm putting candles on top because it is going to be my birthday."

From 5 to 6 Years

Five- and 6-year-olds sound very much like adults when they speak. Their vocabularies are always increasing, and so is the syntactic complexity of their language.

They have vocabularies of approximately 2,500 words, and they are extremely articulate. Many, however, still have difficulty pronouncing some sounds, especially /l/, /r/, and /sh/ at the ends of words. They become aware that a word can have more than one meaning. When they are embarrassed or frustrated at misunderstanding things, they say something silly or try to be humorous. They also tend to be creative in using language. When they do not have a word for a particular situation, they supply their own. The language of 5- and 6-year-olds is interesting, amusing, straightforward, to the point, and delightful (Seefeldt & Barbour, 1986). Children at this age discover bathroom talk and curse words, and they enjoy shocking others by using them. They talk a lot and begin to use language to control situations. Their language reflects their movement from a world of fantasy to that of reality. Two examples of straightforward and to-the-point talk are given in the following two vignettes.

When I visit schools I carry a camera with me to photograph illustrations of good teaching, children in different working settings, and so forth. Over the course of a year, I was a frequent visitor in Jasmine's preschool classroom of 4- and 5-year-olds and took lots of pictures. I snapped a picture of Jasmine engaged in center work, and she looked at me and said, "Okay, already, Dr. Morrow, knock it off with the camera. Enough is enough."

Griffin's mom had a baby when he was 5. He was excited and interested in his new sister. After about a month with the baby at home, Griffin said to his mom, "Okay, so now we got this baby. Isn't it time to take her back to the hospital and leave her there? She cries too much."

STRATEGIES FOR LANGUAGE DEVELOPMENT

ELL   Theory and research suggest how we can help children acquire and develop language appropriately. Children acquire language by emulating adult models, by interacting with others when using language, and by experiencing positive reinforcement for their efforts. Because language is innate to humans, it will develop in some form or other, but it does depend on stages of development and on what happens in the environment. As children mature, they become capable of generating even more complex language structures. They learn language by doing and by acting and within familiar environments. Their first spoken words are those that are meaningful for them within their own experiences. Their earliest language is an expression of needs. They learn language through social interaction with individuals more literate than they are, whether it is adults or older children. Children create their own language; they play with it and engage in monologues.

Table 5.1 presents objectives formulated for a program fostering language development in children from birth through age 5.

TABLE 5.1. Objectives for Receptive and Expressive Language Development from Birth to 5 Years

Objectives for receptive language development

- Provide children with a setting in which they hear varied language.
- Help children to associate language they hear with pleasure and enjoyment.
- Help children to discriminate and classify sounds they hear.
- Expose children to a rich source of new vocabulary on a regular basis.
- Have children listen to others and demonstrate that they understand what is said.
- Provide children with opportunities for following directions.
- Provide children with good models of English.
- Allow children to hear their home language in school.

Objectives for expressive language development

- Encourage children to pronounce words correctly.
- Help children increase their speaking vocabularies.
- Encourage children to speak in complete sentences.
- Give children opportunities to expand their use of various syntactic structures, such as adjectives, adverbs, prepositional phrases, dependent clauses, plurals, past tense, and possessives.
- Encourage children to communicate so they can be understood.
- Give children the opportunity to use language to interpret feelings and points of view and for solving problems, summarizing events, and predicting outcomes.
- Give children opportunities to develop language involving mathematical and logical relations by describing size and amount, making comparisons, defining sets and classes, and reasoning.
- Provide children with the opportunity to talk in many different settings: in the whole group with the teacher leading the discussion, in teacher-led small groups, in child-directed groups for learning, or in conversation in social settings.
- Provide opportunities for children to use their own language freely at any stage of development. This could be a different dialect or mixtures of English and Spanish or other languages.
- Encourage, accept, and respect children's communication.
- Remember that language is best learned when it is integrated with other communication skills and embedded within topics or content areas that have meaning and function for children.

Children are continuously interpreting and making sense of their world based on what they already know. Language is learned through use, as part of our daily and social activities (Au, 1998).

STRATEGIES FOR LANGUAGE DEVELOPMENT FROM BIRTH TO 2 YEARS

Language Development in the Child's First Year

"Hi, Natalie. How's my great big girl today? Let's change your diaper now, upsy-daisy. My goodness, you're getting heavy. Now I'll put you down right here on your dressing table and get a nice new diaper for you. Here, want this teddy bear to hold while I change you? That's a good girl. You really like your teddy bear. You're really yucky; let's clean you up now. This is the way we clean up Natalie, clean up Natalie, clean up Natalie. This is the way we clean up Natalie, so early in the morning. You like that singing, don't you? I can tell. You're just smiling away and cooing. Want to do that again? This is the way we clean up Natalie, clean up Natalie, clean up Natalie. This is the way we clean up Natalie, so she'll feel so much better. Wow, you were singing with me that time. That's right, ahhh-ahhh-ahh, now do it again. Mmmmm, doesn't that smell good? The baby lotion is so nice and smooth."

My granddaughter, Natalie, was 4 months old when I had that conversation with her. In print, it reads like a monologue; in reality, Natalie was a very active participant in the conversation. She stared intently at me. She cooed, she waved her arms, she smiled, and she became serious. I was providing a rich language environment for her. I encouraged her participation in the dialogue and acknowledged her responsiveness in a positive way. I provided her with the environmental stimuli necessary for her language to flourish. I engaged her in this type of conversation during feedings and while changing, bathing, and dressing her. I talked to her even when she was in her crib and I was in another room or in the same room but involved in other things. The baby knew that communication was occurring because she responded to the talk with body movements, coos, babbles, and smiles. When she responded, I responded in turn.

Surround Infants with Sounds

Infants need to be surrounded by the sounds of happy language. Whether they come from mother, father, caregiver at home, a teacher, or an aide in a child care center, sounds and interaction should accompany all activities. Adults who are responsible for babies from birth through the first year need to know nursery rhymes, chants, finger plays, and songs. It is important for children to hear the sounds of language, as well as the meanings. Thus adults can make up their own chants to suit an occasion, as I did when I adapted "Here We Go 'Round the Mulberry Bush" to the situation at hand. Such experiences make the baby conscious of the sounds of language. Children learn that they can have control over language and that oral language can be a powerful, as well as fun, tool.

In addition to the conversation of adults, infants should experience other sounds, such as different types of music—classical, jazz, popular, and so forth. Babies need to hear the sounds of "book language," which differs in intonation, pitch, stress, juncture, and even syntax from normal conversation. They need familiarity with language in all its variety so they can learn to differentiate among its various conventions and patterns. Speaking to infants, singing to them, reading to them, and letting them hear the radio and television provide sources of language that help their own language grow. In addition, there are sounds in the immediate environment that are not prepared and are not the sounds of language but that provide practice in auditory discrimination—the doorbell ringing, the teakettle hissing, the clock chiming, the vacuum cleaner humming, a dog barking, a bird singing, a car screeching, and so on. Bring them to the baby's attention, give them names, and heighten the child's sensitivity to them.

Surround Infants with Sensory Objects

In addition to hearing a variety of sounds, babies need objects to see, touch, smell, hear, and taste. Objects should be placed in the baby's immediate environment—the crib or playpen. The objects will stimulate the baby's activity and curiosity and become the meaningful things within the environment from which language evolves. Some of the objects should make sounds or music when pushed or touched. They can have different textures and smells. They should be easy to grab, push, kick, or pull. They can be placed so they are visible and within the child's reach. At least one item should be suspended overhead: stuffed animals, rubber toys, music boxes made of soft material, mobiles that can be kicked or grasped, mobiles that hang from the ceiling and rotate by themselves, or cardboard or cloth books with smooth edges. Books can be propped open against the side of the crib or playpen when the baby is lying on its back or against the headboard when the baby is on its stomach. Certain familiar objects should always remain, and new objects frequently should be made available. Allow the child to play independently with these objects, but adults should talk about them, name them, join the child in playing with them, and discuss their characteristics.

From 3 to 6 months, the baby gurgles, coos, begins to laugh, and babbles. Adults or caregivers should recognize an infant's sounds as the beginning of language and positively reinforce the infant with responses aimed at encouraging the sounds. When the baby begins to put consonants and vowels together, again adults should reinforce the behavior, imitating what the baby has uttered and urging repetition. When the baby becomes aware of the ability to repeat sounds and control language output, he or she will do the same. Babies also will begin to understand adult language, so it is important to name objects, carry on conversations, and give the baby directions. At the end of the baby's first year, assuming he or she has experienced appropriate sounds of language, as well as encouragement and pleasant interaction, the baby will be on the verge of extensive language growth during the second year.

Language Development at Ages 1 and 2 Years

Throughout the second year of a child's life, the adults in charge need to continue the same kinds of stimulation suggested for developing oral language during the first year. However, because the baby is likely to develop a vocabulary of up to 150 words and to produce two- and possibly three-word sentences during the second year, additional techniques can be used to enhance language growth. As described earlier, one- and two-word utterances by children at this age usually represent sentences. When a 12-month-old points to a ball and says "ball," the child probably means "I want the ball." Parents and caregivers at home or in child care centers can begin to expand and extend the child's language by helping to increase the number of words the child is able to use in a sentence or by increasing the syntactic complexity of their own utterances.

Scaffolding to Help Language Develop

One method for helping a child develop language ability is a kind of modeling called *scaffolding* (Applebee & Langer, 1983). In scaffolding, an adult provides a verbal response for a baby who is not yet capable of making the response him- or herself. In other words, the adult provides a language model. When the baby says "dolly," for instance, the adult responds, "Do you want your dolly?" or "Here is your pretty dolly." In addition to expanding on the child's language, the adult can

Parents expand and extend their babies' language as they play with them.

extend it by asking the youngster to do something that demonstrates understanding and extends his or her thinking. For example, "Here is your nice pretty dolly. Can you hug the dolly? Let me see you hug her." In addition to questions that require action, the adult can ask questions that require answers. Questions that require answers of more than one word are preferable—for example, "Tell me about the clothes your dolly is wearing." *How, why,* and *tell me* questions encourage the child to give more than a yes-or-no answer and more than a one-word response. *What, who, when,* and *where* questions, on the other hand, tend to elicit only one-word replies. As the child's language ability develops, the adult provides fewer and fewer "scaffolds"; the child learns to build utterances along similar models.

New Experiences Help Develop Language

Adults should select songs, rhymes, and books for 1- to 2-year-olds that use language they can understand. They are capable of understanding a great deal of language by now, and the selections should help expand and extend their language. Both vocabulary and conceptual understanding are enhanced by experiences. For the 1- to 2-year-old, frequent outings, such as visits to the post office, supermarket, dry cleaner, and park, provide experiences to talk about and new concepts to explore. Household tasks that are taken for granted by adults are new experiences that enrich children's language. Involve them in activities. For example, an 18-month-old can put a piece of laundry into the washing machine or give one stir to the bowl of food being prepared. During such daily routines, adults should surround the activity with language, identifying new objects for the baby and asking for responses related to each activity (Hart & Risley, 1999).

Overgeneralizations and Language Development

As children become more verbal, adults sometimes want to correct their mispronunciations or overgeneralization of grammatical rules. The child who says "Me feeded fishes," for instance, has simply overgeneralized the rules for forming most past tenses (*feeded* for *fed*), using pronouns (objective *me* for subjective *I*), and forming most plurals (*fishes* for *fish*).

When correcting overgeneralizations, do it in a positive manner. Instead of saying, "No, you should say, I fed the fish," say "Yes, you did a very good job when you fed the fish." Eventually, with positive reinforcement and proper role models in language, the child will differentiate between irregular grammatical conventions and forms. Correcting overgeneralizations negatively as absolute error is likely to inhibit the child from trying to use language. In learning, children need to take risks and make mistakes. Hearing good adult models will eventually enable them to internalize the rules of language and to correct their errors themselves. At least until age 5, children should be allowed to experiment and play with language without direct concern for 100% correctness in syntax and pronunciation. The English language is extremely complex and irregular in many of its rules; in time, children will master these rules in all their complexity if they have good adult models and plenty of verbal interaction. At the same time, encouraging "baby talk" simply because it is cute, for instance, is likely to inhibit growth, because children will use whatever language they believe will please the adults around them.

Materials for Language Development at 1 and 2 Years

Materials for 1- to 2-year-olds should be varied and more sophisticated than those in the first year. Now that the baby is mobile in the home or day care center, books need to be easily accessible to the child. Toys should still include items of various textures, such as furry stuffed animals and rubber balls. Other toys should require simple eye–hand coordination. Three- to five-piece puzzles, trucks that can be pushed and pulled, dolls, a child-size set of table and chairs, crayons and large paper, and puppets are examples. Choose objects that require activity, for activity encourages exploration, use of the imagination, creation, and the need to communicate. The number of books in a child's library should be increasing, and those that they handle alone should be made of cloth or cardboard.

Brain Development and Language and Literacy Development from Birth to 2 Years

Brain research has made it very apparent that what happens to a child from birth to age 3 can affect his or her language and literacy development. Babies are programmed to learn. They search every minute to learn about the environment they are in and to connect to the experiences it has to offer.

At birth, a child's brain has about 100 billion neurons—all of the neurons, or brain cells, the child will ever have. For learning to take place, neurons must make brain connections. Brain connections that are repeated and used become permanent. When brain connections are not used, they disintegrate and vanish. This is referred to as *neural shearing,* or loss of brain cells (Shaywitz, 2003). At birth, the baby's billions of neurons have already formed 50 trillion connections or synapses. By 1 month of age, they have formed 1,000 trillion brain cell connections. The connecting of the brain cells is called *synaptogenesis,* or the rapid development of neural connections. The brain connections form as a result of experiences a baby has, and they become permanent when the same experiences happen again and again. The permanent connections mean that learning has occurred (Newberger, 1997). The right experiences have to occur to help with language and literacy development, and they need to begin at birth.

Different parts of the brain are responsible for different kinds of development. For example, the motor cortex is responsible for the control of movements; the cerebellum for the development of motor skills; the temporal lobe for auditory processes of hearing, including learning, memory, and emotion; Wernicke's area for language understanding; the Broca's area for speech production; the frontal lobe for planning, reasoning, and emotional expression; the somatosensory cortex for body sensations, touch, and temperature; the parietal lobe for perceptions and special processing; and the occipital lobe for visual processing. There are specific moments in time when the different areas in the brain are most sensitive for development. For example, the first year of life is the most critical time for language to be learned. During this time the auditory channels for language develop. At birth, the child has neurons waiting to be connected and can learn any language in the world. Neuron shearing occurs as early as 6 months of age, when the baby can no longer recognize sounds of languages he or she has not heard. By 1 year, babies are programmed to listen to and learn the language they have heard; the neurons for languages they have not been exposed to no longer remain (Kuhl, 1994).

What does this mean for families and child care providers who are engaged with children from birth to age 3? What experiences do they need to provide to create a strong base for language and literacy development so that neurons for language and literacy connect and remain permanent? From the time of birth through age 3, family members and child care providers need to do the following:

- ➢ Provide love, food, and clothing for babies.
- ➢ Talk to babies from the day they are born.
- ➢ Use sophisticated vocabulary with babies.
- ➢ Use complex sentences with babies.
- ➢ Respond to babies' cries, smiles, and other communication attempts.
- ➢ Be playful with language, such as using rhymes.
- ➢ Play with babies.
- ➢ Read books.
- ➢ Sing songs to babies.
- ➢ Play many different types of music.

STRATEGIES FOR LANGUAGE DEVELOPMENT FROM 3 TO 5 YEARS

ELL From ages 3 through 5, a great deal of language development occurs. Children should continue to hear good models of language. They need constant opportunities to use language in social situations with adults and other children. Their oral language production must be reinforced positively. Language should be purposefully integrated into active meaningful experiences with other subjects rather than being taught separately. To accomplish these goals, early childhood teachers provide an environment in which language will flourish. They organize centers of learning, one for each content area, that include materials to encourage language use. A science center, for instance, can include class pets if allowed. Gerbils, for example, are active, loving animals that are fun to watch and handle. Children surround the cage often and generate talk just from watching the animals. Gerbils reproduce in 28-day cycles. When litters arrive, children can observe the birth process. The new babies cause much excitement and inspire questions, comments, and unlimited conversation. Teachers alone could never provide lessons in which language flourishes as much as it does from the events that occur when there are pets in the classroom.

Center Materials for Language Development

Here are some examples of appropriate materials to have in learning centers for generating language with children ages 3 through 5:

➤ *Science:* an aquarium, a terrarium, plants, a magnifying glass, a class pet, magnets, a thermometer, a compass, a prism, shells, rock collections, a stethoscope, a kaleidoscope, a microscope, informational books and children's literature that reflect topics being studied, and blank journals for recording observations of experiments and scientific projects.

➤ *Social studies:* maps, a globe, flags, pictures of community figures, traffic signs, current events, artifacts from other countries, informational books and children's literature that reflect topics being studied, and writing materials to make class books or your own books about topics being studied.

➤ *Art:* easels, watercolors, brushes, colored pencils, crayons, felt-tip markers, various kinds of paper, scissors, glue sticks, pipe cleaners, scrap materials (bits of various fabrics, wool, string, and so forth), clay, play dough, food and detergent boxes for sculptures, books about famous artists, and books with directions for crafts.

➤ *Music:* piano, guitar, or other real instruments, CD and tape players with all types of music, rhythm instruments, songbooks, and photocopies of sheet music for songs sung in class.

➤ *Mathematics:* scales, rulers, measuring cups, movable clocks, a stopwatch, a calendar, play money, a cash register, a calculator, dominoes, an abacus, a number line, a height chart, an hourglass, numbers (felt, wood, and magnetic), fraction puzzles, geometric shapes, math workbooks, children's literature about numbers and mathematics, writing materials for creating stories, and books related to mathematics.

➤ *Literacy:* multiple genres of children's literature, CD players or tape recorders with headsets and stories on tapes or CDs, pencils, writing paper, a stapler, construction paper, 3" × 5" cards for recording words, a hole punch, letter stencils, a computer, puppets, storytelling devices such as a felt board and roll movies, stationery with envelopes, letters (felt, wood, and magnetic) and letter chunks for building words, sets of pictures for different units (e.g. seasons, animals, space, etc.), rhyme games, color games, cards for associating sounds and symbols, alphabet cards, and pictures and words representing out-of-school environmental print. (The literacy center also includes a library corner, a writing center, oral language materials, and language arts manipulatives, all of which are described in later chapters.)

➤ *Dramatic play:* dolls, dress-up clothes, telephone, stuffed animals, a mirror, food cartons, plates, silverware, newspapers, magazines, books, a telephone book, a class telephone book, a cookbook, note pads, cameras and a photo album, a table and chairs, a broom, a dustpan, and child-size kitchen furniture, such as a refrigerator, a sink, an ironing board, and storage shelves. (The dramatic-play area can be changed from a kitchen to a grocery store, beauty shop, gas station, business office, restaurant, etc., with the addition of materials for appropriate themes when they are studied.) Include appropriate materials for reading and writing related to the theme of the dramatic-play area.

➤ *Block area:* blocks of many different sizes, shapes, and textures; figures of people and animals; toy cars and trucks; items related to themes being studied; paper and pencils to prepare signs and notes; and reading materials related to themes.

➤ *Workbench:* wood, corrugated cardboard, a hammer, scissors, screwdrivers, saws, pliers, nails, glue, tape, and a work table.

➤ *Outdoor play:* sand, water, pails, shovels, rakes, a gardening area and gardening tools, climbing equipment, riding toys, crates, a playhouse, balls, tires, and ropes.

Children need opportunities to use such areas for interacting with one another and the teacher. They should be given enough time to touch, smell, taste, listen, and talk about what they are doing. Exploring and experimenting with the materials in the centers provides creative, imaginative, problem-solving, decision-making experiences in which children use language. The opportunity to use language is one of the key elements in language development.

Some materials remain permanently in the centers; others are replaced or supplemented occasionally so that new items of interest become available. Materials added to the centers are often coordinated with thematic units of instruction. For example, if a unit on seasons is introduced, pictures of snow scenes, swimming, growing plants, and autumn leaves are added to the science center and books about the seasons to the literacy center. The different content-area centers provide sources for language use and development; the literacy center is devoted primarily to language development. Thematic units of instruction that integrate all areas make learning more meaningful and expand concepts.

Each new unit of instruction offers specific language experiences that expand vocabulary, syntax, pronunciation, and the ability to understand others and be understood (Tompkins & Koskisson, 1995). With each new unit, similar activities can be adapted to the different topic. The following describes activities designed to aid language growth in early childhood classrooms. For purposes of illustration, assume that the topic throughout is healthy foods.

➢ *Discussion:* Hold discussions about the unit topic. What are some healthy foods? Why are they healthy? Why do we eat healthy foods? What do certain foods do to make our bodies healthy? What are your favorite healthy foods? What do you think might happen to you if you don't eat healthy foods?

➢ *Word lists:* Ask the children to name some favorite healthy foods. The list might include: apples, oranges, chicken, oatmeal cereal, carrots, yogurt, milk, bananas, string beans, or bread. Classify the words into different food groups. Have real food available and discuss how it looks, smells, feels, and tastes. List the words on a chart and hang the chart in the room. Leave the chart hanging when you go to the next unit. When the wall gets full, compile the charts into a class book.

➢ *Pictures:* Provide pictures of different healthy foods for discussion.

➢ *Sharing time (show and tell):* Hold a sharing period during which children bring things from home related to the topic. Give all the children an opportunity to share if they wish, but assign different children for different days. Having more than five or six children speak in one period becomes tedious. Sharing objects from home is an important activity. It gives children confidence because they are talking about something from their environment. The shyest children will speak in front of a group if they have the security of talking about something familiar from home. Encourage children to relate the items to the unit topic if they can. Model language for the children to encourage them to speak in sentences; for example, if a child says, "My truck," the teacher can say, "That is a nice big, red truck. Can you say that?" Coordinate with parents by informing them of topics being discussed.

➢ *Experiments:* Carry out a science experiment related to the topic being studied. Involve the children actively. Discuss the purpose and hypothesize about what is likely to happen. Encourage children to discuss what they are doing while they are doing it. When the experiment is complete, discuss the results with the class. (Example: freeze water outside in the winter, bring it back into the classroom, and let it melt. Discuss what happened and why. Talk about how ice feels and looks and how water feels and looks. How are they the same? How are they different?)

➢ *Art:* Carry out an art activity related to the topic. Allow children to create their own work rather than making them follow specific directions that yield identical results. Discuss the project and the available materials before the activity. Provide materials that children will want to touch, describe, and compare. While children are creating, encourage conversation about what they are doing. For example, provide magazines, construction paper, scissors, and paste. Have the children make a collage of good foods to eat by finding them in the magazines. Discuss why these foods are good. Also, talk about their colors and shapes.

➢ *Music:* Sing songs about food, such as "Do You Know the Muffin Man?" Music is enjoyable, and lyrics help build vocabulary and sensitivity to the sounds and meanings of words. Listen to music without words, music that creates images concerning the topic. Ask the children for words, sentences, or stories that the music brings to mind.

➢ *Food preparation:* Prepare food related to the unit. Prepare different foods for the important food groups. Discuss food textures, smells, taste, and appearance. Follow recipe directions, thus teaching the children about sequencing and quantity. Allow children to help prepare the food, enjoy eating it together, and encourage discussion and conversation throughout. Food preparation can be a source of new vocabulary, especially because many of its terms take on special meanings—stir, blend, boil, measure, dice, and so forth.

➢ *Dramatic play:* Add items related to different topics for the dramatic-play area: empty food boxes, a cash register for ringing up orders, menus to encourage role playing, and language about good food. Introduce the items by placing each in a separate bag and asking a child to reach in, describe what it feels like, and identify it without peeking. Touching elicits descriptive language.

➢ *Outdoor play:* Encourage spontaneous language and frequent problem-solving situations during outdoor play. For example, provide pails for picking berries and shovels and cups during playtime. Discuss outdoor play before going out and again after coming in.

➢ *Morning message:* Discuss weather and the calendar in a daily morning message. Encourage children to share news about themselves: a new pair of sneakers, a new food they tried, a birthday. Make plans for the school day.

➢ *Class trips:* Take the class on a trip, bring in a guest speaker, or show a film. All three activities can generate language and encourage its use.

➢ *Reading stories:* Read stories to the children about the topic under study. *Bread and Jam for Frances* (Hoban, 1964)

Dear Class,
    Today is Monday, February 5, 2007. The weather will be snowy and cold.
    Later, we will work on a Snow activity. I hope you brought your mittens.
    Love,
    Ms. Aguruso

Children and teacher talk about the morning message the teacher has written.

is a story that provides information, expands vocabulary, and addresses issues about food.

➤ *Creating stories:* Provide the children with a title such as "The Big Delicious Dinner" and let them think of a story about it.

➤ *Retelling stories:* Ask children to retell stories. This activity encourages them to use book language and incorporate it into their own language. Retelling is not always an easy task for young children, so props can be helpful—puppets, felt boards and felt characters, roll movies, and pictures in a book. With these same props, children can make up their own stories, as well.

➤ *Very own vocabulary words:* In any of these activities, children should be encouraged to select their favorite Very Own Words about the topic being studied. Very Own Words can be selected from discussions, art lessons, science experiments, songs, books, poems, cooking experiences, or any other activity. After a particular experience, ask children to name a favorite word. Record children's Very Own Words on 5″ × 8″ cards and store them in their own file boxes. When children are capable of writing their own words, assist them with spelling when they ask for help. Very Own Words enhance vocabulary and are a source of reading and writing development.

Children collect Very Own Words they learn and place them in file boxes or in plastic bags to read and write.

➤ *Word walls:* As new class words are learned, especially those related to themes, the teacher can place the words on the class word wall. Word walls have many purposes. In preschool, children's names and thematic words and pictures representing words can be put on word wall cards. In kindergarten and subsequent primary grades, word walls are also used for high-frequency words. Be sure to use the new vocabulary on the word wall by alphabetizing the words, using them in sentences, and creating rhymes and stories with them. If they aren't used, they won't be learned.

➤ *Summary of the day:* Summarize the day's events at the end of the school day, encouraging children to tell what they liked, did not like, and want to do the next day in school.

CHILDREN'S LITERATURE AND LANGUAGE DEVELOPMENT

Research studies have found that children who are read to frequently, with discussion about the story before and after reading, develop more sophisticated language structures and increased vocabulary (Beck & McKeown, 2001). Discussion about the book before and after reading is a necessary part of the experience.

To help develop language skills with children's literature, a teacher can offer preschool children literature that represents varieties of language and experience. Some children's books, such as *Too Much Noise* (McGovern, 1967), feature the sounds of language; they aid auditory discrimination or incorporate additional phonemes into a child's language repertoire. Others help develop the syntactic complexity of a child's language through embeddings and transformations and the use of numerous adjectives and adverbs—for example, *Swimmy* (Lionni, 1963). Craft books require children to follow directions. Wordless books encourage them to create their own stories from the pictures. Concept books feature words such as *up, down, in, out, near,* and *far* or involve children in mathematical reasoning. Realistic literature deals with fears or preschooler's daily problems; discussion of such themes leads to the interpretation of feelings, sensitivity to others, and problem solving using language. Poetry introduces children to rhyme, metaphor, simile, and onomatopoeia and encourages them to recite and create poems. When children hear and discuss the language of books, they internalize what they have heard; the language soon becomes part of their own language.

Two anecdotes illustrate how children incorporate into their own language the language of books that have been read to them.

A group of preschoolers were playing on the playground one early spring day. A few birds circled around several times. Melissa ran up to her teacher and said, "Look, Ms.

Rosen, the birds are fluttering and flapping around the playground." Surprised at first by Melissa's descriptive and sophisticated choice of words, Ms. Rosen remembered that the words Melissa was using came directly from a storybook they had read recently, *Jenny's Hat* (Keats, 1966). In the book, birds flutter and flap around Jenny's hat. Melissa had internalized the language of the book and was using it in her own vocabulary.

One day after a big snowstorm, my daughter asked, "Mommy, can I go out and play? I want to build a smiling snowman." I was surprised and pleased with this sophisticated language being uttered by my 4-year-old. *Smiling snowman* represents a participle in the adjective position, a syntactic structure usually not found in the language of children before the age of 7 or 8. Stephanie was holding *The Snowy Day* (Keats, 1962). In it Peter goes outside and builds a smiling snowman. Stephanie had used the book's language and made it her own.

The activities just suggested can be repeated throughout the school year with each new theme that is studied. Such adaptation and repetition make it possible to introduce children to hundreds of new vocabulary words, concepts, and ideas. They will ensure children opportunities to participate in new kinds of spontaneous language as topics and structured experiences change. Word lists and other materials produced during each unit can be maintained and made available for review and reuse.

Most of the suggestions can be followed at home, as well as at school. Parents should not be expected to create elaborate centers or carry out units of instruction. However, daily living offers holidays, seasons, family events, and other topics of special interest. Parents can tap such meaningful occasions for their potential enhancement of language development. They can discuss events, list words, help children collect favorite Very Own Words, involve children in cooking and household chores, go on outings around town, read stories, sing songs, and generally encourage the use of language as a pleasurable activity and a useful skill.

FORMATS FOR PROMOTING LANGUAGE AND VOCABULARY DEVELOPMENT IN THE CLASSROOM

By the time children come to preschool, they have had varied opportunities for talk in their daily lives. Most of the talk is spontaneous and deals with real-life experiences. Talk with their parents includes questions and answers, either with parents directing the discussion or with the children playing a more active role. I have discussed strategies that initiate talk. Here I offer organizational structures for classrooms that provide different types of talk experiences. These include teacher-directed question-and-answer discussions, small-group conversations for giving and receiving information, and spontaneous discussions that are led by the teacher or children in social settings. In addition, conversations that include different types of talk are described. In structured question-and-answer discussions, teachers need to provide open-ended questions that will encourage talk, such as: What would happen if . . .? What would you do if . . .? and Tell us why.

Conversations occur best in small-group settings that include three to six children. Any number beyond that can no longer be considered a conversation but a large-group discussion. The following guidelines need to be established for conversation to be productive.

Informal Conversations without the Teacher

Children need time to talk without leaders or specific outcomes. This type of conversation is likely to occur during free-play periods, center time, or outdoor play. Although classrooms that encourage this type of talk can be noisy, it is important for children to have the opportunity to use language in social settings at school. In addition to learning the types of organizational structures in which talk should take place, students need to engage in different types of talk, including aesthetic talk, efferent talk, and talk in dramatic activities.

Aesthetic talk typically revolves around children's literature. In this kind of talk, children have the opportunity to interpret what they have read or listened to. Children can participate in aesthetic talk when discussing literature, telling stories, and participating in Readers' Theatre. Aesthetic talk deals with feelings and emotions.

Efferent talk is used to inform; it occurs in discussion of themes being studied. Efferent talk has to do with descriptions, sequencing of ideas, cause and effect, and comparing and contrasting. It can occur in situations such as show-and-tell, morning meeting discussions, or question-and-answer times with a special class visitor, such as asking a firefighter about his or her job.

Small-Group Conversations with the Teacher

Small-group conversations with the teacher should adhere to the following guidelines:

> ➤ Children should listen to others during conversations.

> ➤ Children should take turns talking.

> ➤ Students should raise hands, if necessary, to ensure that everyone gets a turn and that individuals do not interrupt one other.

> ➤ Everyone should keep talk relevant to the topic of conversation.

> ➤ Teachers should help to redirect conversation to its stated purpose if it should stray.

> ➤ Teacher talk should be kept to a minimum as he or she becomes a participant.

> ➤ Teachers should follow the same rules as the children: Listen to others, take turns, do not do all the talking, and so forth.

Dramatic-Play Activities

Dramatic-play activities provide an avenue for many types of talk. When children participate in dramatic activities, they share experiences, explore their understanding of ideas, and interact with peers. Dramatic play can include informal role playing, use of puppets and props, and thematic play. Language literacy learning must be embedded in play. In play settings, children interact and collaborate in small groups. To promote literacy learning, the dramatic-play area can be coordinated with a social studies or science theme that is being studied. Materials for reading and writing are provided to support the play theme, and during play children read, write, speak, and listen to one another, using literacy in functional ways.

Although early childhood educators have realized the value of play for social, emotional, and physical development, in the past it has not been viewed as a means of developing language and literacy. Children have been observed time and time again engaged in meaningful social collaborative language and literacy activities during dramatic thematic play (Morrow, 1990).

To demonstrate the importance of the social, collaborative, and interactive nature of literacy development, I take you into a classroom in which the teacher, Ms. Hart, has designed a veterinarian's office to go along with an animal theme with a concentration on pets. The dramatic-play area was designed with a waiting room and chairs; a table filled with magazines, books, and pamphlets about pet care; posters about pets; office hour notices; a "No Smoking" sign; and a sign advising visitors to "Check in with the nurse when arriving." A nurse's desk holds patient forms on clipboards, a telephone, an address and telephone book, appointment cards, a calendar, and a computer for recording appointments and patient records. Offices contain patient folders, prescription pads, white coats, masks, gloves, cotton swabs, a toy doctor's kit, and stuffed animals to serve as patients.

Ms. Hart guides students in the use of the various materials in the veterinarian's office, for example, by reminding the children to read to pets in waiting areas or to fill out forms with prescriptions or appointment times or with information about an animal's condition and treatment. In addition to giving directions, Ms. Hart also models behaviors by participating in play with the children when the materials are first introduced.

The following anecdotes relate the type of behavior that was witnessed in this setting—a setting that provides a literacy-rich environment with books and writing materials, that models reading and writing by teachers that children can observe and emulate, that provides the opportunity to practice literacy in real-life situations that have meaning and function, and that has children collaborating and performing reading and writing with peers.

> Jessica was waiting to see the doctor. She told her stuffed toy dog, Sam, not to worry, that the doctor wouldn't hurt him. She asked Jenny, who was waiting with her stuffed toy cat, Muffin, what the kitten's problem was. The girls agonized over the

ailments of their pets. After a while, they stopped talking, and Jessica picked up a book from the table and pretended to read *Are You My Mother?* (Eastman, 1960) to her pet dog, Sam. Jessica showed Sam the pictures as she read.

Preston examined Christopher's teddy bear and wrote out a report in the patient's folder. He read his scribble writing out loud and said, "This teddy bear's blood pressure is 29 points. He should take 62 pills an hour until he is better and keep warm and go to bed." While he read, he showed Christopher what he had written so he would understand what to do. He asked his nurse to type the notes into the computer.

Additional play settings that encourage oral language and literacy include the following:

➤ *Newspaper office:* This setting should include telephones, maps, computers, paper, pencils, and areas that focus on sports, travel, general news, and weather.

➤ *Supermarket or local grocery store:* This area can include labeled shelves and sections, food containers with their labels, a cash register, telephone, computers, receipts, checkbooks, coupons, and promotional flyers.

➤ *Post office:* This can be used for mailing children's letters and should include paper, envelopes, address books, pens, pencils, stamps, cash registers, computers, and mailboxes. A mail carrier hat and bag are important for the children who deliver the mail by reading names and addresses.

The play post office engages children in talk about mailing letters, addresses, stamps, writing invitations, birthday cards, and so forth.

➤ *Airport:* An airport setting can be created with signs posting arrivals and departures, tickets, boarding passes, luggage tags, magazines and books for the waiting area, safety messages on the plane, and name tags for the flight attendants. A computer for making Internet reservations is available.

➤ *Gas station and car repair shop:* This can be designed in the block area. Toy cars and trucks can be used for props. There can be receipts for sales, road maps to help with directions to different destinations, auto repair manuals for fixing cars and trucks, posters that advertise automobile equipment, and empty cans of different products that are sold in stations (Morrow & Rand, 1991).

Materials that are used to their fullest potential for language and literacy development should be natural and should come from the child's environment. The materials in the setting must serve a real function and must be familiar to children. It is important not to set up several dramatic themes at once. Instead, have the dramatic-play area match a theme being studied. Change the area when you begin to study a new theme. Teachers need to guide the use of materials initially. This is not a time for teaching specific skills but a time for language and literacy to be initiated by children naturally in the setting provided (Neuman & Roskos, 1993).

The materials in dramatic-play areas should be marked and accessible. All levels of language and literacy development should be accepted. Teachers might find it useful to record anecdotes about the language and literacy activities as an aid in assessing child development.

HELPING ENGLISH LANGUAGE LEARNERS IN YOUR CLASSROOM

ELL English language learners are an important concern. The number of children with different languages and different language proficiencies grows in our classrooms daily. There are children who do not speak any English. These children come from homes in which English is not spoken at all, and some children have very limited English proficiency. The English proficiency of the latter group of youngsters varies; many of them are more proficient in their home language than in English. The goal is for them to become truly bilingual—that is, equally proficient in English and in the home language.

Children also come to school speaking different dialects. A dialect is an alternative form of one particular language used in different cultural, regional, or social groups (Leu & Kinzer, 1991). These differences can be so significant that an individual from a region with one English dialect may have difficulty understanding someone from another region because the pronunciation of letter sounds is so different. Dialects are not inherently superior to one another; however, one dialect typically emerges as the standard for a given language and is used by the more advantaged individuals in a society. Teachers must be aware of different dialects and help youngsters with the comprehension of standard dialects. Children are not to be degraded or viewed as less intelligent for speaking different dialects. Although it is important for children to achieve a level of standard English to help them succeed in society, emphasizing the need to become a standard English speaker before learning literacy is inappropriate and likely to create more difficulties for the children by slowing their literacy development.

There are general strategies that will support the first language of students in regular classrooms. It is helpful if someone in the school speaks the English language learners' first language—either a child or an adult who can provide translation. The following strategies expose children in the class to other languages, thus creating an interest and appreciation for different backgrounds:

> ➤ Include print in the classroom in children's first language.

> ➤ Suggest that students who are English language learners share stories in their first language.

> ➤ Be sure that children from different language backgrounds have the opportunity to read and practice writing with others who speak their own language, such as parents, aides, and other children in the school (Freeman & Freeman, 1993).

> ➤ Along with supporting children's first language, it is also important to support the learning of English. Assign an English-speaking child as a buddy for the English language learner to help with his or her English. The language experience approach provides the following types of activities that are helpful for English language learners:
>
>   ▪ Allow children to talk.
>
>   ▪ Have routine story times.
>
>   ▪ Provide thematic instruction that elicits talk, reading, and writing and that heightens interests in exciting topics.
>
>   ▪ Write charts based on talk about children's home life and experiences in school.
>
>   ▪ Encourage children to copy experience charts, have them dictate their ideas for you to write, and encourage them to write themselves (Lindfors, 1989; Miramontes, Nadeau, & Commins, 1997).

ASSESSMENT OF CHILDREN'S LANGUAGE DEVELOPMENT

It is important to assess children's language development to determine whether it follows expected stages. Assessment also determines how much a child has progressed. The word *assessment* suggests several rather frequent measures by which to judge progress. Assessment should reflect instructional objectives and strategies. It should include evaluation of a wide range of skills used in many contexts. A certain child, for example, may perform better in an interview than on a pencil-and-paper test. Both kinds of evaluation, therefore, should be used. Literacy includes a wide range of skills; it is important to evaluate a child for as many as possible to determine strengths and weaknesses. Unfortunately, many assessment instruments are quite narrow in scope and frequently do not measure a child's total abilities.

There are several ways to measure children's language development in early childhood that are similar to those used for measuring literacy development.

Checklists are practical because they provide concise outlines for teachers and appropriate slots for individual children. They are most effective if used periodically during the school year. Three to four evaluations during the year can provide sufficient data to determine progress. Program objectives offer criteria to include on lists. Figure 5.1 is a checklist for evaluating preschool children's oral language skills.

Anecdotal records are another form of language assessment that can reveal rich information. Loose-leaf notebooks and file cards offer two means of keeping anecdotal records. These records require no particular format. Rather, the teacher or parent simply writes down incidents or episodes on the days they occur. Samples of a child's language and situations involving language can be recorded. Anecdotal samples are necessary periodically to determine growth over a school year.

Tape recordings for evaluating language development can be made from open interviews or as hidden recordings. Videotaping equipment can serve the same purpose, but it may not be readily available in most early childhood classrooms. Children who are unaware that their conversation is being recorded are likely to be more spontaneous and uninhibited (Genishi & Dyson, 1984). It is often difficult, however, to place a tape recorder in the right spot to record language clearly enough to transcribe and analyze. Interviews with children can be more natural when an adult familiar to the child does the interviewing. It is also helpful to allow the tape recorder to become such a familiar tool in the classroom that the child uses it often in the language arts center. Under such circumstances the machine is not threatening when used in an assessment interview.

To record samples of natural language, discuss the child's experiences. Ask about home, favorite games or toys, favorite TV programs, brothers and sisters, trips taken, or birthday parties recently attended. What you should try to collect is a corpus of spontaneous language that provides a typical sample of the child's ability with language.

Tape assessment samples three or four times a year. Let children hear their own recorded voices and enjoy the experience. Then, for assessment purposes, transcribe the tapes and analyze them for such items as numbers of words uttered and numbers of words spoken in a single connected utterance (e.g., "Tommy's cookie" or "Me want water"). The lengths of such utterances can be averaged to determine mean length. Length of utterance is considered a measure of complexity. When children begin to speak in conventional sentences, such as "That is my cookie," measure the length of the T-units. A T-unit is an independent clause with all its dependent clauses, if there are any, attached. It can be a simple or a complex sentence. Compound sentences are made up of two T-units. Length of T-units, like length of utterances, is a measure of language complexity. It typically increases with the user's age, and usually the more words per unit, the more complex the unit (Hunt, 1970).

Further analysis of taped utterances and T-units can determine which elements of language a child uses—number of adjectives, adverbs, dependent clauses,

	Always	Sometimes	Never
Child's Name: _____ Date _____			
Makes phoneme sounds			
Speaks in one-word sentences			
Speaks in two-word sentences			
Identifies familiar sounds			
Differentiates similar sounds			
Understands the language of others when spoken to			
Follows verbal directions			
Speaks to others freely			
Pronounces words correctly			
Is understood by others			
Has appropriate vocabulary for level of maturity			
Speaks in complete sentences			
Uses varied syntactic structures			
Can be understood by others			

FIGURE 5.1. Checklist of language development.

From Lesley Mandel Morrow, *Literacy Development in the Early Years: Helping Children Read and Write,* 5th ed. Published by Allyn and Bacon, Boston, MA. Copyright © 2005 by Pearson Education. Reprinted by permission of the publisher.

negatives, possessives, passives, plurals, and so on. The more complex the transformations, embeddings, and syntactic elements used, the more complex the language overall (Morrow, 1978). Data from several samples over a year can be most revealing.

The following is a verbatim transcription of a taped language sample from a 5-year-old boy at the end of May of his preschool year. The child was presented with a picture book and asked to tell a story from the pictures.

> "He's getting up in the morning and he's uh looking out the window . . . he eats breakfast and he gets dressed and he he's looking out the window with his cat and after he gets out of bed he brushes his teeth then when he gets done brushing his teeth, he eats he eats breakfast and then when he after he eats breakfast he gets dressed and then he puts his bootses on uh he plays he plays with his toys and he plays doctor and he plays cowboys at supper time he plays policeman he dreamed he was on a magic carpet he drived his ship on the waves and and then the ship sanked . . . someone bringed ice cream to the hurted mans then he goes to bed and and then he dreamed about his playing."

After the sample is transcribed, the language is segmented into T-units. Following is a sample of the segmented sample of T-units:

He's getting up in the morning.

And he's looking out the window.

He eats breakfast.

He gets dressed.

He's looking out the window with his cat.

After he gets out of bed he brushes his teeth.

When he gets done brushing his teeth, he eats.

He eats breakfast.

After he eats breakfast he gets dressed.

He puts his bootses on.

He plays with his toys.

He plays doctor.

He plays cowboys.

At suppertime he plays policeman.

He dreamed he was on a magic carpet.

He drived his ship on the waves.

The ship sanked.

Someone bringed ice cream to the hurted mans.

Then he goes to bed.

He dreamed about his playing.

THE RELATIONSHIP BETWEEN LANGUAGE DEVELOPMENT AND READING

The relationship between reading and language is evident in studies of children who are early readers. It has been found, for instance, that early readers score higher on language screening tests than children who were not reading early. Early readers come from homes in which rich language and a great deal of oral language are used (Dickinson & Tabors, 2001). When interviewed, parents of early readers revealed that their children tended to use very descriptive language and sophisticated language structures. These youngsters invented words, used humor, and talked a lot. The mother of a 4-year-old early reader reported her son's description of a friend of his. He said, "Jenny is a pink girl with orange hair and sprinkles on her nose." Another mother reported that her 3-year-old son said, "The sun came out and ate up all the rain."

In the learning environment described throughout this chapter, language development is spontaneous and also encouraged. Modeling, scaffolding, and reinforcement make this environment interactive between child and adult, and they guide and nurture language development to an extent that children are not likely to achieve on their own. The strategies discussed are appropriate for children who have language differences and minimal language disorders. These youngsters, however, may need additional attention on a one-to-one basis from the classroom teacher or a resource room teacher (Burns, Snow, & Griffin, 1999; Dickinson & Tabors, 2001).

REFERENCES

Applebee, A. N., & Langer, J. A. (1983). Instructional scaffolding: Reading and writing as natural language activities. *Language Arts, 60,* 168–175.

Au, K. H. (1998). Constructivist approaches, phonics, and the literacy learning of students of diverse backgrounds. In T. Shanahan & F. V. Rodriguez-Brown (Eds.), *Forty-seventh yearbook of the National Reading Conference* (pp. 1–21). Chicago: National Reading Conference.

Beck, I. L., & McKeown, M. G. (2001). Text talks: Capturing the benefits of read-aloud experiences for young children. *Reading Teacher, 55,* 10–20.

Berk, L. (1997). *Child development.* Boston: Allyn & Bacon.

Bloom, L. (1990). Developments in expression: Affect and speech. In N. L. Stein &

T. R. Trabasso (Eds.)., *Psychological and biological approaches to emotion* (pp. 215–245). Hillsdale, NJ: Erlbaum.

Brown, R., Cazden, C., & Bellugi-Klima, U. (1968). The child's grammar from one to three. In J. P. Hill (Ed.), *Minnesota symposium on child development*. Minneapolis: University of Minneapolis Press.

Burns, M. S., Snow, C. E., & Griffin, P. (Eds.). (1999). *Starting out right: A guide to promoting children's reading success*. Washington, DC: National Academies Press.

Cox, C. (2002). *Teaching language arts: A student- and response-centered classroom* (4th ed.). Boston: Allyn & Bacon.

Dickinson, D. K., & Tabors, P. O. (Eds.). (2001). *Beginning literacy with language*. Baltimore: Brookes.

Freeman, D., & Freeman, Y. (1993). Strategies for promoting the primary languages of all students. *Reading Teacher, 46,* 18–25.

Gaskins, I. W. (2003). A multidimensional approach to beginning literacy. In D. M. Barone & L. M. Morrow (Eds.), *Literacy and young children: Research-based practices* (pp. 45–60). New York: Guilford Press.

Genishi, C., & Dyson, A. (1984). *Language assessment in the early years*. Norwood, NJ: Ablex.

Halliday, M. A. K. (1975). *Learning how to mean: Exploration in the development of language*. London: Arnold.

Hart, B., & Risley, T. R. (1999). *The social world of children learning to talk*. Baltimore: Brookes.

Hunt, K. W. (1970). Syntactic maturity in children and adults. *Monograph of the Society for Research in Child Development* (Vol. 25). Chicago: University of Chicago Press.

Jewell, M., & Zintz, M. (1986). *Learning to read naturally*. Dubuque, IA: Kendall/Hunt.

Kuhl, P. (1994). Learning and representation in speech and language. *Current Opinion in Neurobiology, 4,* 812–822.

Leu, D. J., & Kinzer, C. (1991). *Effective reading instruction K–8* (2nd ed.). New York: Merrill.

Lindfors, J. (1989). The classroom: A good environment for language learning. In P. Rigg & V. Allen (Eds.), *When they don't all speak English: Integrating the ESL student into the regular classroom* (pp. 39–54). Urbana, IL: National Council of Teachers of English.

Miramontes, O. B., Nadeau, A., & Commins, N. L. (1997). *Reconstructing schools for linguistic diversity: Linking decision making to effective programs*. New York: Teachers College Press.

Morrow, L. M. (1978). Analysis of syntax in the language of six-, seven-, and eight-year olds. *Research in the Teaching of English, 12,* 143–148.

Morrow, L. M. (1990). Preparing the classroom environment to promote literacy during play. *Early Childhood Research Quarterly, 5,* 537–554.

Morrow, L. M., & Rand, M. (1991). Promoting literacy during play by designing early childhood classroom environments. *Reading Teacher, 44,* 396–405.

Neuman, S., & Roskos, K. (1993). *Language and literacy learning in the early years: An integral approach*. Orlando, FL: Harcourt, Brace.

Newberger, J. J. (1997). New brain development research: A wonderful window of opportunity to build public support for early childhood education. *Young Children,* 52(4), 4–9.

Pflaum, S. (1986). *The development of language and literacy in young children* (3rd ed.). Columbus, OH: Merrill.

Piaget, J., & Inhelder, B. (1969). *The psychology of the child.* New York: Basic Books.

Seefeldt, C., & Barbour, N. (1986). *Early childhood education: An introduction.* Columbus, OH: Merrill.

Shaywitz, S. (2003). *Overcoming dyslexia.* New York: Knopf.

Tompkins, G. E., & Koskisson, I. K. (1995). *Language arts content and teaching strategies.* Englewood Cliffs, NJ: Prentice Hall.

Vygotsky, L. S. (1978). *Mind in society: The development of psychological processes.* Cambridge, MA: Harvard University Press.

CHILDREN'S LITERATURE

Eastman, P. D. (1960). *Are you my mother?* New York: Random House.

Hoban, R. (1964). *Bread and jam for Frances.* New York: Harper & Row.

Keats, E. (1962). *The snowy day.* New York: Viking.

Keats, E. (1966). *Jenny's hat.* New York: Viking.

Lionni, L. (1963). *Swimmy.* New York: Pantheon.

McGovern, A. (1967). *Too much noise.* Boston: Houghton Mifflin.

CHAPTER 6

KNOWLEDGE ABOUT PRINT

Ms. Dunston's class was studying nutrition. The dramatic-play area was set up like a supermarket, with products displayed separately in the following food groups: dairy; breads and cereals; meat, poultry, and fish; and fruits and vegetables. From time to time Ms. Dunston encouraged the children to identify the letters in their names on the food box labels. Specials were listed on the blackboard for children to notice in the dramatic-play center. Additionally, children had access to pencils and paper so they could copy food labels to create their own shopping lists. Occasionally children would pick a food, make a rhyme about it, and clap as they sang. For example, "This is the way we eat our bananas, eat our bananas, eat our bananas. This is the way we eat our bananas so early in the morning. This is the way we drink our juice, drink our juice, drink our juice. This is the way we drink our juice, so early in the morning." Ms. Dunston might ask how many claps were in the word *banana,* and the children would count out three. Then she would ask how many claps were in the word *juice,* and the children would count one.

As a result of this dramatic play, students in Ms. Dunston's classroom are developing their sight vocabulary, letter recognition, and phonemic awareness. Ms. Dunston has purposefully prepared the classroom environment for the play theme and as one in which knowledge about print can occur.

DEVELOPMENTAL TRENDS IN LITERACY ACQUISITION

Becoming literate is a process that begins at birth and continues throughout life. Children differ in their rates of literacy achievement. Therefore, they should not be pressured into accomplishing tasks or placed on a predetermined time schedule. According to researchers, learning that print has functions is one of the first steps children take toward reading and writing (Mason, 1980; Smith, 1971). The first words a child speaks, reads, and writes are those that have meaning, purpose, and function in his or her life, such as family names, food labels, road signs, and names of fast-food restaurants. Later, the child becomes interested in forms of print. As a result, details about letter and word configurations, names, and sounds serve the child's learning more than does a simple understanding of how print functions. The child then learns the conventions of print: that we read and write from left to right, that punctuation serves a purpose in reading and writing, and that spaces demarcate letters and words. Although the first stages of reading and writing are dominated by the functions of print, at the same time, children develop an interest in and ideas about the forms and conventions of print, although to a lesser degree. Researchers warn that children do not systematically go from one developmental stage to the next. In early reading and writing, for example, children often go back to earlier stages (Morrow, 2005).

Studies of young children's responses to story readings reveal developmental trends. Children's initial questions and comments during story readings are related to the pictures and the meanings of the stories. However, as they gain experience, their questions and comments begin to concern the names of letters, the reading of individual words, or attempts to sound out words (Morrow, 2005; Roser & Martinez, 1985; Yaden, 1985). Again, the function of print dominates early responses, and the form of print becomes more important in later responses.

Some children have gained considerable information about reading and writing before they enter school for formal instruction. Some are reading and writing before they come to school, whereas others have had little literacy exposure. Some children who come to school have had almost no exposure to print and have no books in their homes. Children who have been exposed to print and a literacy-rich environment know the difference between drawing and writing, associate books with reading, can read environmental print, and realize the functional purposes of reading and writing. They expect that reading and writing activities will make sense because their knowledge about literacy, to this point, is based on meaning and function. Children without this exposure do not have these concepts about books and print.

Efforts to expand children's reading abilities into reading fluency initially need to build on their strengths and on what they already know and expect of reading (Harste, Woodward, & Burke, 1984). Early writing, similar to early reading, is embedded in real-life experience. Many families do things together that involve meaningful literacy. They write each other notes, lists, holiday greetings, and directions. Many children, however, do not have these same opportunities. Therefore, all children will not have developed the same skills at the same age.

Children are likely to become involved in literacy activities if they view reading and writing as functional, purposeful, and useful (Mason & McCormick, 1981; Taylor, 1983). Grocery lists; directions on toys, packages, household equipment, and medicine bottles; recipes; telephone messages; school-related notices; religious materials; menus; environmental print inside and outside the home; mail; magazines and newspapers; storybook readings; TV channel listings; telephone numbers; conversations among family members; and letters represent but a sample of the functional literacy information that a child comes into contact with on a daily basis. Children are familiar with such forms of literacy and participate in them, pretend to use them at play, and understand their purposes. Parents and day care and preschool teachers need to provide experiences with reading similar to the experiences children have already had. Some children know certain information necessary for reading. These children know the difference between letter characters and pictures in books, how to handle a book, and how to turn pages. They also know that books are sources of meaning through printed words. Children also have awareness of environmental print in familiar contexts and literacy-rich environments can make learning to read as natural as language acquisition (Morrow, 2005).

READING READINESS

Reading readiness programs in the past have viewed getting ready to read as a set of social, emotional, physical, and cognitive competencies. Social and emotional development was and still is enhanced with periods of play. During these play periods, children can select materials in dramatic-play, art, and science centers that consist of literacy materials, blocks, and manipulative toys. The goal is for children to learn to share and cooperate and to develop self-control, good self-concept, and appropriate school behavior. Discussions often focus on sharing and getting along with others.

Physical development of large and fine motor control was and still is seen as a factor in literacy development. Teachers should have indoor and outdoor periods designed specifically to teach children to hop, skip, trot, gallop, jump, throw a ball, and walk in a straight line. Often there is music to accompany these activities.

To develop fine motor coordination, children can use clay and can play with toys that require fitting pegs into holes or snapping things together. These activities supply the strength little hands need to develop the coordination necessary to write letters. Teachers ask children to draw and trace to develop eye–hand motor coordination. Children also trace pictures and letters with their fingers. Children practice cutting to enhance fine motor ability, which is needed to write letters.

Cognitive development is equally important to social, physical, and emotional development. In a reading readiness program, cognitive development means developing auditory and visual discrimination skills in preparation for reading. Visual discrimination activities involve children in seeing likenesses and differences between shapes and pictures. Visual discrimination activities are more useful when real objects are used and classroom discussion about the similarities and differences between objects ensues.

Another visual discrimination activity is color identification. In this activity children are asked to classify objects into color groups or to make a collage from magazine pictures that are all, for example, red, blue, or green. Identifying like and different shapes, such as squares, circles, and rectangles, is another activity used for developing visual discrimination. Finally, children are taught left-to-right eye progression, because this is not a natural activity but one that is necessary for reading.

After working on these visual discrimination skills, teachers ask children to identify letters of the alphabet. Children memorize the alphabet, trace and copy letters, and learn to identify upper- and lowercase letters. All of these activities are seen as preparation for reading and are useful with real materials that actively involve children.

Auditory discrimination prepares children to learn auditory decoding skills. Teachers ask children to identify sounds that are alike and different. Listening to rhymes, identifying rhyming words, and creating rhyming word lists are auditory discrimination activities. Matching rhyming puzzle pieces (see Figure 6.1) or real

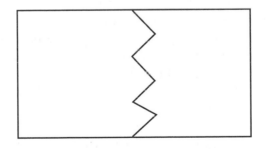

FIGURE 6.1. Rhyming puzzle game.

objects are activities that work well for young children. From rhyme exercises, the teacher progresses to associating letters with their sounds. Some activities that can help children do this include collecting objects that begin with the sound featured or cutting pictures from a magazine in order to make a collage for a specific letter. For example, children could make a collage for the letter *M*.

RESEARCH ON HELPING CHILDREN FIGURE OUT WORDS

Word-study skills and knowledge about print involve learning strategies that will help children figure out words and become independent readers. Word-study skills begin with phonemic awareness, which is the ability to recognize that words are made up of individual speech sounds. To decode words, children can use the context and syntax of a sentence to help identify an unknown word, can develop sight vocabulary, and can use the configuration or the shape of a word. The most well-known word-study strategy is the use of phonics, which involves learning letter sounds and combinations of letter sounds (referred to as *phonemes*) associated with their corresponding letter symbols (referred to as *graphemes*). One of the problems with phonics is that the English alphabet has at least 44 different sounds, and sound–symbol correspondence is not consistent—there are many irregularities and exceptions to many rules.

Phonemic awareness, which is discussed later in this chapter, is the ability to recognize that words are made up of individual speech sounds. This is different from phonics, which includes knowledge about the relationship between letters and sounds. Phonological awareness, which is different from phonemic awareness, involves identifying and manipulating larger parts of spoken language, such as whole words, syllables, and initial consonants and word chunks at the ends of words (referred to as *onsets* and *rimes*). These are considered to be precursors to phonics and are needed in order to learn phonics.

Research concerning early literacy has demonstrated the importance of meaningful experiences in early literacy instruction (Teale, 2003). There is considerable evidence, from both experimental and longitudinal studies, that phonemic and phonological awareness and knowledge of phonics are necessary for success in learning to read and write alphabetic languages (Adams, 1990; Juel, 1994).

Concerns about word study in early literacy deal with such questions as exactly what skills should be taught, when to introduce them, how to teach them, and how much time to spend dealing with them. Although there are no definitive answers to all these questions, we have found that teaching word-study skills in a variety of ways seems to be the best approach. For example, word-study skills should be taught through direct systematic and spontaneous instruction and in meaningful contextually based settings.

SKILLS AND OBJECTIVES FOR WORD STUDY

The following are objectives for word study to enhance literacy development in preschool. The child should be able to do these things (see also Figure 6.2):

1. Demonstrate that print is read from left to right.
2. Demonstrate that oral language can be written down and then read.
3. Demonstrate what a letter is and point to one on a printed page.
4. Demonstrate what a word is, point to one on a printed page, and know that there are spaces between words.
5. Demonstrate that print in the environment has a message, and read some of this print on signs and logos.
6. Recognize high-frequency words and other words by sight.
7. Identify rhyming words he or she hears and make up a rhyme.
8. Identify and name some upper- and lowercase letters of the alphabet.
9. Blend and segment phonemes in words.
10. Begin to associate letters with their initial consonant sounds, such as *b—bear, t—train.*
11. Begin to associate letters with corresponding long and short vowel sounds, such as *a—acorn, apple; e—eagle, egg; i—ice, igloo; o—oats, octopus; u—unicorn, umbrella.*
12. Use context, syntax, and semantics to identify words.
13. Clap the number of syllables in words.
14. Attempt to read by attending to picture clues and to print.

TEACHING STRATEGIES FOR FIGURING OUT WORDS

Instructional activities designed to help youngsters learn about the function, form, structure, and conventions of print should involve a wide variety of learning experiences. Children need to be socially interactive when they are learning about print, they need direct instruction with models to emulate, and they need to learn through experiences that are meaningful and connected to real life and that incorporate what children already know.

The following sections describe strategies to help children learn about print in direct, meaningful, and functional ways. The strategies are intended for preschoolers who range from being at risk to advanced in their literacy development; the teacher simply adjusts the activity for the children he or she

ELL

	Always	Sometimes	Never	Comments
Name _____ Date _____				
Demonstrates that print is read from left to right				
Demonstrates that oral language can be written down and then read				
Demonstrates what a letter is and points to one on a written page				
Demonstrates what a word is, points to one on a printed page, and knows that there are spaces between words				
Reads some print in the environment, such as signs and logos				
Recognizes high-frequency words and other words by sight				
Identifies rhyming words he or she hears and can make up a rhyme				
Identifies and names some upper- and lowercase letters				
Blends and segments phonemes in words				
Begins to associate letters with their initial consonant sounds, such as *b—bear, t—train*				
Begins to associate letters with corresponding long and short vowel sounds, such as *a—acorn, apple; e—eagle, egg; i—ice, igloo; o—oats, octopus; u—unicorn, umbrella*				
Uses context, syntax, and semantics to identify words				
Claps the number of syllables in words				
Attempts to read by attending to picture clues and to print				

FIGURE 6.2. Checklist of word-study skills.

is working with. The learning of these skills should be connected to content-area material and functional activities. Teachers can help children develop knowledge about print through the following activities: reading to children; pointing out words in the environment and noting their letters and sounds; taking a child's dictation; encouraging children to write in their own ways; allowing youngsters to see print being read from a Big Book and that it is tracked from left to right across the page; using predictable books that rhyme or have patterned language; and allowing children to guess about and share in the reading (Invernizzi, 2003). Through these experiences children learn that print is read from left to right, that words in a book are oral language that has been written down and can be read, that letters have sounds, that letters make up words, that words have meaning, that pictures hold clues to what the print says, and that words can be predicted based on the meaning of the text. In addition, explicit instruction in phonological and phonemic awareness, alphabetic knowledge, and phonics is needed.

When explicit instruction is used, lessons should teach skills as strategies for children to use. In these lessons the teacher does the following:

1. Begins with an explanation and rationale for the children by letting them know what is being taught and why it is being taught.

2. Models and demonstrates how to use the skill and when to use the skill.

3. Gives students the opportunity to practice the skill taught with the teacher's guidance.

4. Encourages students to practice and apply the skill.

Children can read several words and simple books through their knowledge of syntax, semantics, and acquired sight vocabulary before phonics is emphasized. Children may also be able to read simple books because the book has been repeated often and they have learned to pretend read. When youngsters have experienced success with initial reading, they will seek information about forms of print because they will want to read independently.

USING ENVIRONMENTAL PRINT

Several researchers have found that children as young as 2 can read familiar environmental print (Strickland & Snow, 2002). Others, however, have shown that a child often is reading the sign rather than its print. When the print is separated from its familiar environmental context, the young child sometimes can no longer identify it (Mason, 1980). Even so, when very young children associate the McDonald's logo with the word *McDonald's* and read it, they are learning that a group of letters makes up a word that can be read

ELL

and thus provides information. The ability to read environmental print also gives the child a sense of accomplishment and usually elicits positive reinforcement from caring adults.

Parents can make children aware of environmental print from the first year of life. During daily routines, parents can point out and read words and labels on food boxes, road signs, stores, and restaurants. The world is filled with environmental print. Our early childhood classrooms need to contain environmental print from outside, and teachers should label items in their child care centers and preschools. The labels must be used, or they will serve no purpose. They should be traced, copied, read, and discussed. Such print, once familiar, becomes part of a child's sight vocabulary.

The environmental print that children tend to know best appears on food containers—especially those for cereal, soup, milk, and cookies—and on detergent boxes and bottles. Among common signs, they recognize fast-food logos, road signs, traffic signals, and names of popular store chains, supermarkets, and service stations. Collect such logos and trade names and make them available in your classroom by posting them on charts, pasting them onto index cards, and creating loose-leaf books of environmental print. Most firms distribute various printed materials free, complete with logos. Photograph environmental print in your neighborhood and bring the photos to your classroom. Suggest that children read the words, copy them, and write them in a sentence or a story.

Start including environmental print in your classroom at the beginning of the school year with only a few signs, such as children's names on their cubbies and the names on centers, such as "block center," to identify that area of the room. Make labels with 5″ × 8″ index cards and dark felt-tip markers. Begin each word with a capital letter and continue with lowercase manuscript, thus providing youngsters with configuration clues. Hang labels at heights easy for children to see. Point out the labels to the children and suggest that they read them to friends and copy them. As the school year progresses, label new items that are added to the classroom. Refer to the labels as part of your normal routine so that they are used and will be added to the child's sight vocabulary. Label items because they are of interest to the class and serve a function, such as identifying important classroom materials and learning centers. Use labels for relating messages such as "wash your hands before snack." Refer to the labels often so the children identify them as useful and functional.

Label items related to content-area topics. For example, if your class is studying dinosaurs, display and label model dinosaurs. Even long, difficult words, such as *brontosaurus* and *tyrannosaurus,* immediately become sight words for many young children. It is not uncommon to observe preschool children reading labels to themselves or to each other. I observed a preschool class after the teacher had posted two new labels in the science center, which featured a lesson on the sense of touch and focused on items that were hard and soft. I watched Josh take Jennifer by the hand and heard him say, "See, Jen. See this. This bunny is soft. This word says soft." Josh continued, "See this, Jen. This is a rock and this word says hard. Touch it. It is hard." The two children stroked the bunny, pointed to the label, and said in unison, "soft." They then touched the rock, pointed to the label, and said, "hard." They repeated the sequence several times.

THE MORNING MESSAGE

ELL
Another way to make print part of the classroom environment is to communicate with it, even with preschool children. Post messages and assignments for children daily. Select a permanent spot on the chalkboard or on chart paper. Use rebus or picture writing, along with print, to help children make sense of the message. Here is an example of an appropriate message:

> Dear Boys and Girls,
> It is a rainy day today.
> It is a cold day today.
> We are going on a trip to the town library later.
> Love,
> Ms. Dunston

This routine will teach children to look automatically at the chalkboard each day for a special message. From the messages they will learn that print carries meaning that is interesting and useful. Some teachers have formalized this "morning message" into a lesson when the school day begins (Morrow, 2003).

Morning messages are used at morning meetings, when the class gets together to discuss what will happen during the school day. Write the same message at the beginning of the school year with only small changes to it. Write at least some of the message with the children watching, so that you provide a writing model for them. Use the message to develop various concepts about print. Emphasize specific words or letters, pursue questions about meaning, or let children add sentences to the original message. When working with preschool children, look for letters in the message that are in their names or in the Burger King sign, or look for an *M* for *mommy*. Find the same letter more than once in a message. Talk about words that might rhyme in a message such as:

> Dear Boys and Girls,
> We have a cake for Kate.
> It is her birthday today.
> Love,
> Ms. Dunston

Clap the words in the message, noting which ones have one clap and which ones have two or three claps.

After children are used to the routine and have repeatedly read similar morning messages, Ms. Dunston can purposefully make spelling errors or leave a letter out of the morning message and ask the children to find the mistakes. These can be corrected and filled in by the children. Entire words can be left out, as well.

In Ms. Fassi's preschool class, the children gather around the morning message chart daily. Early in the year her message is almost the same every day. It says:

> Dear Boys and Girls,
> Today is Wednesday, September 10, 2007.
> The weather is warm.
> The sun is out.
> We are learning about jungle animals.
> We talked about lions, tigers, monkeys, and giraffes.
> Love,
> Ms. Fassi

Because the message is similar every day, the children begin to be able to read it. Soon Ms. Fassi leaves out a word or letters in the message for children to fill in, such as:

> Dear Boys and _____,
> Today is Thursday, December 10, 2007.
> The weather is _____.
> It is _____ outside.
> Love,
> Ms. Fassi

DEVELOPING SIGHT VOCABULARY

In *Teacher* (1963), Sylvia Ashton-Warner described Very Own Words as a method for developing sight vocabulary. She encouraged children to have a parent or teacher write their favorite words on 5" × 8" index cards with pictures that depicted what the words said. On the other sides the words were written without pictures. Very Own Words often come from a child's home life—mommy, daddy, grandpa, grandma, cookie. They also reflect emotional feelings—naughty, nice, good, no, punish. After Very Own Words are recorded on index cards (just one word per card), they are stored in a child's file box, in a coffee can, in a plastic bag, or on a loose-leaf ring.

Teachers have devised many other methods for storing Very Own Words. Helping children start their collections of Very Own Words is an exciting experience in school and one that can come from the study of a theme. Before an activity or exercise, let the children know that at its completion you will ask them to name their favorite words from the activity. The activity should be a pleasant one that produces interesting language. Perhaps the class is studying farm animals and visited a farm. The teacher may ask children to name their favorite farm animals for their Very Own Words collection. Children also can choose a favorite word from a storybook or words generated from the study of themes in art, music, play, social studies, and science. Soon children will request their Very Own Words without being asked.

Encourage children to do things with their words, such as read them to friends or to themselves, copy them, and dictate them to the teacher to use in a sentence. Due to the fact that words are based on a child's expressed interests in situations at home and in school, the collection of Very Own Words is a powerful technique for developing sight vocabulary.

Children can compare the Very Own Words they have collected to see whether any of their words have the same letters. They can clap the sounds or syllables in the words. Very Own Words are also useful with bilingual children. The index card

Children compare their Very Own Words to see whether any of their words have the same letters. They can say and clap the number of sounds or syllables in the words.

should include a child's Very Own Word in English and can have the word written in his or her native language, as well.

WORD WALLS

A word wall typically features the letters of the alphabet posted at a level that children can easily see. The first words to put on a word wall in preschool are the names of the children in the class. Each name goes under the letter it begins with. A picture of the child can accompany the name. The words are placed on index cards. Sometimes words are written and then cut out into the shape of the word, providing visual configuration clues for remembering it. When putting words up, be sure to name the word and recite the letters of the word. Children can copy them, read them, and trace them in the air. Other words that can go up on the wall are words that mean something to the class, such as words featured in a theme. If they are studying winter, words such as *snowball, snowman,* or *sled* could go up on the word wall. The teacher should use the word wall to play word games. For example, if the teacher wants to work with rhymes, he or she can point to a child's name, such as Kim, and say, "the word I am thinking of rhymes with Kim, but begins with a Tuh." Many different lessons and directions for using the wall independently can be provided (Cunningham, 1995; Moustafa, 1997). With preschoolers, limit the number of words that are put on the word wall.

Use the word wall often by having children identify words, clap the number of sounds in the words, copy the words, and so forth (Allington & Cunningham, 1996). An additional word wall activity the teacher can lead is the Secret Word game, which provides the student with a series of clues such as:

The secret word has four letters.
It is the name of a boy in this class.
The first letter is *B* and the last letter is *d.*
The word is _____.

USING THE LANGUAGE EXPERIENCE APPROACH

ELL The language experience approach (LEA) has been used for many years in reading instruction. It can help children associate oral language with written language, specifically teaching them that what is said can be written down and read. The LEA illustrates the left-to-right progression of our written language. In practice, the LEA demonstrates the formation of letters plus their combination into words. It helps build sight vocabulary. It is a source of

Children read their friends' names on the word wall, figure out rhyming words on the wall, and look for letters they know.

meaningful teaching of phoneme–grapheme correspondence, as well as other knowledge about print, and it is based on the child's interests and experiences.

Many educators have been associated with developing and articulating the LEA, among them R. V. Allen (1976), M. A. Hall (1976), and J. Veatch and colleagues (Veatch, Sawicki, Elliot, Barnett, & Blackey, 1973). The LEA is based on the following premises, from the learner's point of view:

➢ What I think is important.

➢ What I think, I can say.

➢ What I say can be written down.

➢ What is written down can be read by me and by others.

The LEA builds on interests and experiences that come from children's home and school lives. It is particularly well suited for use with ELL students because it incorporates their lives and vocabulary into the learning process. Children can also use their own words to create their own books. In school the teacher needs to plan experiences, for example, class trips, cooking projects, the use of puppets, guest speakers, class pets, and holiday events or plan to study topics that are exciting to young children, such as dinosaurs, outer space, and other cultures. The language experience lesson is usually carried out with an entire class, but it also can take place with a small group or an individual child.

An LEA lesson begins with oral language. A discussion is usually generated from an interesting or exciting class experience, for instance, a recent trip to the zoo or the pet gerbil's new litter. To begin the discussion, ask open-ended questions that will encourage descriptive responses rather than yes-or-no answers. For example, if the topic is a trip to the zoo, ask children to name their favorite animal. Why was it their favorite animal? What did the animal look like? What did the animal do while they were watching it at the zoo? It is important to accept all the children's responses. Accept nonstandard English without correction, but provide a language model by using standard English to paraphrase what the child has said.

After a discussion has generated several ideas, write them down on a large sheet of paper (approximately 24″ × 36″) to create an experience chart. It can be taped to the wall or mounted on an easel. Print with a dark felt-tip marker of medium thickness, allowing ample spacing between words and between lines so that the chart is easily readable. Use manuscript in upper- and lowercase letters, following the conventions of regular print. This gives configuration to words that uppercase manuscript alone cannot give. Word configuration aids children in word identification.

In recording language on experience charts, teachers should write quickly and legibly, providing good manuscript samples for children to read and copy. When creating a new chart, try to remember which children have not contributed in the past and encourage them to contribute to the new chart. It is a good idea to identify who said what. The chart is more interesting to youngsters whose names are included. For example, "Jacob said, 'I liked the gorilla at the zoo,' and Jordanna said, 'I liked the baby deer.'" Try to accompany each sentence with an illustration; this will help children read the charts.

Experience charts should not be very long. Charts dictated by 2- and 3-year-olds can simply be lists of words, such as names of animals with illustrations next to them. Used occasionally, lists of words make appropriate charts for older children, as well. They are a quick way to record and reinforce vocabulary associated with topics being studied. Small-group and individual dictation of experiences can be made into books by the teacher or the child. While writing a chart, take the opportunity to point out concepts about print. For example, "Now I am writing the word *gorilla—g-o-r-i-l-l-a*. See, it begins here with a *g* and ends here with an *a*." Ask children to point out where you should begin to write on the chart. Like the morning message and the word wall, the LEA lesson can have a specific skill objective.

The last step in the LEA lesson is to read the chart to the class. Use a pointer to emphasize left-to-right progression. Let the class read the chart in unison, or ask individual children who contributed different sentences to read them. Leave the chart in a visible spot in the room. Encourage the children to read the chart, copy parts of it, copy words they like, or add words to their Very Own Word collection. Vocabulary charts and experience charts representing different topics discussed in

As teachers write words on the experience chart, they will ask children to help spell some by listening to the sounds of the words.

school can be left hanging in the room if space permits, then made into Big Books for children to look at throughout the school year. If a laminating machine is available, it is wise to preserve charts.

Pocket chart activities are associated with the LEA. (Pocket charts are wall hangings that have long, transparent pockets attached to them. They are made of sturdy fabric and come in a variety of standard sizes, such as 24″ × 36″; see Figure 6.3.) Words associated with class experiences are featured on the chart. Short stories, poems, and songs also are printed on individual sentence strips—long, thin strips of paper on which the teacher or child writes sentences—that students chant together. The charts can be copied, and the sentence strips can be scrambled and sequenced into the pocket chart. Sentence strips can also be cut up so that students can learn about individual words. They can identify and practice new words or use the words to create sentences.

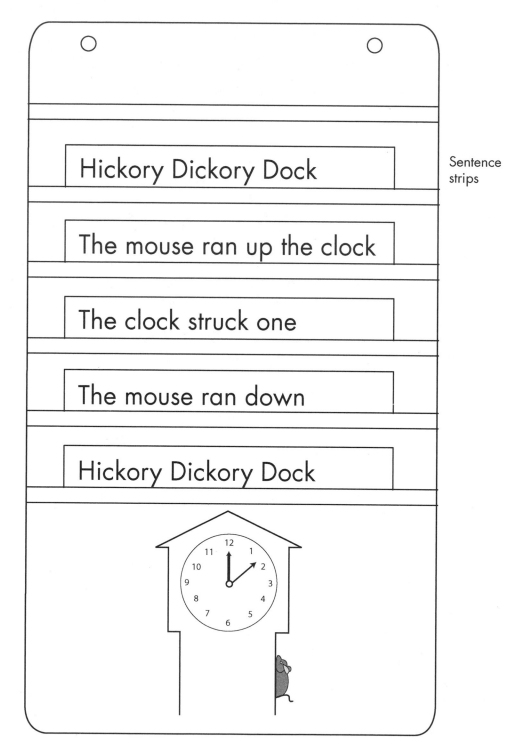

Sentence strips

FIGURE 6.3. Pocket chart.

The children were working on rhyming and also listening for sounds in words, such as the /k/ sound at the end of *clock*. Ms. Healey reinforced the skill by chanting the poem "Hickory Dickory Dock":

Hickory Dickory Dock,
The mouse ran up the clock.
The clock struck one,
The mouse ran down!
Hickory Dickory Dock.

Ms. Healey wrote the words of the poem on chart paper and then on sentence strips. She cut a second set of sentence strips into individual words. This provided the children with activities to practice matching the sentence strips with the chart paper, sequencing whole sentences, and identifying the letter *k* within the context of the poem. Children also were able to practice new vocabulary that appeared in the poem. Pocket chart activities are often used to practice new skills during independent center time.

The LEA, which is appropriate throughout early childhood and beyond, can be used similarly to the morning message and Very Own Words. LEA charts help children learn that print is written and read from left to right with familiar and meaningful information. Occasionally prepare a chart in the languages of bilingual children in your class. If necessary, solicit help from bilingual parents or colleagues. This strategy will guide bilingual youngsters in making connections between their languages and English.

LEA materials are inexpensive and easy to use. They include chart paper, sentence strips, colored construction paper, white paper, index cards, scissors, staplers, pencils, markers, and crayons. With directions from the teacher, these simple classroom materials record precious words and pictures created by children from their own meaningful, real-life experiences. The LEA should be central, not supplemental, to literacy instruction in early reading programs.

USING CONTEXT AND PICTURES TO FIGURE OUT WORDS

ELL Experiences with literature can lead children to use contextual print and illustrations to recognize that words have meaning. Contextual print and illustrations can also help children figure out what a word says. Again, those experiences can take place in whole-class, small-group, or one-to-one settings and through such techniques as shared book experiences and repeated readings of stories. For example, select a story that is predictable, in which the text and illustrations are closely related. Ask children to look at the pictures on a page before reading it to them. Ask them what they think the words will say. Then read the page to demonstrate that print and illustration are closely related and that the pictures provide information that can help the children as they read the story.

The syntax and semantics of a sentence (its grammatical structure and meaning) also help children identify words. Encourage children to use these elements of written language by stopping your oral reading at predictable points in a story and asking them to fill in words. For example, when reading *The Little Red Hen* (Galdone, 1973), first read the complete repetitive phrase "I won't, said the dog; I won't, said the cat; I won't, said the pig." Then have children fill in the blanks: "I won't, said _____ dog," and the next time, "I won't, _____ _____ cat," and lastly, "I _____, _____ _____ pig." This technique is most effective with a Big Book, because you can point to the words as the children say them. As the children begin to understand the concept of filling in words, choose more difficult passages for your pauses. Prepare charts and sheets with predictable text and leave out words to be filled in as you read. Children use their prior knowledge of syntax and context in predicting words. They will eventually assimilate and use the strategy when they are able to read themselves.

In addition to these general suggestions, specific experiences in figuring out words can be varied so that students have many different strategies for using context. A common way to determine words from context is through the meaning of the text. For example, in the sentence "The King and _____ lived in a castle together," it is apparent that the missing word is *Queen*. We need to show children how to use the meaning of the text to figure out a word that might be unknown to them.

PHONOLOGICAL AWARENESS AND PHONEMIC AWARENESS DEFINITIONS

Phonological and phonemic awareness instruction in early literacy helps students to become independent readers. These skills should be taught concurrently with other strategies for learning to read, such as acquiring sight words and learning how to use context clues and picture clues. Children need to have a holistic view of books and reading, as well as the more abstract skills, as they work on decoding unknown words. As mentioned earlier, phonemic awareness is the ability to recognize that words are made up of individual speech sounds (Burns, Snow, & Griffin, 1998). The words *hat* and *chat* contain three speech sounds, referred to as *phonemes*. The phonemes are not letters; they are sounds. This is different from phonics, which includes knowledge of the relationship between letters and sounds. Phonological awareness is the awareness of the sound structure of language. Phonological awareness involves identifying and manipulating larger parts of spoken language, such as whole words, syllables, onsets, and rimes. The segmenting and blending of these sounds is the important skill children need to develop. Phonemic awareness is a subset of phonological awareness. Phonemic awareness and phonological awareness are considered precursors to phonics, and they are needed to learn phonics. They are important to achieving successful reading ability. However, they are just one part of a comprehensive program in learning to read (National Reading Panel, 2000). It is the concurrent use of several of the word-study skills mentioned that creates a proficient reader (Reutzel & Cooter, 2004). Also according to the National Reading Panel (2000), a child needs 18 hours of phonemic awareness instruction during the kindergarten school year to learn the skills. In a 180-day school year, that would be about 6 minutes a day.

PHONOLOGICAL AND PHONEMIC AWARENESS INSTRUCTION

Instruction in phonemic and phonological awareness should be playful, as teachers read and tell stories, play word games, and use rhymes and riddles. In addition, instruction in the area should be purposeful and planned. We must make sure children get the necessary experiences. In the past this instruction was spontaneous and incidental. Of course, it still can be spontaneous when the moment arises, and it should be; however, this instruction cannot be left to chance. It must be systematically written into daily plans. Try as much as possible to make your instruction meaningful and purposeful (Adams, 2001). It is easiest for young children to learn to deal with whole words or larger parts of words first and then smaller parts. The teacher can begin by exposing children to rhyming activities. This is considered to be the easiest task, as it deals with whole words. Rhyming activities can be done in preschool and kindergarten. Simply chanting nursery rhymes and reading stories that rhyme help children to develop the skill. Next, children can deal with segmenting sounds, such as listening for and counting syllables in words. Help children learn about segmenting sounds in words by asking them to clap the sounds in their names. The most difficult skill in phonological awareness is segmenting and then blending words together. For this, we work with onsets and rimes. An *onset* is the beginning sound in a word; the *rime* is the ending chunk or group of letters in a word. Work in this area, for example, asks children to listen for the beginning sound in the word *cat,* which is *c,* and then to put it together with its ending sound, *at,* to make the whole word *cat* (Yopp, 1992). When teaching activities that help to learn rhyming, segmenting, and blending, we ask children to match sounds, work with sounds in isolation, and make sound substitutions and deletions. These activities help children to learn about sounds in words.

When asking children to match, I may ask them to identify whether two words start with the same sound, such as *big* and *boy.* When working with words in isolation, I will ask children what sound they hear at the beginning of the word *cow.* I am not asking for the letter name; I am asking for the sound.

When I ask children to substitute sounds, I change the beginning sound of a word like *bat* to *mmm*. Then I ask children, "What is the word now, *mat*?" When I ask children to delete, I might say, "Tell me what word we have when we say the word *snowman* without the *man*," or "*hat* without the *h*." Remember that, with all of these exercises, we are saying sounds, not identifying them with the letters. They are oral exercises.

The easiest phonemic awareness task is working with rhymes. Teachers can help children to hear, identify, and match to similar word patterns. Early work in this area should be playful. Exposing children to books that contain rhymes, such as *Green Eggs and Ham* (Dr. Seuss, 1960), *Goodnight Moon* (Brown, 1947), and *The Queen of Hearts* (Hennessy & Pearson, 1989) helps develop the skill. Teachers can recite rhyming and nonrhyming words from the books and ask children to differentiate between them. For additional practice with rhyme, children can do the following:

1. Make up words that rhyme with their names.
2. Sing songs that rhyme and separate out the rhyming words.
3. Act out well-known nursery rhymes, such as Jack and Jill.
4. Make up new rhymes for a story, such as "I Know an Old Lady Who Swallowed a Fly" (Westcott, 1980). Let the children decide what else she could swallow and what would happen to her if she did. For example, "I know an old lady who swallowed a frog; she began to jog when she swallowed a frog."

It is a good idea to have some routine rhymes and songs that the class chants repeatedly. The chant should allow them to change, to match, and to substitute rhymes. The following chant will allow children to make up rhymes and substitute rhymes:

Let's Make a Rhyme
When it's cold outside, and you want to play,
Let's make a rhyme, my teacher would say.
Did you ever see a *dog*
Pushing a *log*
On a cold and winter's day?

When it's cold outside, and you want to play,
Let's make a rhyme, my teacher would say.
Did you ever see a *moose*
Pushing a *goose*
On a cold and winter's day?

The next step is for each child to think of an animal to make a rhyme with, for example:

Did you ever see a *cow*
Saying *bow wow*
On a cold and winter's day?

Segmenting is an important skill and a more difficult one than rhyming for children. It is easier for a child to segment the beginning sound, or onset, and then the ending chunk, or rime. If this is done with the word *man,* for example, the child should be guided to say *mmm* for the onset /m/ and then *annn* for the rime /an/.

Syllabication is a way of segmenting words or working on phonological awareness. Children can clap the syllables in their names and in the names of their friends.

Name Chant
If your name has a beat and the beat is one,
Say and clap your name and then Run, Run, Run.

If your name has a beat and the beat is two,
Say and clap your name and hop like a kangaroo.

If your name has a beat and the beat is three,
Say and clap your name, then buzz like a bee.

If your name has a beat and the beat is four,
Say and clap your name and stamp on the floor.

After segmenting words, ask children to blend them back together again. The goal is for children to be able to identify each sound within a word, to know the number of sounds heard, and to be able to blend the word back together. We can ask them to stretch the word out like a rubber band, which would be asking them to segment, and then say it really, really fast as the elastic springs back to blend. The following are some activities that will help children learn to segment and blend:

1. Sing the song "Bingo." In the song, each letter is chanted and then blended together. Change the words from "There was a farmer had a dog and Bingo was his name-o," to "There is a pretty girl [or handsome boy] that I know and Jenny is her name-o, J-e-n-n-y, J-e-n-n-y, J-e-n-n-y, and Jenny is her name-o."

2. Play a riddle substitution of onsets game. Say, "I'm thinking of a word that

sounds like *head,* but begins with the /b/ sound," or "I'm thinking of a word that sounds like *fat,* but has an /mmm/ sound at the beginning."

3. A good song for segmenting and blending is sung to the tune of "This Old Man." You can use the name of the letter featured or use the letter sounds.

This Old Man
This old man sings *N* songs
He sings *N* songs all day long
With a Nick, Nack, Nackie Nack
He sings his silly song
He wants you to sing along

This old man sings *B* songs
He sings *B* songs all day long
With a Bick, Back, Backie Back
He sings his silly song
He wants you to sing along

Now make up your own verse with a new sound.

4. Elkonin boxes are used to engage children in segmentation and blending. Select and write words on a piece of paper. Draw square boxes next to each word. Have chips for students to put into the squares. Say the word on the paper, such as *duck,* and have the children put the number of chips in the boxes that represent the number of sounds in the word. For the word *duck,* children would put three chips into the boxes, because the *ck* in the word has one sound (Invernizzi, 2003; Fitzpatrick, 1997; Johns, Lenski, & Elish-Piper, 1999).

LEARNING ABOUT THE ALPHABET

Many young children who cannot yet identify individual letters of the alphabet are able to read. As noted, they read sight words from environmental print, from classroom labels, and from Very Own Words lists. They learn other sight words from repeated readings and shared book experiences. It is not necessary to be able to identify and name the letters of the alphabet in order to develop an initial sight-reading vocabulary. It is easier for a young child initially to learn whole words that are already familiar through oral language than to learn abstract letters. Familiar words carry meaning for them, whereas isolated letters do not.

Children, of course, need to learn the alphabet to become independently fluent readers and writers. However, there is no evidence that alphabet identification should be treated as the first skill in early literacy; it makes more sense for children to learn to identify letters after they have learned several sight words. Traditionally, the alphabet has often been the first thing parents try to teach their children at home, and knowledge of it is usually high on any list of reading-readiness skills in preschool and kindergarten curricula. Teaching the alphabet will always be prominent in early literacy programs because it is difficult to depart from deeply rooted tradition.

Allow children to explore letters by using manipulative materials available in the literacy center. Be sure to stack the center with alphabet puzzles, magnetic upper- and lowercase letters and a magnetic board, a set of wooden upper- and lowercase letters, tactile letters made of sandpaper, alphabet games, felt letters and a felt board, letter stencils, alphabet flash cards, and a long alphabet chart posted along the wall of the classroom at the children's eye level. In addition to these materials, a large supply of alphabet books and taped songs about the alphabet should be in the classroom library. (See Appendix C for a list of alphabet books.) Encourage children to explore these materials through play. Later, they will begin to identify the letters they are playing with and teach letters they know to other children. Provide chalk and a chalkboard so they can make letters themselves. Children also enjoy finger-painting letters, painting them on easels, shaping them out of clay, and eating them in alphabet soup or as cookies or pretzels. Shaping letters with their fingers and their whole bodies is an activity often used in early childhood rooms.

Systematic teaching of the alphabet, one letter per week, is not as successful as teaching children letters that are meaningful to them. Many teachers help children identify the letters in their own names first. When teaching thematic units, select a few letters to feature that are used in the context of the theme. For example, in a unit on transportation, feature *b* for boat and *t* for train. When children have learned to identify several different letters, ask them to look for the same letters in other contexts, such as magazines, newspapers, and books. Check children individually by using flash cards to determine which letters they know and which they do not know. Ask children which letters from their Very Own Words they would like to learn. Give children flash cards of the letters they choose to learn and encourage them to use those letters in all the activities just mentioned. They need to practice letters all year through.

Additional ideas for learning and reinforcing what is known about the alphabet include the following:

1. Sing the alphabet song often and point to the letters on a poster as they are sung.

2. Play letter bingo, which involves cards filled with letters and markers to

cover them. Call a letter and hold up a card with the letter on it to help children with letter identification. When a child covers one row of letters on the card, he or she gets bingo.

3. Provide children with alphabet journals. On each page is another letter of the alphabet. On the different letter pages, children can trace the letter, write the letter, and find words in a magazine that use the letter and paste them on the page.

4. Create an alphabet center with many different alphabet materials such as those already mentioned (magnetic letters, wooden letters, matching-letter games, alphabet puzzles, alphabet books, alphabet stamps, alphabet flash cards). Children will identify this area with the alphabet, and they should be encouraged to use the materials often.

Alphabet books also help children to learn the alphabet. For example, read different books throughout the year and do different activities based on the book. The book *Chicka Chicka Boom Boom* (Martin, Archambault, & Ehlert, 1989) is perfect for helping children to learn the alphabet. Before reading the book aloud to the class, the teacher should have each child make a sign for one letter of the alphabet. Signs should include the letter in both upper- and lowercase writing. When the story is read to them, the children put their signs around their necks and pop into

Using manipulative letters and with the help of a teacher, the child spells his name.

After several practice sessions the child can spell his name alone.

the story when their letter is called. Each letter is mentioned twice in the story. When the story is repeated, the children trade signs. Photograph the children as the story is read, and then make a book of the photos for them to read. *The Handmade Alphabet* by Laura Rankin (1991) is an alphabet book that signs the letters. The children are shown how to sign them as they say them. *Potluck* (Shelby & Travis, 1991) is an alphabet book about children going to a picnic and each bringing something. It starts with "Acton appeared with asparagus soup; Ben brought bagels." It ends with "Yolanda brought yams and yogurt and Zeke and Zelda zoomed in with zucchini casserole." We make food in our class based on the book.

State standards declare that, by the end of kindergarten, children must be able to name and recognize the letters of the alphabet. Teachers need to check children's knowledge of the alphabet and provide instruction based on the findings. If more direct instruction is needed to help students, then it should be provided. The letters of the alphabet must be practiced regularly. Students should be exposed to letters on a daily basis and in different settings.

STRATEGIES FOR TEACHING PHONICS

Phonics is the connection of sounds and symbols. The use of phonics requires children to learn letter sounds and combinations of letter sounds or phonemes, associated with their corresponding letter symbols, or graphemes. The English alphabet contains 26 letters; however, there are at least 44 different sounds in English. Sound–symbol correspondence is not always consistent in English. There are many irregularities and exceptions to many rules. This makes it difficult for children. Therefore, we must help children learn words by sight that cannot be sounded out, and we need to give them strategies for figuring out words. For the most part, preschool teachers do not explicitly teach phonics, but there are teachable moments to take advantage of.

How can we help children recognize the sound–symbol relationships in a meaningful context? Science and social studies themes lend themselves to featuring letters that appear in units. For example, the letter *p* is used frequently when studying farm, pet, and zoo animals. The following types of activities can be done:

1. Read *The Pig's Picnic* (Kasza, 1988), *Pet Show* (Keats, 1974), and *The Tale of Peter Rabbit* (Potter, 1902) during the unit and point out words that begin with the letter *p*.

2. Make word charts using words from the books that begin with the letter *p*.

3. On a field trip, bring peanuts to the zoo to feed the animals.

4. Make lists of animals that begin with the letter *p*.

5. Collect sensory items about animals that begin with the letter *p*, such as Puppy Chow to smell, peanuts to eat and to feed to elephants when you visit the zoo, peacock plumes to touch, a purring kitten to listen to, and the book *Petunia* (Duvoisin, 1950) to look at and read.

6. List words from the unit that begin with the letter *p*.

7. Write an experience chart of activities carried out during the unit, and highlight the letter *p* when it appears in the chart.

8. Ask children to add to their Very Own Word collection with favorite words from the unit that begin with the letter *p*.

9. Make a collage of pictures featuring things from the unit and mark those that begin with the letter *p*.

10. Have children help make nonsense rhymes for featured letters, such as:

    > My name is Penelope Pig.
    > I pick petals off of petunias.
    > I play patty cake
    > and eat pretzels with pink punch.

11. Add a page for the letter *p* to a class Big Book titled *Our Own Big Book of Letters, Sounds, and Words*. Have children draw pictures or paste in pictures of words that begin with the letter *p*.

12. Encourage children to write something and include the letter *p*. Think about the letter *p* in songs sung, stories told, and activities participated in. At the end of his preschool year, at 5 years old, Matthew wrote a story about *The Pig's Picnic*. He wrote "Pig wanted the picnic to be perfect" as PG W PCNC PRFT.

Children's literature is an excellent source of letters that are attached to themes. Be careful not to abuse the stories by overemphasizing the sounds featured; however, do not pass up the opportunity to feature letters in this natural book setting. For example, in a unit on food, Ms. Aguruso emphasized the letter *b* and read *Blueberries for Sal* (McCloskey, 1948), *Bread and Jam for Frances* (Hoban, 1964), and *The Berenstain Bears and Too Much Birthday* (Berenstain & Berenstain, 1987).

Alphabet books can be used for sound–symbol relationships, as they introduce each letter. Do not try to teach phonics in any formal manner. Answer questions and play games that are fun and that the children can do. Learning corresponding sounds and symbols is not a skill that must be learned in preschool.

A CENTER FOR WORD-STUDY ACTIVITIES

A center that contains materials for word study is necessary in the preschool classroom. The activities for sorting pictures and letters discussed earlier can be game like if they are presented with interesting manipulative materials. Have magnetic letters and a magnetic board to work on. Students can use wooden moveable letters, rubber foam letters, an alphabet puzzle, and flash cards with letters on them. The flash cards can be used to match and classify on a table or a pocket chart. Children enjoy working with letter stamps and white slates with Magic Markers. Board games such as Bingo, Lotto, Concentration, and Candyland and card games can be constructed so that children have to identify letters or pictures that match in sounds. All materials must be modeled by the teacher and played with as a large or small group before they are placed into a center for children to use independently. Games for centers can be purchased from teacher-supply stores and large school-supply companies. Teachers also can create numerous word-study activities that children can learn from, use to reinforce knowledge, and use independently when teachers are engaged in small-group instruction. Teachers can make materials and seek the help of parents, aides, and upper-grade children to make materials.

ASSESSING KNOWLEDGE ABOUT PRINT

Numerous skills concerning print knowledge are discussed in this chapter. Initially, teachers should be concerned with a child's phonemic awareness. The Yopp–Singer Test of Phoneme Segmentation (Yopp, 1992) is widely used to determine how well children can segment phonemes in words. The directions specify ensuring that the child says the sounds, not the letters, in the word, because these are two different skills.

In addition to daily performance samples of children's writing and activity sheets, observations and descriptions of children's emergent reading behaviors should be included in word-study assessment. Checklists are also important materials for testing children on word-study skills. For example, to test for knowledge of the alphabet, the teacher can name particular letters and ask a child to circle them on a sheet of paper containing upper- and lowercase letters. A checklist of skills can be found in Figure 6.2. Teachers can also use flash cards of letters for students to identify. Some sight words and Very Own Words can be checked in a similar manner to alphabetic knowledge by being circled on a sheet of paper or by using flash cards. To determine the ability to rhyme, the teacher says pairs of words and asks children to identify rhyming and nonrhyming words. Knowledge of phonic sounds, such as consonants, is checked by having the child identify the letter a word begins with. When asking children to determine the beginning letter of an object in a picture, ensure that the object is clear and easy to identify. For example, some children may mistake a donkey for a horse and choose the initial letter *h,* instead of *d.* Besides the assessments mentioned, some of the same game-like activities used for instruction and practice materials for reinforcement are used for assessing children's knowledge of word-study skills.

REFERENCES

Adams, M. J. (1990). *Beginning to read: Thinking and learning about print.* Urbana: University of Illinois Center for the Study of Reading.

Adams, M. J. (2001). Alphabetic anxiety and explicit systematic phonics instruction: A cognitive science perspective. In S. B. Neuman & D. K. Dickinson (Eds.), *Handbook of early literacy research* (pp. 66–80). New York: Guilford Press.

Allen, R. V. (1976). *Language experience in communication.* Boston: Houghton Mifflin.

Allington, R. L., & Cunningham, P. M. (1996). *Schools that work: Where all children read and write.* New York: HarperCollins.

Ashton-Warner, S. (1963). *Teacher.* New York: Bantam.

Burns, M. S., Snow, C. E., & Griffin, P. (1998). *Preventing reading difficulties in young children.* Washington, DC: National Academy Press.

Cunningham, P. (1995). *Phonics they use.* New York: HarperCollins.

Fitzpatrick, J. (1997). *Phonemic awareness.* Cypress, CA: Creative Teaching Press.

Hall, M. A. (1976). *Teaching reading as language experience.* Columbus, OH: Merrill.

Harste, J., Woodward, V., & Burke, C. (1984). *Language stories and literacy lessons.* Exeter, NH: Heinemann.

Invernizzi, M. (2003). Concepts, sounds, and the ABC's: A diet for the very young reader. In D. M. Barone & L. M. Morrow (Eds.), *Literacy and young children: Research-based practices* (pp. 140–157). New York: Guilford Press.

Johns, J., Lenski, S. D., & Elish-Piper, L. (1999). *Early literacy assessments and teaching strategies.* Dubuque, IA: Kendall/Hunt.

Juel, C. (1994). Teaching phonics in the context of the integrated language arts. In L. Morrow, J. K. Smith, & L. C. Wilkinson (Eds.), *Integrated language arts: Controversy for consensus* (pp. 133–154). Boston: Allyn & Bacon.

Mason, J. (1980). When do children begin to read? An exploration of four-year-old children's letter and word reading competencies. *Reading Research Quarterly, 15,* 203–227.

Mason, J., & McCormick, C. (1981). *An investigation of pre-reading instruction: A developmental perspective* (Tech. Rep. No. 224). Urbana: University of Illinois, Center for Study of Reading.

Morrow, L. M. (2003). *Organizing and managing the language arts block.* New York: Guilford Press.

Morrow, L. M. (2005). *Literacy development in the early years: Helping children read and write* (5th ed.). Boston: Allyn & Bacon.

Moustafa, M. (1997). *Beyond traditional phonics: Research discoveries and reading instruction.* Portsmouth, NH: Heinemann.

National Reading Panel. (2000). *Teaching children to read.* Washington, DC: National Institute of Child Health and Human Development.

Reutzel, D. R., & Cooter, R. B. (2004). *Teaching children to read: Putting the pieces together* (4th ed.). Upper Saddle River, NJ: Pearson/Merrill Prentice Hall.

Roser, N., & Martinez, M. (1985). Roles adults play in preschool responses to literature. *Language Arts, 62,* 485–490.

Smith, F. (1971). *Understanding reading.* New York: Holt, Rinehart, & Winston.

Strickland, D., & Snow, C. (2002). *Preparing our teachers: Opportunities for better reading instruction.* Washington, DC: Joseph Henry Press.

Taylor, D. (1983). *Family literacy.* Exeter, NH: Heinemann.

Teale, W. (2003). Questions about early literacy learning and teaching that need asking—and some that don't. In D. M. Barone & L. M. Morrow (Eds.), *Literacy and young children: Research-based practices* (pp. 140–157). New York: Guilford Press.

Veatch, J., Sawicki, F., Elliot, G., Barnett, E., & Blackey, J. (1973). *Key words to reading: The language experience approach begins.* Columbus, OH: Merrill.

Yaden, D. (1985, December). *Preschoolers' spontaneous inquiries about print and books.* Paper presented at the annual meeting of the National Reading Conference, San Diego, CA.

Yopp, H. K. (1992). Developing phonemic awareness in young children. *Reading Teacher, 45,* 696–703.

CHILDREN'S LITERATURE

Berenstain, S., & Berenstain, J. (1987). *The Berenstain bears and too much birthday.* New York: Random House.

Brown, M. (1947). *Goodnight moon.* New York: HarperCollins.

Dr. Seuss. (1960). *Green eggs and ham.* New York: Random House.

Duvoisin, R. (1950). *Petunia.* New York: Knopf.

Galdone, P. (1973). *The little red hen.* Boston: Houghton Mifflin.

Hennessy, B. G., & Pearson, T. C. (1989). *The queen of hearts.* New York: Picture Puffins.

Hoban, R. (1964). *Bread and jam for Frances*. New York: Harper & Row.

Kasza, K. (1988). *The pig's picnic*. New York: Putnam.

Keats, E. J. (1974). *Pet show*. New York: Aladdin Books.

Martin, B., Jr., Archambault, I., & Ehlert, L. (1989). *Chicka chicka boom boom*. New York: Scholastic.

McCloskey, R. (1948). *Blueberries for Sal*. New York: Viking Press.

Potter, B. (1902). *The tale of Peter Rabbit*. New York: Scholastic.

Rankin, L. (1991). *The handmade alphabet*. New York: Dial Books.

Shelby, A., & Travis, I. (1991). *Potluck*. New York: Orchard Books.

Westcott, N. B. (1980). *I know an old lady who swallowed a fly*. Boston: Little Brown.

CHAPTER 7

COMPREHENDING AND ENJOYING CHILDREN'S LITERATURE

t is an early autumn day. Ms. Aguruso and the 3- and 4-year-olds in her pre-school class take a walk outside to collect colorful leaves. Four-year-old Richey becomes very excited when he finds a cricket. He cups it in his hands, yelling, "Come and look!" Everyone gathers around to inspect the cricket. Richey care-fully puts the cricket on a nearby rock, and the children clap as it hops away.

When they return to the classroom, Ms. Aguruso, taking advantage of this event, thumbs through the bookshelf to find *Quick as a Cricket* (Wood, 1982). She remembers that the cover has a wonderful picture of a cricket and that the book features many animals and rich, descriptive language ("happy as a lark," "cold as a toad," "strong as an ox"). It takes her several minutes to find the book; she knows the power of literature, and the shelves in her classroom are filled with fables, folktales, picture storybooks, informational books, wordless books, easy-to-read books, and poetry. Finally, she locates *Quick as a Cricket*.

The children are excited when Ms. Aguruso holds up the book and says, "Look what I found!" Several children see the cover and chant, "A cricket! A cricket!" They then gather around Ms. Aguruso, and she begins to read *Quick as a Cricket* aloud. As she reads, Ms. Aguruso shows the children the book's large and beautiful illustrations. After reading a page or two, so that the children get the rhythm of the story ("I'm as quick as a cricket, I'm as slow as a snail, I'm as small as an ant . . ."), she reads "I'm gentle as a lamb." She then points to the little boy in the illustration and says, "He's . . ." and the children begin to repeat the text in unison, " . . . as gentle as a lamb."

When Ms. Aguruso and the children finish reading the book, she asks the children which animal they think is most like them. One very small boy speaks up in a big voice and says, "I'm strong as an elephant." A little girl then chimes in, "I'm loud as a lion." Richey then volunteers, "I'm quick as a cricket—because I caught a cricket!" With that remark the teacher and the children cheer and applaud. As the children begin to wander off, Richey leans over and whispers to his teacher, "Can I have that book?" Ms. Aguruso beams as Richey clutches the book to his chest and wanders over to the reading corner.

When a teacher reads a good piece of children's literature aloud, children are exposed to much more than an oral rendering of the book in a storybook reading event. The language of the text is expanded by the discussion and social interaction that takes place among the adults and children (Sulzby & Teale, 1987). During the "talk about the text" that occurs during storybook reading, children seek to understand and negotiate the meaning of the text. This construction of meaning that occurs during storybook reading may account for the powerful influence that exposure to children's literature has on literacy development. Because teachers play such an important role in the literacy development of young children, their primary concerns regarding read-alouds are practice and attitude. Reading good literature aloud is perhaps the major way in which teachers share their enthusiasm for reading with their students. Sharing literature with young children sparks the imagination, provides language models, and shapes cognitive development (Cullinan, 1987).

THE IMPORTANCE OF USING CHILDREN'S LITERATURE

Parents and teachers of young children agree that it is vitally important to read high-quality literature to young children. Sharing books with young children has always been acknowledged as a critical aspect of early literacy development. According to the National Institute of Education, "the single most important activity for building the knowledge required for eventual success in reading is reading aloud to children" (Anderson, Hiebert, Scott, & Wilkinson, 1985, p. 23). Sharing books with children in preschool is crucial to literacy development. Reading aloud to young children is associated with increased vocabulary, language complexity, good comprehension skills, and success in beginning reading (Cosgrove, 1989; Cullinan, 1992; Elley, 1989).

When the teacher shares books, children have the opportunity to hear the rich and diverse language of books, as well as the rhythm and flow of book language. Read-aloud time provides an opportunity for children to hear and enjoy books that may be related to a topic or theme being explored in the classroom. There is a strong relationship between storybook reading in the home and beginning literacy development (Morrow, 2005). Early readers come from homes in which they were read to frequently beginning when they were only months old (Clark, 1984; Morrow, 1983; Teale, 1981). Although many children come from homes rich in literacy events, we know that many children, especially those from economically disadvantaged communities, have less exposure to literacy. Most educators agree that the preschool years are an especially critical time for providing rich literacy experiences for all young children.

Preschool teachers need to take advantage of teachable moments, as Ms. Aguruso did. They also need to be explicit in their teaching. When they have specific skills to teach in literature, such as putting the events of the story in sequential order, teachers need to:

➢ Explain the skill that is being taught to the children.

➢ Model how to put the skill into practice.

➢ Provide guided practice through assistance by scaffolding for children who need the help.

➢ Provide time for independent practice and application of the skill in different contexts.

➢ Teach parents how to use this model so they can provide good learning experiences at home.

Using Children's Literature with Children from Diverse Backgrounds

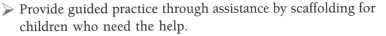

ELL   The use of children's literature provides the opportunity for teachers to be sensitive to children in our diverse society. Diversity is more apparent than ever before. One out of every seven children in our classrooms in the United States is an English language learner, that is, a child whose first language is something other than English. This number increases daily. We need to acknowledge diversity by being sensitive toward cultural and language differences. To help students who are English language learners, include books in their native language, as well as stories in English about their countries. Everyone will enjoy informational books about the different cultures, as well. Learn about customs of the diverse cultures in your classroom and learn a few words in the languages represented in your class. Using some key phrases and sharing books related to a child's background will make him or her feel welcome and more comfortable. If possible, assign a bilingual child, one who speaks both English and the language of the English language learner, as a buddy. This child can help the English language learner understand more of what is happening in the classroom. Preschoolers who are able to speak their first language well are likely to acquire English through immersion in an English-speaking classroom; this is something that older children cannot do. Moreover, it is important that students hear their own languages, as well as English.

To help students who are learning English to understand English, speak slowly and in simple language. Repeat phrases you want them to learn, and use gestures and visual references when communicating (Shore, 2001). Teach them functional language that will help them participate in classroom activities. Make a book for the child filled with pictures of different parts of the classroom. For example, include a picture of the block center, the dramatic-play area, the library corner, and so forth, and label the pictures in the book in English and in the child's native language. The book can illustrate predictable daily routines that the teacher follows. This book will help to make the child feel safe and confident. The book can include drawings or photographs. In addition to functional book making, creating other books about topics of interest to children is a recommended activity. For example, making a book about fruit with an illustration on a page and the word underneath it will help with vocabulary. High-interest picture books and books with predictable patterns are particularly useful in helping the English language learner learn English. Reading the same book repeatedly is a useful approach. Also recommended is dramatic play and the use of props with stories to visually represent language.

Throughout this book I discuss good strategies for all children. Strategies that use props and visual cues, such as those listed here, are particularly good for students who are learning English. You will learn more about these techniques as you read about them.

> ➤ Reading to children and showing the illustrations.
> ➤ Discussing stories read.
> ➤ Reading the same stories repeatedly.
> ➤ Using Big Books when reading stories.
> ➤ Reading to children in small groups and one-to-one.
> ➤ Engaging children.
> ➤ Retelling stories.

➢ Using buddy reading (e.g., looking at books with an older student).

➢ Using partner reading (e.g., looking at books with peers and children who have the same cultural background).

➢ Using choral reading (e.g., reciting a poem together).

➢ Using echo reading (e.g., the teacher reading one line and the children repeating it).

➢ Using tape-assisted reading.

➢ Integrating storybooks into content areas, in particular, art, music, and play.

➢ Engaging children in independent reading.

➢ Engaging children in independent use of story props for retelling stories.

➢ Modeling for parents of English language learners ways they can share books with children in their own language.

COMPREHENDING AND RESPONDING TO BOOKS

Whenever Ms. Fassi reads to the class, she starts reading by saying, "The title of this book is _____, the author is _____, and the illustrator is _____." She does this to encourage her children to do the same before looking at the rest of the book. One day during literacy center time, Max placed the Big Book, *Chicka Chicka Boom Boom* (Martin, Archambault, & Ehlert, 1989) on the Big Book stand. Max had gathered some children in front of him to read to. He started by saying, "I'm going to read this book to you." He turned to the first page and acted as if he was the teacher and began pretend reading the book to the children. Aiden popped up and said, "Max, you can't read the book yet; you forgot to read the title." Max put his hand to his forehead, looked somewhat annoyed with himself, and said, "How could I forget that? The title of the book I'm going to read is *Chicka Chicka Boom Boom*." Children need to learn concepts about books and to comprehend what is read to them. Through activities that ask them to respond to literature, they will learn to understand different types of text.

LEARNING CONCEPTS ABOUT BOOKS

We often assume that children naturally know concepts about books. If they have had little experience with books, they will not know them; therefore, we need to teach them. When children are very young, teachers discuss how to handle books, the parts of a book, and the difference between pictures and print. Knowledge of concepts about books is important in the road toward becoming literate. Children who know concepts about books:

> Are aware that a book is for reading.

> Can identify the front, back, top, and bottom of a book.

> Can turn the pages of a book properly in the right direction.

> Know the difference between print and pictures.

> Know that pictures on a page are related to what the print says.

> Look at the pictures to grasp meaning.

> Know where to begin reading on a page.

> Know what a title is.

> Know what an author is.

> Know what an illustrator is.

Activities That Develop Concepts about Books

Take every opportunity available to help children learn concepts about print. Point out concepts about print during reading activities. Introduce a story by pointing as you say, "The title of the story that I'm going to read is *If You Give a Mouse a Cookie* [1985]. This print that I am pointing to is called the title of the book and is on the front cover."

On another day say, "The author of the book is the person who wrote it. The author of *If You Give a Mouse a Cookie* is a lady named Laura Numeroff. I am pointing here where her name is on the cover of the book."

On a different day, talk about the illustrator. "The illustrator of a book is the person who draws the pictures. The illustrator for *If You Give a Mouse a Cookie* is Felicia Bond. I am pointing to her name here on the cover of the book."

Repeat these little lessons often. Remind the children that all books have titles and authors and that if books have pictures they also have illustrators. If the book has photographs, they have a photographer. You will need to discuss the difference between photographers and illustrators—one draws the pictures, and the other takes the photos with a camera.

After you have discussed these concepts frequently, suggest to the children that they look for the title every time they look at a book. It is always on the front cover. It is also usually on the title page at the beginning of the book. Eventually, when you introduce a book, you can talk about the title, author, and illustrator all at the same time.

The repetition of such dialogue will help the children to learn the concepts just mentioned. Similar dialogue helps to explain other concepts. For example:

1. Point to a picture and say, "The picture helps us predict what the book is about."

2. Point to the print and say, "The print is what we read to find out what the book is about."

3. After identifying the print and the pictures, ask, "Which do we read? Do we read the picture or the print?"

4. We need to ask, "Show me one word. See how it is made up of many letters? Look, there are spaces between each word. Count the words on this page."

As you get ready to read to the children, ask them to point out the top and bottom of the book and where you should begin reading on a page. Not only will you give the children the opportunity to learn the concepts, but at the same time you can also determine which children know the concepts and which need help. These discussions can be carried out during story readings to whole groups, to small groups, or to individual students. A child's independent exploration of books will reinforce what you have explained. As a result of this type of teacher behavior, the following will begin to happen when reading stories to children:

When children are taught to point to print, they learn that print is different from pictures, they see the spaces between words, and they learn that words are made up of letters.

"After I read *Horton Hatches the Egg* (Dr. Seuss, 1940) to a small group of 4-year-olds, Jovanna said to me, 'Show me where it says "I meant what I said and I said what I meant, an elephant's faithful one hundred percent." I want to see it in the book.' When I showed her and the other children the words, they repeated them. I pointed to them as they chanted. When we finished, they asked to see them again in another part of the book. We proceeded to search through the rest of the book, reading with great enthusiasm each time we found the line 'I meant what I said and I said what I meant, an elephant's faithful one hundred percent.'"

Big Books Help Preschoolers with Concepts about Books

Big Books are an important part of early literacy instruction. They are oversized picture storybooks that measure from 14″ × 20″ up to 24″ × 30″. Enlarged print and pictures in these books help get children involved with concepts about books, print, and the meaning of text. Big Books are appropriate for preschoolers and for children in the primary grades. Active involvement is encouraged when using Big Books in small- and large-group settings. When using a Big Book, a teacher places it on a stand, because it is difficult to handle otherwise. It is positioned so the children can see the pictures and text. Big Books can be purchased or made by teachers and students. When they are made, children become even more aware of book concepts because they are engaged in creating a book.

Materials for Making a Big Book

➢ 2 pieces of oak tag for the cover (14″ × 20″ to 20″ × 30″)

➢ For the pages in the book, 10 pieces or more of tagboard or newsprint the same size as the oak tag used for the cover

➢ 6 loose-leaf rings (1")

➢ Hole punch

Directions for Making a Big Book

➢ Punch three sets of holes in top, middle, and bottom of the cover and paper that is to go inside of the book.

➢ Insert a loose-leaf ring in each hole. The Big Book should have about 10 pages.

➢ Print should be 1″ to 2″ high.

Big Books are effective for developing concepts about books mainly because of their size. As the teacher reads the book and tracks the print from left to right across the page, children see that books are for reading and where we begin to read on a page. They also learn to differentiate the print from the pictures. Children make the connection that the oral language they hear from their teacher is being read from the book. The correct way to turn pages is easy to see and learn with Big Books because they are so large. We take the top corner of the right-hand page and turn it. The title of the book is prominently displayed on the front of the book and on the title page inside, as are the names of the author and the illustrator.

DEVELOPING COMPREHENSION WITH PRESCHOOL CHILDREN

Comprehension is the ability to read or listen and understand text. Understanding what is read is one of the major goals of reading instruction. Learning to comprehend should be an active process when preschoolers listen to stories. Based on prior knowledge, children need to learn to interpret and construct meaning from what they listen to (Pressley & Hilden, 2002). Comprehension development is enhanced as a result of children's social interactions with others during reading. For example, children benefit from early experiences with books and from the interaction with adults who read to them. The child is asked to respond, and the adult offers information when necessary. Comprehension depends on the difficulty of the text for the listener or reader. Therefore, when reading to children, keep in mind the following characteristics of the text that will determine how well a child will comprehend:

> The familiarity of the content in the text.

> The background knowledge required to understand the text.

> How interesting the topic is to the listener.

> The syntactic complexity of the sentences.

> The amount and difficulty of vocabulary included.

> The length of a selection (Graves, Juel, & Graves, 1998).

In a study by Dolores Durkin (1978–1979), it was found that comprehension was rarely taught in early childhood. During the 1980s a great deal of research about comprehension was carried out by the Center for the Study of Reading at the University of Illinois. As a result of that work and other research that followed, more attention has been paid to teaching comprehension to young children. The Rand Reading Study Group report (2002) and the National Reading Panel report (2000) discuss what comprehension strategies need to be taught to students and how to teach them. These reports draw on research about successful comprehension practices. The strategies discussed here reflect some of the findings from these reports that are appropriate for preschool children.

To help children learn to comprehend narrative and expository text we need to:

> Read materials to children from beginning to end.

> Refer back to the text to clarify some difficult parts.

> Slow down when we come to information that is relevant to what we want children to remember.

> Provide background information so that children have some prior knowledge of the text before it is read to them.

> Ask children to anticipate and predict what might happen in a story.

> Discuss the text with children after reading so they can reflect on ideas and summarize what was read (Pressley & Afflerbach, 1995). This might sound sophisticated for preschool, but children can participate in these types of discussions.

COMPREHENSION STRATEGIES

The Directed Listening and Thinking Activity

When children are read to, or when they read themselves, there should be a purpose for reading or listening. The format of the directed listening and thinking activity (DLTA) and the directed reading and thinking activity (DRTA) sets a purpose for reading and listening, thus helping to direct thought. This strategy, when internalized by children as a result of frequent use by the teacher, will be transferred and used by students when new material is read or listened to (Morrow, 1984; Stauffer, 1980). I talk about the DLTA in this book because we are dealing with preschoolers. The strategy provides the listener with a framework for organizing and retrieving information. In the following DLTA for the story *Peter's Chair* (Keats, 1967) the following two skills are being developed:

1. Sequencing the events of the story after it is read.

2. Making inferences related to the text.

Preparing Students for Listening with Prequestions and Building Background Knowledge

It is crucial to build children's background knowledge related to what is going to be read when introducing a story. It helps children focus their thinking about the story topic and aids comprehension. Ask prequestions that build additional background knowledge and set a purpose for listening. Relate the questions to real-life experiences whenever possible. The following is a sample discussion from a preschool classroom:

"Today I'm going to read a story titled *Peter's Chair.* Let's look at the pictures to see if you can tell what the story is going to be about." The teacher encourages the children to discuss the pictures as she turns the pages of the book from beginning to end. She calls this a "book walk." After the children offer their ideas, she says:

> "This story is about a little boy named Peter whose mommy and daddy just brought home a new baby sister. Many of Peter's things, such as his baby toys, high chair, and crib, are being painted pink for his sister. Peter gets upset thinking that his family doesn't love him anymore. Do you have a younger brother or sister? Do you have to share your toys with your little brother or sister? How does that make you feel? Do you have to give them some of your things, such as your crib and high chair? Were you sad or happy about that and why? When I read the story you will hear about how Peter feels about his new baby sister and having to share his belongings with her. While I'm reading try to decide if you think you would feel as Peter did."

When the children have gained enough experience with your prequestions on a daily basis, they will begin to think of their own. For example, you could say, "Now that I've told you a little about the story, what do you want to find out about Peter, his baby sister, and his mom and dad?"

Reading the Story

Be sure to show the children the pictures as you read the story. Stop just one or two times for reactions, comments, or questions. Do not interrupt the story for a lot of discussion because it interferes with the storyline. Save the discussion for the end.

Discussion after Reading

The postdiscussion should be guided by the objectives or purpose set for listening to the story, such as:

1. "What things that belonged to Peter did his parents prepare first, second, and third for the new baby?" Children can retell the story. Retelling will demonstrate their knowledge of sequence. Allow children to use the pictures in the book to help them follow sequence.

2. Finally, focus on the second goal, making inferences, and ask: "What would you have done if you were Peter? Do you think Peter's parents were right to take Peter's things and give them to his baby sister? How would you feel if your parents took your things and gave them to your baby sister or brother if you had one or have one?"

A DLTA can have many different objectives. The framework, however, is always the same: (1) preparation for listening or reading—prequestions and discussion; (2) reading the story with few interruptions; and (3) discussion after reading. All three steps are focused on the DLTA's specific objectives. A DLTA can focus

ELL

on both literal responses (such as recall of facts and sequencing) and inferential responses (such as interpreting characters' feelings, predicting outcomes, and relating the story to real-life experiences). It can focus on identifying elements of story structure, whether narrative or informational text. Research has demonstrated that a DLTA can increase the story comprehension of young listeners (Morrow, 1984), just as a DRTA can increase the story comprehension of young readers (Baumann, 1992; Pearson, Roehler, Dole, & Duffy, 1992). Provide a workshop to teach parents these techniques for reading to children.

The directed listening and thinking activity (DLTA) used when reading to children creates a purpose for them to listen.

Shared Book Experiences

The shared book experience (Holdaway, 1979) is usually carried out in a whole-class setting, although it may be carried out in small groups as well. During this activity, teachers model fluent reading for children. They also help children to develop listening skills by asking them to participate in the story reading.

Shared book reading often involves reading from a Big Book designed so that everyone in the group can see the pictures and words clearly while it is being read. If the book is a new one for the class, the children are asked to listen during the first reading. If it is being read for the second time or is already familiar, immediate participation is encouraged. Often the teacher uses a pointer during the reading to emphasize left-to-right progression with younger children in addition to the correspondence of spoken and written words.

Ways to gain children's participation during a teacher's reading in a shared book experience include chanting together repeated phrases in the story, stopping at predictable parts and asking children to fill in words and phrases, or reading key words that are special to the story. Shared book experiences could also include echo reading, in which the teacher reads one line and the children repeat it. Big Books and regular-size copies of the same book should be available for children to use independently after a first Big Book reading.

Shared book readings can be tape-recorded and made available in the listening center. This provides a familiar and fluent model for reading with good phrasing and intonation for children to emulate. Shared book experiences can be adapted to the DLTA format, with one of the objectives being to provide a participatory and enjoyable read-aloud event. Research indicates that shared book reading benefits the acquisition of reading and writing. It enhances background information and sense of story structure and familiarizes children with the language of books (Cullinan, 1992; Morrow, 1985). Book language is different from oral language. It introduces new syntax and vocabulary. The following excerpt from *Swimmy* (Lionni, 1963) makes this clear:

> One bad day a tuna fish, swift, fierce and very hungry, came darting through the waves. In one gulp he swallowed all the little red fish. Only Swimmy escaped.

Predictable stories are ideal for shared book experiences because they allow children to guess what will come next, thereby encouraging participation. Predictability takes many forms. The use of catch phrases, such as " 'Little pig, Little pig, Let me come in" from *The Three Little Pigs* (Brenner, 1972), encourages children to chant along. Predictable rhyme enables children to fill in words, as in *Green Eggs and Ham* (Dr. Seuss, 1960). Cumulative patterns contribute to predictability. In books with predictable patterns, new events are added with each episode and then repeated in the next, as in *I Know an Old Lady Who Swallowed a Fly* (Hoberman & Westcott, 2004). This book repeats phrases and episode patterns as the story continues, for example:

> I know an old lady who swallowed a fly,
> I don't know why she swallowed a fly I guess she'll die
> I know an old lady who swallowed a spider
> That wiggled and jiggled and tickled inside her
> She swallowed the spider to catch the fly,
> I don't know why she swallowed a fly, I guess she'll die
> I know an old lady who swallowed a bird,
> How absurd to swallow a bird.
> She swallowed the bird to catch the spider
> That wiggled and jiggled and tickled inside her
> She swallowed the spider to catch the fly
> I don't know why she swallowed the fly
> Perhaps she'll die. . . . (pp. 1–5)

Conversation can contribute to predictability, as in *Goldilocks and the Three Bears* (Izawa, 1986) or *The Three Billy Goats Gruff* (Brown, 1957). All books become predictable as children become familiar with them, so repeating stories builds a repertoire for shared book experiences. Books that carry familiar sequences, such as days of the week, months of the year, letters, and numbers, are predictable. Eric Carle's *The Very Hungry Caterpillar* (1969) is a good example of this. Books gain predictability through good plot structures and topics familiar to children. Books in which pictures match text page by page tend to be predictable to children, especially if everyone in the group can see the pictures as the story is being read. Predictable books are excellent for emergent and conventional readers in shared book experiences, as well as in independent reading. They allow the child's first experience with reading to be enjoyable and successful. This success encourages the child to continue efforts at reading.

Repeated Storybook Reading

Children enjoy repetition. Being familiar with an experience is comfortable, like singing a well-known song. Besides offering the pleasure of familiarity, a repeated story helps develop concepts about words, print, and books. In a study with 4-year-olds, one group listened to three repeated readings of the same story, and the other group listened to three different stories. After the stories were read, the discussions consistently revealed that the children in the repeated-reading group increased the number, kind, and complexity of responses made. In addition, their responses differed significantly from those of the different-story group. The repeated-reading group's responses became more interpretive, and they began to predict outcomes and make associations, judgments, and elaborative comments. Children also began to narrate stories as the teacher read, to focus on elements of print, and to ask names of letters and words. Even children of low ability seemed to make more responses with repeated readings than with a single reading (Kuhn & Stahl, 2003).

Repeated readings are important for youngsters because they can engage in the activity on their own. Children who are able to read by themselves or to participate in pretend reading behaviors often will select the same book to look at or read over and over again. Teachers should repeat readings of stories to children and encourage youngsters to read stories and look at books more than once. They should carry out discussions about books that have been read and discussed previously.

The following dialogue (from Morrow, 2005) is from a transcription of a 4-year-old child's responses to a third reading of *The Three Little Pigs* (Brenner, 1972). This excerpt primarily includes the child's comments and questions and the teacher's responses. Most of the story text has been omitted.

> TEACHER: Today I'm going to read the story *The Three Little Pigs*. It is about three pigs who wanted to leave home and build their own houses and take care of themselves. (*She begins to read the story. When she gets to the part where the wolf says to the first little pig "Little pig, little pig, let me come in," Marcy chimes in.*)
>
> MARCY: "Not by the hair on my chinny chin chin." "Then I'll huff and I'll puff and I'll blow your house down."
>
> TEACHER: Very nice, Marcy. You are helping me with the reading. (*She continues to read.*)
>
> MARCY: I want to read that part, but I don't know how.
>
> TEACHER: Go ahead and try. I bet you can. I'll find the part and help you.
>
> MARCY: (*Pretend reads parts she remembers from the repeated readings.*) The little pig ran to his brother's house; the one who had the house made of sticks.

TEACHER: (*Continues reading.*) "The wolf got to the pig's house that was made of bricks and sand."

MARCY: (*Chants with the teacher and points to the words on the page.*) "Little pigs, little pigs let me come in," said the wolf. "Not by the hair of my chinny chin chin," said the pigs. "Then I'll huff and I'll puff and I'll blow your house down," said the wolf.

TEACHER: You're right again, Marcy. (*She reads to the end of the story.*) Did you want to say anything else about the story?

MARCY: The wolf scared the pigs. But they learned they need to have strong houses. I want to see the part again when the pigs leave home. (*She searches through the pages.*)

TEACHER: Show me the part you are talking about.

MARCY: There it is, at the beginning. The pigs are packing their bags and saying good-bye to their mommy and daddy.

TEACHER: How do you think their mommy and daddy felt when they all left home together?

MARCY: I bet they were sad. I want to look at the part when the wolf falls down the chimney into the pot of boiling water.

TEACHER: Here it is.

MARCY: "The wolf fell, jumped down the chimney and ended up in a pot of boiling water and ran out the door and never came back again."

Sophisticated discussions about storybooks occur as children interact with adults about a book that has been read to them a repeated number of times.

TEACHER: That's terrific.

MARCY: That's what the story said.

TEACHER: You're right.

This type of sophisticated response can happen only when a child has heard a story that has been repeated many times. Children enjoy hearing the same book read to them over and over again. As adults we often tire of the repetition; however, it has great value in early reading development. There should be a repertoire of books considered favorite stories that are read repeatedly to children at home and in school. To study emergent reading behaviors, Sulzby (1985) observed children from ages 2 to 6 attempt to read their favorite storybooks. They could participate in the activity because they knew the stories so well. Although they were not yet readers in the conventional sense, the children were asked, "Read me your book." Sulzby found that in their "reading" the children produced speech that could indeed be categorized as a first act of reading. That is, the speech they used as they "read" was clearly different in structure and intonation from their typical conversation. In addition to this, different developmental levels could be observed in these "oral readings."

To use the classification scheme (Figure 7.1), ask a child to read a story that is well known to him or her. Preschoolers will not conventionally read; however, from their attempts at storybook reading, we can determine characteristics of their emergent reading behavior.

Small-Group and One-to-One Storybook Readings

The importance and benefits of reading to small groups and to individuals must not be overlooked. Too often considered impractical in school settings, one-to-one and small-group readings yield such tremendous benefits that they must be incorporated into preschool programs.

The most striking benefit of one-to-one storybook readings at home—often called the lap technique—is the interactive behavior it involves, along with the direct information it gives the child. It also provides the adult with insight into what the child already knows and wants to know. Preschoolers do well participating in small-group and one-to-one readings, because they need the attention that this setting provides. It is much easier to get the attention of preschoolers in small groups than in a large-group setting.

It has been found that one-to-one readings are beneficial for preschoolers and especially for those from homes with little exposure to books (Morrow, 1988). When reading in small groups or in a one-to-one setting, it is important for teachers to encourage children to be interactive. Teachers need to manage storybook reading by introducing the story and providing background information. When teachers read frequently to children and initiate interactive discussions, the num-

The child "reads" by labeling and commenting on the pictures in the book but does not "weave a story" across the pages.	YES ____ NO ____
Attends to pictures and forms oral stories.	YES ____ NO ____
The child "reads" by following the pictures but weaves a story across the pages through wording and intonation like those of someone telling a story.	YES ____ NO ____
Attends to a mix of pictures, reading, and storytelling. The child "reads" by looking at the pictures. The majority of the child's "reading" fluctuates between the oral intonation of a storyteller and that of a reader.	YES ____ NO ____
Attends to pictures but forms stories (written-language-like). The child "reads" by looking at the pictures. The child's speech sounds like reading, both in wording and intonation. The listener rarely needs to see the pictures in order to understand the story. With his or her eyes closed, the listener would think the child was reading print. The "reading" is similar to the story in print and sometimes follows it verbatim. There is some attention to print.	YES ____ NO ____
Attends to print. This category has two divisions: The child reads the story mostly by attending to print but occasionally refers to pictures and reverts to storytelling. The child reads in a conventional manner.	YES ____ NO ____

FIGURE 7.1. Sulzby's classification scheme for children's emergent reading of favorite storybooks. Adapted from Sulzby (1985). Copyright 1985 by the International Reading Association. Adapted by permission.

ber and complexity of the children's responses increases. The youngsters will offer many questions and comments that focus on meaning. They label illustrations initially and then give more attention to details. Their comments and questions become interpretive and predictive, and they draw from their own experiences. They also begin narrating—that is, "reading" or mouthing the story along with the teacher. When frequently involved in small-group or one-to-one storybook readings, children begin to focus on structural elements in a story, remarking on titles, settings, characters, and story events. After many readings the children begin to focus on print, reading words, and naming letters and sounds (Morrow, 2005). Reading to small groups of children seems to encourage many responses. Children tend to repeat one another's remarks, and they are motivated to respond to and elaborate on what their peers have said.

Teacher Interactions with Children during Storybook Reading

1. Manage.
   a. Introduce the story.
   b. Provide background information about the book.
   c. Redirect irrelevant discussion back to the story.
2. Prompt responses.
   a. Invite children to ask questions or comment throughout the story when there are natural places to stop.
   b. Model responses for children if they are not responding. For example, "Those animals aren't very nice. They won't help the little red hen."
   c. Relate responses to real-life experiences. ("I needed help when I was preparing a party, and my family shared the work. Did you ever ask for help and couldn't find anyone to give it to you? What happened?")
   d. When children do not respond, ask questions that require answers other than yes or no. ("What would you have done if you were the little red hen and no one helped you?")
3. Support and inform.
   a. Answer questions as they are asked.
   b. React to comments.
   c. Relate responses to real-life experiences.
   d. Provide positive reinforcement for children's responses (Morrow, 1988).

The following segments from transcriptions of small-group storybook readings in preschool illustrate the various questions and comments children make when they are involved in the activity. They illustrate the rich information children receive from the responding adult. The transcriptions also illustrate what the children already know and what their interests are, which helps us design instruction.

Story: The Very Busy Spider (Carle, 1985)

The child asks about book concepts.

JEROME: (*He points to the picture on the front of the book.*) Why does it have a picture on it?

TEACHER: The cover of the book has a picture on it so you will know what the story is about. Look at the picture. Can you tell what the book is about?

JEROME: Ummm, I think that's a spider. Is it about a spider?

TEACHER: You're right, very good. The book is about a spider, and the name of the story is *The Very Busy Spider.* When you look at the pictures in a book they help you find out what the words say.

Story: Where the Wild Things Are (Sendak, 1963)

The child asks for a definition.

> TEACHER: I'm going to read a story called *Where the Wild Things Are*.
>
> JOVANNA: What are wild things?
>
> TEACHER: They are people or animals that act angry, scary, a little crazy, cause trouble, are too excited or much too active. See, there is a picture of a wild thing in the book.
>
> JOVANNA: I never knew that before. They look scary.

Story: The Pigs' Picnic (Kasza, 1988)

The child attends to the print.

> COLIN: Wait, stop reading. Look at all the *p*'s on the page. See, here is one, here is one. What does that say?
>
> TEACHER: This word is *pig*, and this is *picnic*, and this is *perfect*. You are right, they all begin with a *p*.

Story: Mr. Rabbit and the Lovely Present (Zolotow, 1962)

The child predicts.

> DORENE: I wonder what the present will be.
>
> TEACHER: I don't know. Look at the pictures before I start reading and see if you can get an idea.
>
> DORENE: Well, I see them picking apples, and pears, and grapes. Maybe they will give her mother some fruit for her birthday.
>
> TEACHER: That is a good thought. Let's read the book and find out.

These segments reveal understanding of text. The children's comments and questions relate to literal meanings, discuss interpretive and critical issues by associating the story with their own lives, make predictions about what will happen next in a story, or express judgments about characters' actions. In these examples the children's comments and questions also relate to matters of print, such as names of letters, words, and sounds.

Although whole-class readings are more practical and have tremendous value in simply exposing children to literature, the interactive behavior between adult and child in one-to-one readings and small-group readings does not occur in the large-group setting. If we review transcripts of story readings in all three settings, several things become apparent. In whole-group settings, a child cannot ask questions or comment throughout the story because it would interfere with the story line for the other children. In addition, the teacher might never get through a coherent reading. In a whole-group setting, the discussion has to be managed by the teacher to such an extent that he or she often says more than the children. A truly interactive situation does not exist because of the size of the group. In small-group and one-to-one readings, by contrast, a teacher initially may manage and prompt often but only to encourage and model responses for children. The roles reverse in a short time, when most of the dialogue is initiated by the children (Morrow, 2005).

Teacher- and Child-Generated Questions

Productive discussions result from good questions. Discussions from questions must include more than a few words by participants and should include questions that ask for clarification, explanations, predictions, and justifications.

Literal questions ask students to:

➤ Identify details such as who, what, when, and where.

➤ Classify ideas.

➤ Sequence text.

➤ Find the main idea.

Inferential and critical questions ask students to:

➤ Draw information from their background knowledge.

➤ Relate text to life experiences.

➤ Predict outcomes ("What do you think will happen next?").

➤ Interpret text ("Put yourself in the place of the characters.").

➤ Compare and contrast.

➤ Determine cause and effect.

➤ Apply information.

➤ Problem solve.

Discussion questions should reflect children's interests and have many appropriate responses rather than just one correct answer. Occasionally, questions with one correct answer can be asked. Most questions, however, should stimulate discussion and elicit responses that reflect children's thoughts and feelings about what was read to them. These questions are asking children to deal with feelings, sensations, and images. Other questions can deal with facts, details of the story, and main ideas. When asking questions, have students look back into the book to find pictures that could answer the questions. After they have been asked questions, children should be encouraged to ask their own questions about a story that was read to them.

Story Retelling

Encouraging a listener or reader to retell a story helps develop a child's vocabulary, syntax, comprehension, and sense of story structure (Ritchie, James-Szanton, & Howes, 2003). Retelling engages children in holistic comprehension and organization of thought. It also allows for original thinking, as children mesh their own life experiences into their retelling (Gambrell, Pfeiffer, & Wilson, 1985). With practice in retelling, children come to assimilate the concept of narrative or informational text structure. They learn to introduce a narrative story with its beginning, setting, theme, plot episodes, and resolution. They also learn to retell narrative text in their particular structure, such as a sequence structure, cause and effect, or problem solution. In retelling stories, children demonstrate their comprehension of story details and sequence. They also infer and interpret the sounds and expressions of characters' voices. In retelling informational text, children learn to sequence events, describe in detail the information presented, and determine cause and effect.

Retelling is not an easy task for children, but with practice they improve quickly. To help children develop the practice of retelling, let them know before they listen to a story that they will be asked to retell it (Morrow, 1996). Further guidance depends on the teacher's specific purpose for the retelling. If the immediate intent is to teach sequence, for instance, then children are asked to think about what happened first, second, and so on. If the goal is to teach the ability to make inferences from the text, ask the children to think of things that have happened to them that are similar to those that happened in the story. Props, such as feltboard characters or the pictures in the book, can be used to help students retell. Pre- and post-discussion of text helps to improve retelling ability, as does the teacher's modeling a retelling for children. Retelling is used to develop comprehension, and it also allows adults to evaluate children's progress. If you plan to evaluate a retelling, tell the child during your introduction of the selection that he or she will be asked to retell it after the reading. If you are assessing a retelling, do not offer prompts beyond general ones, such as "Then what happened?" or "Can

As James retells a story to his baby sister that was previously read to him, he remembers details, reviews the sequence of the story, and demonstrates that he comprehends.

you think of anything else about the selection?" Retellings of narrative text can reveal a child's sense of story structure, focusing mostly on literal recall, but they also reflect a child's inferential thinking. To assess the child's retelling for sense of story structure, first divide the events of the story into four categories—setting, theme, plot episodes, and resolution. Use a guide sheet and the outline of the parsed text to record the number of ideas and details the child includes within each category in the retelling, regardless of their order. Do credit the child for partial recall or for recounting the "gist" of an event (Pellegrini & Galda, 1982). Evaluate the child's sequencing ability by comparing the order of events in the child's retelling with the proper order of setting, theme, plot episodes, and resolution. The analysis indicates not only which elements the child includes or omits and how well the child sequences but also where instruction might be focused. Comparing analyses of several retellings over a year will indicate the child's progress.

Story Retelling Guidelines

1. Ask the child to retell the story. "A little while ago, I read the story [name the story]. Would you tell [retell] the story as if you were telling it to a friend who has never heard it before?"

2. Use the following prompts, if needed:
   a. If the child has difficulty beginning the retelling, suggest beginning with "Once upon a time" or "Once there was."
   b. If the child stops retelling before the end of the story, encourage continuation by asking, "What comes next?" or "Then what happened?"
   c. If the child stops retelling and cannot continue with general prompts, ask a question that is relevant at the point in the story at which the child has paused—for example, "What was Jenny's problem in the story?"

3. When a child is unable to retell the story, or if the retelling lacks sequence and detail, prompt the retelling step by step. For example:
   a. "Once upon a time" or "Once there was. . . ."
   b. "Who was the story about?"
   c. "When did the story happen?" (day, night, summer, winter)
   d. "Where did the story happen?"
   e. "What was [the main character's] problem in the story?"
   f. "How did [he or she] try to solve the problem? What did [he or she] do first [second, next]?"
   g. "How was the problem solved?"
   h. "How did the story end?" (Morrow, 1996)

The following example uses an outline of the narrative story *Franklin in the Dark* (Bourgeois, 1987). The outline is followed by a transcription of the retelling of the story by a 4-year-old child named Philip (Morrow, 1996).

Story Outline for Story Structure

> ➤ Setting: Once upon a time there was a turtle named Franklin.

> ➤ Characters: Franklin (main character), Franklin's mother, a bird, a duck, a lion, a polar bear.

> ➤ Theme: Franklin is afraid to go into his shell because it is dark inside the shell.

> ➤ Plot episodes:
>   - First episode: Franklin decided to look for help to solve his problem.
>   - Second episode: Franklin meets a duck and asks for help. The duck tells Franklin that he wears water wings because he is afraid of the water.
>   - Third episode: Franklin meets a lion who wears earmuffs because he is afraid of his own roar.
>   - Fourth episode: Franklin meets a bird who is afraid to fly so he uses a parachute.
>   - Fifth episode: Franklin meets a polar bear who wears a hat, mittens, and a scarf because he doesn't like the cold.
>   - Sixth episode: Franklin shares his experiences with his mother.

> ➤ Resolution: Franklin and his mother put a night-light in his shell. Now Franklin will go inside his shell.

Verbatim Transcription

TEACHER: What's the title of the story I read to you today?

PHILIP: I don't know.

TEACHER: *Franklin in the Dark.*

PHILIP: *Franklin in the Dark.* One time Franklin didn't want to go in his shell. He was too scared. But his Mama says, there's nothing in there. But Franklin didn't want to go in the shell because he thought there was monsters in there. He didn't like to go in because he was scared. It was dark. At the end he went in, he turned on a little night-light and went to sleep. That's it.

Retellings can be evaluated for many different comprehension tasks. The directions for students prior to retelling and the method of analysis should match the goal. Figure 7.2 provides an analysis form for evaluating a retelling. The teacher checks for the elements a child includes and to determine progress over time.

In his retelling, Philip names the main character, Franklin, and Franklin's mother. Philip does state the problem of the main character or the theme. He does get the resolution of the story and ends it. The parts of the story that Philip included are told in sequential order. In his retelling Philip does not begin the story with an introduction. Aside from mentioning Franklin and his mother, he does not talk about any of the other four characters. There is no statement of time and place. Philip does not

Setting

- Begins story with an introduction. ☐

- Names main character. ☐

- List other characters named. _____

_____

_____

- Includes statement about time and place. ☐

Theme

- Refers to main character's primary goal or problem to be solved. ☐

Plot Episodes

- Recalls episodes. ☐

- List episodes recalled. _____

_____

_____

Resolution

- Includes the solution to the problem or the attainment of the goal. ☐

- Puts an ending on the story. ☐

Sequence

- Tells story in sequential order. ☐

FIGURE 7.2. Analysis of story retelling and rewriting.

recall any of the plot episodes in the story. The teacher knows from this evaluation that Philip is able to recall the theme of the story and the resolution. The teacher especially needs to work on helping Philip to remember details of a story, such as characters and plot episodes, and also to begin the story with more of an introduction.

SOME COLLABORATIVE STRATEGIES TO DEVELOP COMPREHENSION

The National Reading Panel (2000) report suggested that collaboration is an important strategy for developing comprehension. Collaborative settings allow children to engage in productive conversations as they exchange ideas and learn to listen to each other. Teachers model the behaviors for collaborative activities before children participate in them with peers.

Buddy Reading

Buddy reading involves a child from an upper grade paired with a child in preschool or other primary grades. The child in the upper grade is instructed on how to read to children. At specified times during the school week, buddies get together for storybook readings and discussions.

Partner Reading

Partner reading involves peers reading together. This may simply mean that the children sit next to each other and share the same book. They take turns discussing the pictures or narrating the text.

Mental Imagery and Think-Alouds

Mental imagery asks children to visualize what they see after they have been read to. We ask children to "make a picture in your mind" to help remember and understand what was read to them. After the mental imagery, we ask children to "think aloud" and talk to peers about their images. We also ask children to predict what will happen next in the story. We tell children to ask themselves questions about the story and to look back at the pictures if they need to remember forgotten details. We often ask children to personalize the text by asking them if they have ever been in a similar situation as the main character and what they did. Visualizing ideas and relating those visualizations orally to a peer helps clarify information and increase understanding (Gambrell & Koskinen, 2002).

Strategies to Develop Fluency

Fluency is a skill that needs more emphasis in literacy instruction. According to the National Reading Panel (2000), helping children to become fluent readers is crucial for literacy development. When a child is a fluent reader, he or she is able to automatically and accurately decode text. In addition, the child reads with the appropriate pace and expression (Kuhn & Stahl, 2003). The ultimate goal for reading instruction is that students be fluent readers. Preschoolers can participate in fluency activities as listeners. Research has shown that particular strategies are useful in helping to develop fluency. These include echo reading, choral reading, and tape-assisted reading. With preschool children we adapt the strategies as echo chanting, choral chanting, tape-assisted listening, and repeated readings.

Echo Reading

When we involve children in echo reading, the teacher reads one line of text, and the child then reads the same line after. Preschoolers can listen and echo chant what has been read to them. When reading to the children, model with good accuracy, pace, and expression. Try to echo chant a few times a week.

Choral Chanting

In choral reading the entire class, or a small group of children, reads or chants a passage together. The teacher provides a model for pace and expression. Preschoolers who are not yet conventional readers can choral chant poems they have learned, such as "Humpty Dumpty," "Jack and Jill," and so forth. When choral chanting, children will experience the correct pace and expression necessary to read fluently. Try to choral chant a few times a week.

Tape-Assisted Listening

Listening to fluent reading on audiotapes while following the pictures in a book provides children with an excellent model of good reading. Tapes can be purchased but also made by teachers, parents, and older students who present fluent models for reading.

Children should participate in fluency activities daily. They are easy to do, do not take much time, and are fun (Rasinski, 1990). Repeating stories is a way to enhance fluency as well.

ASSESSMENT OF CONCEPTS ABOUT BOOKS AND COMPREHENSION

Three techniques described in this chapter are designed to develop concepts of books and comprehension of story through the use of informational and narrative text. The skills listed in Figure 7.3 for assessing concepts about books and comprehension of text can be used to check student progress. To determine how much

Child's Name _____ Date _____

Concepts about Books

	Always	Sometimes	Never	Comments
Knows a book is for reading				
Can identify the front, back, top, and bottom of a book				
Can turn the pages properly				
Knows the difference between print and pictures				
Knows that pictures on a page are related to what the print says				
Knows where to begin reading				
Knows what a title is				
Knows what an author is				
Knows what an illustrator is				
Pretend reads storybooks, resulting in well-informed stories				
Participates in story reading by narrating as the teacher reads				

(continued)

FIGURE 7.3. Checklist of comprehension skills. From Lesley Mandel Morrow, *Literacy Development in the Early Years: Helping Children Read and Write,* 5th ed. Published by Allyn and Bacon, Boston, MA. Copyright © 2005 by Pearson Education. Reprinted by permission of the publisher.

	Always	Sometimes	Never	Comments
Retells stories and includes elements such as: Setting				
Theme				
Plot episodes				
Resolution				
Recognizes informational text structures: Description				
Sequence				
Details/facts				
Problem and solution				
Responds to text after listening with interpretive comments or questions				
Participates in: Partner reading				
Buddy reading				
Mental imagery				
Participates in fluency activities such as: Echo chanting				
Choral chanting				
Tape-assisted reading				

FIGURE 7.3. *(continued)*

children know about books (such as a book's front, back, top, and bottom; differentiating print from pictures; how pages are turned; where reading begins; and what titles, authors, and illustrators are), one can observe how youngsters handle books. Have one-to-one interviews with children. Also question and encourage responses in whole-group, small-group, or individual interaction. Children's comprehension of story can be demonstrated and evaluated through their story retelling, attempted reading of favorite storybooks, role playing, picture sequencing, use of puppets or felt boards to reenact stories, and their questions and comments during storybook readings. When possible, keep periodic performance samples of activities, such as audio- or videotapes of retellings.

Throughout this chapter assessment tools for evaluating strategies have been provided. These materials should be placed in a child's portfolio to evaluate his or her concepts of books and comprehension of text. Baseline data from children should be collected early in the school year, with assessment measures repeated a few times a year.

REFERENCES

Anderson, R. C., Hiebert, E. H., Scott, J. A., & Wilkinson, I. A. G. (1985). *Becoming a nation of readers.* Washington, DC: U.S. Department of Education.

Baumann, J. F. (1992). Effect of think-aloud instruction on elementary students' comprehension monitoring abilities. *Journal of Reading Behavior, 24*(2), 143–172.

Clark, M. M. (1984). Literacy at home and at school: Insights from a study of young fluent readers. In J. Goelman, A. A. Oberg, & F. Smith (Eds.), *Awaking to literacy* (pp. 122–130). London: Heinemann.

Cosgrove, M. S. (1989). Read out loud? Why bother? *New England Reading Association Journal, 25,* 9–22.

Cullinan, B. E. (1987). *Children's literature in the reading program.* Newark, DE: International Reading Association.

Cullinan, B. E. (1992). *Invitation to read: More children's literature in the reading program.* Newark, DE: International Reading Association.

Durkin, D. (1978–1979). What classroom observations reveal about reading instruction. *Reading Research Quarterly, 14,* 481–533.

Elley, W. (1989). Vocabulary acquisition from listening to stories. *Reading Research Quarterly, 24,* 174–187.

Gambrell, L., Pfeiffer, W., & Wilson, R. (1985). The effect of retelling upon comprehension and recall of text information. *Journal of Educational Research, 78,* 216–220.

Gambrell, L. B., & Koskinen, P. S. (2002). Imagery: A strategy for enhancing comprehension. In C. C. Block & M. Pressley (Eds.), *Comprehension instruction: Research-based best practices* (pp. 305–319). New York: Guilford Press.

Graves, M. F., Juel, C., & Graves, B. B. (1998). *Teaching reading in the 21st century.* Boston: Allyn & Bacon.

Holdaway, D. (1979). *The foundations of literacy.* Sydney, Australia: Ashton Scholastic.

Kuhn, M. R., & Stahl, S. A. (2003). Fluency: A review of developmental and remedial strategies. *Journal of Educational Psychology, 95,* 3–21.

Morrow, L. M. (1983). Home and school correlates of early interest in literature. *Journal of Educational Research, 76,* 221–230.

Morrow, L. M. (1984). Reading stories to young children: Effects of story structure and traditional questioning strategies on comprehension. *Journal of Reading Behavior, 16,* 273–288.

Morrow, L. M. (1985). Retelling stories: A strategy for improving children's comprehension, concept of story structure and oral language complexity. *Elementary School Journal, 85,* 647–661.

Morrow, L. M. (1988). Young children's responses to one-to-one story readings in school settings. *Reading Research Quarterly, 23*(1), 89–107.

Morrow, L. M. (1996). Story retelling: A discussion strategy to develop and assess comprehension. In L. B. Gambrell & J. F. Almasi (Eds.), *Lively discussions: Fostering engaged reading* (pp. 265–285). Newark, DE: International Reading Association.

Morrow, L. M. (2005). *Literacy development in the early years: Helping children read and write* (5th ed.). Boston: Allyn & Bacon.

National Reading Panel. (2000). *Teaching children to read.* Washington, DC: National Institute of Child Health and Human Development.

Pearson, P. D., Roehler, L. R., Dole, J. A., & Duffy, G. G. (1992). Developing expertise in reading comprehension. In S. J. Samuels & A. E. Farsturp (Eds.), *What research has to say about reading instruction* (2nd ed., pp. 145–199). Newark, DE: International Reading Association.

Pellegrini, A., & Galda, L. (1982). The effects of thematic fantasy play training on the development of children's story comprehension. *American Educational Research Journal, 19,* 443–452.

Pressley, M., & Afflerbach, P. (1995). *Verbal protocols of reading: The nature of constructively responsive reading.* Hillsdale, NJ: Erlbaum.

Pressley, M., & Hilden, K. (2002). How can children be taught to comprehend text better? In M. L. Kamil, J. B. Manning, & H. J. Walberg (Eds.), *Successful reading instruction* (pp. 33–53). Greenwich, CT: Information Age.

Rand Reading Study Group. (2002). *Reading for understanding: Towards a research and development program in reading comprehension.* Washington, DC: Author/OERI/Department of Education.

Rasinski, T. (1990). Effects of repeated reading and listening while reading on reading fluency. *Journal of Educational Research, 83,* 147–150.

Ritchie, S., James-Szanton, J., & Howes, C. (2003). Emergent literacy practices in early childhood classrooms. In C. Howes (Ed.), *Teaching 4- to 8-year-olds* (pp. 71–92). Baltimore: Brookes.

Shore, K. (2001). Success for ESL students: 12 practical tips to help second-language learners. *Instructor, 1,* 30–32, 106, 110.

Stauffer, R. G. (1980). *The language-experience approach to the teaching of reading* (2nd ed.). New York: Harper & Row.

Sulzby, E. (1985). Children's emergent reading of favorite storybooks. *Reading Research Quarterly, 20,* 458–481.

Sulzby, E., & Teale, W. H. (1987). *Young children's storybook reading: Hispanic and Anglo families and children* (Report to the Spencer Foundation). Ann Arbor, MI: University of Michigan.

Teale, W. H. (1981). Parents reading to their children: What we know and need to know. *Language Arts, 58,* 902–911.

CHILDREN'S LITERATURE

Bourgeois, P. (1987). *Franklin in the dark.* New York: Scholastic.

Brenner, B. (1972). *The three little pigs.* New York: Random House.

Brown, M. (1957). *The three billy goats Gruff.* New York: Harcourt Young Classics.

Carle, E. (1969). *The very hungry caterpillar.* New York: Philomel.

Carle, E. (1985). *The very busy spider.* New York: Philomel.

Dr. Seuss. (1940). *Horton hatches the egg.* New York: Random House.

Dr. Seuss. (1960). *Green eggs and ham.* New York: Random House.

Hoberman, M. A., & Westcott, N. B. (2004). *I know an old lady who swallowed a fly.* New York: Little, Brown.

Izawa, T. (1986). *Goldilocks and the three bears.* New York: Grosset & Dunlap.

Kasza, K. (1988). *The pigs' picnic.* New York: Putnam.

Keats, E. J. (1967). *Peter's chair.* New York: Harper & Row.

Lionni, L. (1963). *Swimmy.* New York: Knopf.

Martin, B., Jr., Archambault, I., & Ehlert, L. (1989). *Chicka chicka boom boom.* New York: Scholastic.

Numeroff, L. (1985). *If you give a mouse a cookie.* New York: HarperCollins.

Sendak, M. (1963). *Where the wild things are.* New York: Harper & Row.

Wood, A. (1982). *Quick as a cricket.* Singapore: Child's Play

Zolotow, C. (1962). *Mr. Rabbit and the lovely present.* New York: Harper Collins.

CHAPTER 8

WRITING IN
THE PRESCHOOL CLASSROOM

At the beginning of an interactive preschool writing session during the month of May, Ms. Callister read the story *Alexander and the Terrible, Horrible, No Good, Very Bad Day* (Viorst, 1972). In the story Alexander has one difficult thing after another happen to him. The purpose of the lesson was to have children engaged in open-ended, problem-solving thinking to tell about a terrible thing that happened to them one day. She helped them out by telling them how she had had a difficult day when she missed her train to get home and her son had forgotten his house key and had to stand outside in the rain. She felt terrible. Josh raised his hand and said, "I broke my favorite game at home and

170

felt really sad." Janice said, "I fell once and really hurt my knee. I had to go to the hospital and get stitches." Emily said, "When my mommy was driving us to the park, we got a flat tire and it took so long for the men to come and fix it, that we never got to the park." Ms. Callister wrote down what the children said on a flip chart and drew a picture representing what they had to say. She took a pointer and asked all the children to read aloud together what their friends had said. Each child was given a white board to copy one word they liked from all the ideas that she had written down. The class talked about which experience they thought was the worst of all. This turned into an interactive writing experience with lots of ideas and sharing of thoughts.

THEORY AND RESEARCH ABOUT WRITING DEVELOPMENT

The purposes of reading and writing are similar. We read and write to construct meaning. Readers deal with meaning by responding to what has been read. Writers deal with meaning by constructing text (Bromley, 2007). When reading and writing, children engage in similar activities. Readers and writers:

> Organize ideas.

> Generate ideas.

> Monitor their thoughts.

> Problem solve.

> Revise how to think about the ideas.

Children learn about reading and writing in similar ways. They experiment, pretend play at reading and writing, and engage in trial and error as they practice the literacy skills they have learned. Children are inventive when learning to read and write as they decorate letters, symbols, and words. They mix drawing and writing and they invent messages in various forms and shapes. Similarly, when they read, they invent what they think the text may say by reading the pictures; they invent the voices of the characters in the books; and they predict outcomes in stories and create their own endings. We teach children phonics skills so they can decode text independently. When children write, they use the same phonics skills to create their writing pieces. When preschoolers begin writing using invented spelling, they are using sound–symbol relationships, or phonics. It is important to realize how similar reading and writing are and to engage children in both reading and writing daily. When a child engages in reading-like behaviors, he or she is strengthening beginning writing skills. When a child engages in emergent writing, he or she is strengthening reading skills.

HOW EARLY WRITING IS ACQUIRED

Children's early writing experiences are embedded in the familiar situations and real-life experiences of family and community (Ritchie, James-Szanton, & Howes, 2003). In fact, we have discovered that because these events are so natural many parents do not recognize them as important writing experiences until it is pointed out to them (Taylor, 1983). Many things family members do on a regular basis involve writing. They write each other notes, make to-do lists, send greeting cards, and write directions.

Early writing development is characterized by children's moving from playfully making marks on paper to communicating messages on paper to creating texts. Children are at first unconcerned about the products of their "writing"; they lose interest in them almost immediately after they have completed them. However, once they begin to understand that the marks made can be meaningful and fun to produce, they are determined to learn how to write (Tompkins, 2000).

When observing children scribbling and inventing primitive "texts," researchers have noted that children seem to know what writing is for before they know much about how to write in correct forms. The letters to friends or relatives, greeting cards, and signs they produce are not conventional forms of writing. Yet the child is demonstrating an understanding of the function of written texts (Bromley, 2007; Gundlach, McLane, Scott, & McNamee, 1985).

Children's writing develops through constant invention and reinvention of the forms of written language (Graves, 1994). Children invent ways of making letters, words, and texts, moving from primitive forms to closer approximations of conventional forms (Hansen, 1987). Parents and teachers of preschool children need to show an interest in children's early writing and accept and support their youngsters' production of the primitive forms. Children learn about writing through instruction from teachers, by observing others more skilled than themselves engaging in writing, and by participating in writing experiences alone or with others. People who are more proficient writers play an important modeling role in children's writing development (Temple, Nathan, Burris, & Temple, 1988).

In writing, as in talking, story making is a primary impulse and activity. As humans, we share a deep need to turn our experiences into stories. Story making is a fundamental means by which we learn and shape our intellectual development. Making and telling stories play central roles in the development of literacy (Ritchie et al., 2003).

Children need to write independently. When they write independently they are involved in practicing aspects of writing—letter formation and differentiation, similarities or differences between drawing and writing, spelling, punctuation, and so forth. When children engage in independent writing they become more conscious of what they know.

Children also need to write in social settings. When children write with each other, with a teacher, or with a more literate peer, they talk about what they write, share each others' writing, and imitate the more literate other. Social interaction is crucial when learning to write.

Writing development is a part of a child's journey to literacy development. Literacy learning starts with drawing, then writing, and then reading (Vygotsky, 1978). Children's main resource for literacy learning is their knowledge of ways to express experiences and to communicate through the use of symbols.

For most children, the process of writing development occurs as a continuum. Under normal circumstances, children's early literacy development begins with learning to communicate—first nonverbally, then by talking, next through symbolic play, and finally by drawing. Each new phase is rooted in earlier phases and forms a new network of communication resources.

Literacy learning begins to develop quite naturally in the interactions of family and community life. In the process, children move from playing with written language to using it to communicate. They invent and reinvent forms. When children first begin making marks on paper, most do so with no knowledge of the alphabetic nature of the written language's symbol system. Shortly thereafter, they view letters as referring to actual people or things. It is quite a bit later when children realize that writing represents language (Spandel, 2001).

THE DEVELOPMENT OF WRITING ABILITY

Children learn a lot about literacy through play. This is especially true in literate societies in which they imitate adult models by making their own pretend play marks on paper. Soon the marks become written messages, from which children achieve a sense of identity in their own eyes and in the eyes of others. The continuum, from playing with drawing and writing to communicating through written messages to writing narrative and expository text, reflects the basic theories of early literacy development (Dyson, 1993; Halliday, 1975).

Researchers have recorded varied descriptions of developmental stages of writing in early childhood (Dyson, 1993). Most agree, however, that if there are stages, they are not well defined nor necessarily sequential. Dyson (1993) describes children's writing development as having two broad phases. From birth to about age 3, children begin to explore the form of writing by scribbling. Then, as children progress from 3 to 6, their controlled scribbling begins to look like writing and they will tell you what they have written says. Increasingly, the child's writing looks like real print written across the page and in rows.

Sulzby (1985) identified six broad categories of writing development that span the time from children's first beginning to make marks on a page until conventional writing begins. She cautions that these should not be considered a reflection of developmental ordering. They do, however, describe children's early attempts at writing.

1. *Writing via drawing.* The child will use drawing to stand for writing. The child is working out the relationship between drawing and writing, not confusing the two. The child sees drawing/writing as communication of a specific and purposeful message. Children who participate in writing via drawing will read their drawings as if there is writing on them (see Figure 8.1).

2. *Writing via scribbling.* The child scribbles but intends it as writing. Often the child appears to be writing and scribbles from left to right. The child moves the pencil as an adult does, and the pencil makes writing-like sounds. The scribble resembles writing (see Figure 8.2).

3. *Writing via making letter-like forms.* At a glance, shapes in the child's writing resemble letters. However, close observation reveals that they only look like letters. They are not just poorly formed letters; they are creations (see Figure 8.3).

4. *Writing via reproducing well-learned units or letter strings.* The child uses letter sequences learned from such sources as his or her own name. The child sometimes changes the order of the letters, writing the same ones many different ways, or reproduces letters in long strings or in random order (see Figure 8.4).

5. *Writing via invented spelling.* Children use many varieties and levels of invented spelling. Children create their own spelling for words when they

FIGURE 8.1. Writing via drawing: James, age 2½.

FIGURE 8.2. Controlled scribble writing: Matthew, age 3.

FIGURE 8.3. Letter-like forms.

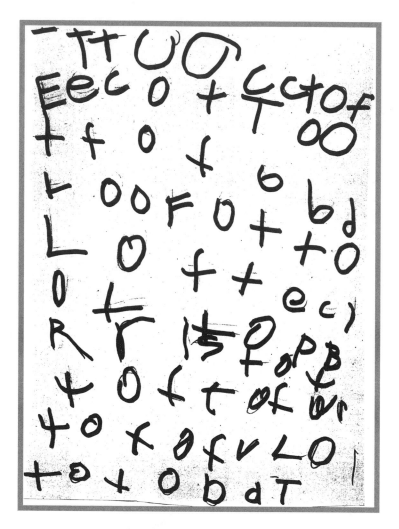

FIGURE 8.4. Letter strings.

do not know the conventional spellings. In invented spelling, one letter may represent an entire word, and words sometimes overlap and are not properly spaced. As the child's writing matures, the words look more like conventional writing, with perhaps only one letter invented or left out (see Figure 8.5).

6. *Writing via conventional spelling.* The child's writing resembles adult writing. Sulzby's general description of early writing is helpful for teachers and parents when they are observing and describing children's writing. As noted, however, Sulzby (1985) emphasizes that these categories are not necessarily sequential.

FIGURE 8.5. Invented spelling. ("We went to see the balloons go up. The balloons were pretty.")

OBJECTIVES FOR PROMOTING WRITING DEVELOPMENT

Parents and teachers can use various strategies to encourage and respond to children's self-initiated writing efforts. They can create situations that will engage children in producing and learning about written language. These situations reflect our growing understanding that children's literacy develops within the context of family and school events that involve writing and reading.

Our current way of thinking about writing development changed enormously in the 1970s. We always encouraged children to use crayons and paper to develop motor coordination in preparation for writing, but we never thought of their using writing to convey meaning or of writing as being an integral part of an early literacy program for children as young as 2. We now integrate strategies for writing into the daily routines of babies, toddlers, preschoolers, and kindergartners. We consider even the youngest child's marks on paper as early attempts at writing, rather than as random marks. This perception is necessary in programs for early literacy development.

Generally, the best way to assist young children in language and literacy development is to provide instruction and to create situations that are meaningful. This principle applies equally in the home, in the child care center, in preschool, and in kindergarten. The following objectives for promoting language and literacy development take the perspective that children learn language, including writing and reading, by using it purposefully in many situations.

> ➢ Children will be provided with an environment in which they are regularly exposed to many kinds of print.

> ➢ Children will experience print as a source of pleasure and enjoyment.

> ➢ Children will regularly observe adults writing for work and for leisure.

> ➤ Children will be given opportunities and materials for writing.

> ➤ Children will be assisted in deciding what to write about but encouraged to make their own decisions.

> ➤ Children's attempts at writing, whatever the form, will be responded to as meaningful communication (e.g., scribble writing, letter-like forms, random letters, invented spelling).

> ➤ Children will be taught some manuscript writing.

> ➤ Teachers will take the opportunity through children's writing to point out sound–symbol correspondences as the spoken word is transformed into the written.

> ➤ Children will be exposed to concepts such as left-to-right progression in writing, spaces between words, and writing one line after the other.

> ➤ Children will be exposed to some aspects of punctuation: periods, question marks, and quotation marks.

> ➤ Children's invented spelling will be accepted as working toward conventional writing.

> ➤ Students will participate in discussing their own work.

> ➤ Children will be encouraged to use writing for many purposes, such as writing stories, conveying information, journal writing, and functional writing, such as lists and letters.

> ➤ The use of writing will be integrated throughout the curriculum.

STRATEGIES FOR WRITING DEVELOPMENT FROM BIRTH TO 2 YEARS

I have watched my grandson begin his adventure into the world of literacy. We have large newsprint in the house and fat crayons for him to use that are always placed in the same spot. At 18 months, he began to make marks on the paper. When he began scribbling, his productions sprawled all over the page. At 20 months, he made more controlled sprawls, dots, and wavy lines. He watched his parents and me writing often, and by 23 months his writing began to resemble cursive writing. The length of time he was able to engage in writing increased as he reached 2 years. Now he could spend 10 minutes writing. He also began to babble in his own way while he wrote, as if he was telling a story about what he was writing. Next he began to attempt to write letters in familiar words such as his name or the *M* in *McDonald's* or in *Mommy*. It is important to observe the literacy development of a child so that we can remember milestones for future reference. This attention to literacy behaviors is important for parents, child care providers, and preschool teachers to observe and record.

If we interact with children in this way, especially from their second year on, we are ready to support them when, as a part of their scribble writing, they try to write one or more of these environmentally learned letters. In fact, some children may make their first attempts to do this between 18 and 24 months, though most children will not begin until they are 2 or 3. We can assist children in their first attempts to make marks on paper. Often, when children begin scribbling, they bang on the paper with their writing implements. As they become more familiar with writing, they will begin using smoother, more deliberate and coordinated movements to make their marks. When children are in their first primitive stages of scribbling, we can show them how to hold markers or crayons. We can guide their hands to paper, not making marks for them but helping them understand that the paper is the place for writing.

Our responses to children's early scribbling are important. It is better not to urge children to write particular things. They should make marks spontaneously and decide for themselves when these marks are intended to represent something. It is important not to press them to tell us what their marks mean or represent. It is better to say, "I like that, can you tell me about what you are writing? Can you write more?" than to ask, "what is it?" Don't insist on answers if the child says no. Expressing genuine pleasure in children's early markings, whether they resemble writing or not, and seeing them as an important step in a long developmental process are positive responses that will encourage children to continue. By continuing their "writing," they will incorporate in it what they are learning about print from daily literacy events.

Beyond responding supportively to children, we can model writing for them. We can let them see us writing letters, lists, and notes and filling out forms, and we can interact with them about what we are doing. For example, "I'm writing a letter to invite your parents to school. Do you have ideas of what I should say? Do you want to write something on the paper to them?" When writing, invite the youngsters to sit with you, watch you, ask questions, and try their own hand at writing. This gives children opportunities to see how we go about writing and to begin to understand that the marks we make convey meaning.

An important way that we can support children's writing development is to provide experiences with environmental print, including print they see on television, on food cans and boxes, on signs, in stores, on the computer, and so forth. We need to talk with children about experiences with environmental print by commenting, asking questions, and encouraging them to identify and remember signs, letters, and bits of print out of their normal contexts; for instance, understanding that the letter *D* is used in other places besides Dairy Queen.

Junk mail is a form of environmental print that can arouse interest in writing. Children enjoy writing or making marks on flyers, brochures, ads, announcements, and forms. They will write over the print and in the blank spaces. Apparently, the look and arrangement of the print gives them the model and inspiration to make their own marks.

ELL   Repeating rhymes and singing songs also can contribute to children's early writing. So can the use of hand puppets to tell a story. Puzzles that can be taken apart and put back together and manipulative toys that require dexterity help with the motor development needed to shape letters. Playing with clay or play dough, finger-painting, using chalkboards, and painting on easels help build motor coordination as well. Of course, reading to children not only develops oral language and promotes early reading attempts, as discussed earlier, but also can motivate children to want to write and make their own books, no matter how crude the first attempts. Parents and caregivers in child care centers can display children's early writings on walls, doors, and appliances to be enjoyed and not judged.

Homes, child care centers, and preschools should provide environments for writing—comfortable spots with rugs and child-size tables and chairs—and storage for writing materials. The latter should include felt-tip markers, pencils, crayons, and chalk. There should be ample supplies and varied sizes of large unlined paper (newsprint works well) and a chalkboard. Materials should be stored consistently in the place provided for writing so that the child can learn how to select materials and put them away independently.

WRITING IN PRESCHOOL CLASSROOMS

Parents and teachers can expect to see rapid development in writing in children from 2 to 8 years of age. As we have seen, it is during this period that most children move from scribbling to producing random letters to writing letters to writing words with invented spellings to beginning to use conventional writing. They will begin to space properly between words and use some marks of punctuation. They tend to write longer pieces, and their productions often represent wider ranges of functions and forms. This is a time when children show intense bursts of writing activity, perhaps alternating these with intense bursts of reading activity. It is important, therefore, that teachers have a sense of children's writing needs and interests at this time and know how to interact with them to support their efforts, learning, and growth. Like younger children, preschoolers and kindergartners take more pleasure in the process of writing than in its products. The act of writing is their center of interest, although they gradually develop concern for the products. When they play waiter or waitress, for example, and take an "order," they may be concerned that others can "read" it. The same thing might happen with notes or greeting cards sent to relatives or friends. Children begin to express concerns that recipients are able to read their messages, perhaps so they can write back. Children who have had little experience in pretending to write might be reluctant to make marks on paper even by kindergarten age, possibly because they have become aware that their marks are not conventional writing and thus might not be accepted. It is important to let them know that writing that is not conventional will be accepted. Some children may request conventional spellings and will not write unless they know it is correct. They should be given the help they request.

We must realize that what young children write about and how they approach writing is more important initially than their mechanics of writing (spelling, handwriting, punctuation, and spacing). Learning to write involves learning to compose texts that convey meaning. As children gain experience with writing, they will learn the skills and mechanics of writing through instruction and practice.

When children are free to write in unconventional ways, such as using invented spellings, they are enhancing phonemic awareness and, eventually, knowledge of phonics. When children write, they have to transform the spoken word into written language. This fosters understanding of the structure of spoken language and how it is related to written language. The more children write, the better they become at segmenting sounds and blending them into words, which develops not only their ability to write but also their ability to read independently.

Young children choose to write if a situation has meaning for them. If we impose on them our selection of what they should write about all the time, we are not likely to see positive results. With these basic ideas in mind, we can create strategies and appropriate environments for helping children write.

The Writing Center

The literacy area in the classroom should include a place designated for writing. It should be easily accessible, attractive, and inviting. This area can be a part of the library corner. It should be furnished with a table and chairs and a rug for youngsters who want to stretch out and write on the floor. Writing implements should include plenty of colored felt-tip markers, large and small crayons, large and small pencils (both regular and colored), and chalk and a chalkboard. Various types of paper should be available, lined and unlined, plain white or newsprint, ranging from 8" × 11" to 24" × 36".

Index cards for recording Very Own Words should be stored in the writing area, as should the children's collections of Very Own Words. Each child should have a writing folder to collect samples of his or her written work during the school year. Several computers for word processing are also necessary. Materials for making books should be available, including colored construction paper for covers, plain white paper for inside pages, a stapler, and scissors. Teachers can prepare blank books, keyed to special occasions, for children to use. For example, a blank Valentine's Day book shaped like a heart and made of red construction paper with five or six sheets of plain white paper stapled inside provides inviting space that

After putting his Very Own Words into a sentence, James will copy the sentence onto a piece of paper. The sentence says, "I like James."

children can fill with their written greetings. Stock bare books (books with hard covers but no print inside) for special projects. Blue books, used for college examinations, are perfect for young children's writing. They can be purchased inexpensively from school supply companies. They come with 12 or 16 pages, which is usually just right for an original story by a young child. Try to purchase blue books with the name of a university or college that is close to your school, or select a university well known to your children. It makes children feel special about writing in them. Keep a supply of interesting pictures, posters, magazines, and newspapers; these can stimulate, decorate, or illustrate children's writing.

An alphabet chart in easy view helps children identify and shape letters they may need while writing. Plastic, magnetic, wooden, and felt letters should be among the language arts manipulatives. These help develop eye–hand coordination and aid in letter recognition and formation. Small white slates are good for practicing new words learned and for writing sentences that feature these words. A bulletin board should be available on which children can display their own writing, with a space for posting notices or sending and receiving private messages. "Mailboxes" for youngsters' incoming and outgoing "mail" can be placed in the writing center. (Mailboxes for a pen-pal program are discussed later, in the section on functional writing.) The writing center should be labeled with a sign that says "Author's Spot" or with a name selected by the children. Basic implements and supplies for writing should be stocked in every other learning center in the room as well. The accessibility of these materials will encourage writing (Bromley, 2007). A child might want to record the outside temperature on a chart in the science center, to protect a construction of blocks with a "Do Not Touch" sign, or to copy a Very Own Word in the social studies or science area. A group might decide to turn the dramatic-play corner into a dentist's office, including in it an appointment book for recording dates, times, and patients' names, appointment cards, patient records, and a prescription pad for medication.

The activities described for the writing center should be introduced to the entire group. They are used during writing workshop and at center time for independent writing. The activities are done independently once the teacher has modeled for the children how to use the materials. With this preparation, students will participate quite naturally in the writing activities as a means of communication.

Taking Dictation

Much of the writing that will occur early in preschool will involve the teacher taking dictation from the child. We must, however, also realize that we need to encourage them to write by themselves in their own unconventional way. Taking dictation does play an important role in writing development, in that we model conventional writing for the children. When teachers take dictation, children see more of their own thoughts written on a page, and they can attempt to read them back. The following are important when you take dictation:

1. Begin with discussion to encourage ideas.
2. Write exactly what the child says, but write it correctly in sentences.
3. Make sure the child can see you write.
4. Write legibly.
5. Read the dictation back to the child when finished, tracking the print as you read it.
6. Encourage the child to read what was written back to you, to another child, or to him- or herself.

As the child dictates to the teacher, she writes it down.

Writing Workshop

Writing workshop is a period of time set aside for writing instruction of any kind, such as independent writing, interactive writing, journal writing, and so forth. During writing workshop the teacher can provide a mini-lesson, a time for writing, and a time in which writing is shared. Writing Workshop should occur daily, or at least a few times a week.

Mini-Writing Lessons

A mini-writing lesson takes place with the whole class or with a small group of children to teach a particular type of writing skill, such as writing a letter to someone. The lesson lasts about 5 to 10 minutes. It prepares the children so they can then practice the new writing skill. We want children to learn that writing involves thinking, prewriting, discussions, organizing, and maybe rewriting (Fletcher & Portalupi, 2001; Calkins, 1986).

Prewriting is probably the most important part of the writing process. It helps students select a topic to write about, figure out the purpose for writing, think of ideas related to their topic, and decide for whom the piece is being written. During prewriting activities a decision can be made as to the form that the writing will take—such as a poem, a letter, a narrative, and so forth (Tompkins, 2003). Prewriting activities include brainstorming related to the topic and making outlines. Prewriting can take place with the entire class, with a friend, with the teacher, or alone.

Ms. Keri gives a mini-writing lesson that involves children in prewriting activities. After reading *The Snowy Day* (Keats, 1962), Ms. Keri asks the children to draw a picture about the part of the story they liked best. She also asks them to think of a word or words to write about their picture. They discuss what parts they liked best and the words they liked. Ms. Keri writes the words, with a drawing next to the word so that children can read them. The words and ideas generated by the children are *snowman, snow fight, stick, angels, mountain climber, snowball,* and *snowsuit,* among others.

Writing Time

The children can do the writing task alone or sometimes with a peer. The writing activity is tied to the mini-lesson about the story *The Snowy Day*. While the children are writing, the teacher meets with an individual child or with pairs for a conference or discussion about the writing they are doing. When they work with peers, children are encouraged to confer with each other about their work. Sometimes Ms. Keri prefers to walk around and talk to the children about their work instead of having them come to her.

Shared Writing

The writing time ends with children sharing their work with a partner, a small group, or the class. With the sharing come constructive comments, such as, "I also liked the part in the book where the little boy made angels." Teachers may have small groups come together who need help with the beginnings of writing. One of the most difficult things to teach young children is to stay on task and to spend as much time as they can with their work.

Teaching Children to Write in Different Ways

Children need to learn to write for many purposes. The following are types of writing they should be taught, with experiences to help in practicing the genre. The writing workshop format can be used with all of these ideas.

Narrative Writing

Narrative writing is probably the most popular form of writing that we ask children to engage in. Narrative writing involves writing original stories or retelling or rewriting a story that was read to the child. Narrative stories could be about incidents in the child's life, as well. Good narrative stories have a beginning, a middle, and an end. They follow a basic story structure, with a setting at the beginning that introduces the characters, time, and place. The theme, which is the problem or goal of the main character, comes next. Then there are the plot episodes, or the events that help the main character solve his or her problem or accomplish his or her goal. Finally there is the resolution, which involves the solving of the problem or the accomplishing of the goal and an ending to the story. Young children have limited ability to do a lot of writing, but they can dictate their original stories or retell a story for the teacher to write. They can draw a picture and then write one or two words or a letter related to the retelling or the original story.

Informational Writing

Informational writing usually involves content-area topics from social studies or science. Informational writing has to do with facts. For example, when the class was learning about fish, they wrote down the different parts of a fish, such as the fins, tail, scales, mouth, and eyes.

Functional Writing

Functional writing is writing that serves clear, real-life purposes. Class writing projects that are particularly purposeful include greeting cards to parents, grandparents, sisters, brothers, friends, and relatives for birthdays, holidays, and other occasions. Write thank-you notes to guest speakers who come to class, to adults who help on class trips, to the director of the zoo you visited, or to the librarian who spent time with the class at the public library. Prepare lists of things to remember to do in preparing a party, a special program, or a class trip. Make address and telephone books with entries from class members. Write notes to parents about activities in school. Encourage individual children to write to their parents about specific things they are doing in school. Children need to be reminded that their Very Own Words offer the opportunity to copy words they need, as does classroom environmental print.

Some preschools and kindergartens have established mail service and pen-pal programs (Edwards, Maloy, & Verock-O'Loughlin, 2003; Martinez & Teale, 1987). Children are offered pen pals to write to regularly, about once every 2 weeks. Teachers or aides help children write their letters or take dictation. Encourage children to use what writing capabilities they have, even if they can only write a scribble or a single letter. Teachers talk about the letters that come from the pen pals with the children.

With more and more schools having Internet capabilities, the use of e-mail for pen pals (called "key pals") is another way for children to communicate with others. E-mail gives children the opportunity to write to others around the world, and the sending and receiving of messages is almost immediate. Children can simply type a few letters from the keyboard, copy their names on the computer keyboard, and send the e-mail.

A notice board for exchanging messages also motivates functional writing (Newman, 1984). Children can tack up pictures for each other as beginning messages. The teacher should provide a model by leaving messages for individuals and for the entire class. Notices about school or class events are appropriate. It is important to draw attention to the board when posting a class message or when leaving messages for individuals so children get into the habit of looking for messages and leaving them themselves. There also needs to be a place for private messages. These can be posted on the notice board in an envelope or in student mailboxes. Some teachers have taped brown bags to each child's desk with their names on them for giving and receiving private messages. Messages by preschoolers can be a scribble, a letter, their names, or a picture.

Interactive Writing

ELL Interactive writing provides a model for children so they will know what to do when writing on their own. Interactive writing is a joint effort, as the teacher and the children create the writing together. The teacher guides the lesson and writes on large chart paper in a whole-class or small-group setting. Sometimes the children are writing as the text is being created, either on regular lined paper or on their own white boards. White boards work well in this activity, as they make it easy to edit. Any type of writing can be done in the interactive setting, such as letters, a narrative story, or some informational material (McCarrier, Pinnell, & Fountas, 2000). Interactive writing demonstrates what good writing looks like and how it is created.

The topic for writing is decided on by the teacher or by the children. It is good to select writing that has a purpose for the class and that includes a part of the writing curriculum. If the class is studying water, for example, they might want to make a list of the uses of water as a summary of the unit. In addition to recording what they learned, they will also learn about writing lists.

Anyone can begin the writing. That is, the teacher can start the writing with a sentence on the chart. When a student contributes an idea, the teacher writes it down; with older children, the child who contributes the idea will write at least some of what he or she said. When a child does write (this could come at the end of the preschool year just before kindergarten), the teacher guides the student almost word by word if he or she needs help with spelling, with an idea, or with a better way to say something. The entire class can contribute to the conversation to improve the writing. White correction tape is used for changes during interactive writing. Instead of crossing out, the teacher or child puts white tape over the part to be changed, and the change is made by writing it on the tape.

Ms. Jenkins wanted to teach her preschoolers about being courteous and writing thank-you notes. She wanted to teach them about the content of thank-you notes. As part of their study of good health habits, a student's mother, who was a nurse, was invited to be a guest speaker. Ms. Jenkins wanted the class to write a thank-you note to the nurse, and she decided to present the lesson in an interactive writing experience. They discussed things to say in a thank-you note besides thanking the person. They decided that they could say what they liked about the presentation and could ask her if she might come again. They discussed different ways to end the letter, such as using "Love," "best wishes," and so forth. The activity accomplished two tasks: the need to write a thank-you note to teach courteous behavior and the need to learn about the content and format of thank-you notes.

Independent Writing

Independent writing gives children the opportunity to write alone or in collaboration with others. When children engage in independent writing, they can select what they would like to write. Teachers can provide ideas, or children can select what to do on their own. Some activities teachers can list are:

➢ Writing alone or with a partner.

➢ Listening to a story on a headset and writing about it in a picture or in words.

➢ Writing a story by dictating it to a teacher, an aide, a parent, or an older child.

➢ Taking a blank book from the writing center shaped to represent the theme being studied. If the theme is good nutrition, the book might be shaped like an apple, with a red cover and blank white pages within. The children can draw and write about the good foods they have learned about.

Journal Writing

Ethan is 3, and he has begun to keep a journal in his nursery school. At first his inclination was to scribble something on a page, then turn to the next and do the same, as the journal was a spiral notebook with many pages. His teacher worked with him alone for several entries, asking him to think about something that happened to him recently that he would like to write about. Ethan said, "I got my knee stuck in the bars on my swing set tree house. It hurt and my mommy couldn't get it out. She sprayed soapy stuff and other yucky stuff so maybe it would get out and it didn't. She called the police, and he took a big stick and pushed on the wood and my knee got out. I cried after. The policeman gave me a teddy bear. We made him cookies and took them to the police house with a note to say thank you." The teacher asked Ethan what part of the story he would like to draw and write about. Ethan said, "I want to draw the cookies we brought." He drew the cookies and told the teacher to write, "These are the cookies for the policeman who helped me get my knee unstuck." Ethan wrote his name on the page, the teacher wrote his dictation, and he also copied the word *cookies*. After a few weeks of this type of practice, Ethan understood that when he writes in his journal, he uses only one page, and that he should write about something that happened to him.

Journal writing can be carried out successfully in early childhood classrooms, with entries made daily or a few times a week. Journals can be written in notebooks or on pages stapled together to create a book. Children write in their journals at their developmental level. No corrections are made in journals. Some children's journals might include pictures and no writing, scribble writing, random letters, or invented spelling (see Figure 8.6). The teacher models different types of journal writing. She may model an entry about her personal life: "I'm very excited. My daughter is going to be in a play tonight, and I'm going to watch her." By example, children are being given an idea about the kinds of entries they can make in their journals. Journal entries can be related to topics studied, such as recording the growth of a seed that was planted, charting daily temperature, or reacting to a

story that was read. Journal writing should include private experiences in a child's life, and some entries can be written in response to literature. When used regularly in preschool throughout the school year, journal writing improves in length and sophistication (Gunning, 2003). Preschoolers need help

James writes about his afternoon at the pool in his journal.

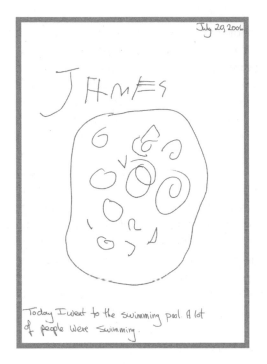

FIGURE 8.6. In James's journal entry, he drew and dictated: "Today I went to the swimming pool. A lot of people were swimming."

with journal writing. Families should be encouraged to keep journals with their children at home.

Using Children's Literature to Motivate Writing

Children's literature is as natural a medium for encouraging writing as it is for encouraging oral language and reading (Vukelich, Evans, & Alberson, 2003; Tompkins, 2000). Reading several books by the same author or illustrator can prompt a class letter asking the author how he or she gets ideas to write or asking the illustrator what kind of art materials he or she uses. It is best to identify authors or illustrators who are likely to respond, for it is important to receive a response, even if it comes from a publisher's representative.

Old favorites and series books—those that use the same character in several different books, such as *Madeline* (Bemelmans, 1939), *Curious George* (Rey, 1941), and *Harold and the Purple Crayon* (Johnson, 1955)—can motivate children to write their own books or a class book about the character. Books such as *Swimmy* (Lionni, 1963) and *Alexander and the Terrible, Horrible, No Good, Very Bad Day* (Viorst, 1972) involve the main character in a series of adventures or incidents as the story proceeds. Children can be asked to write still another episode or adventure for the character.

Shared book experiences and small-group story readings can lead to writing experiences. Predictable books provide patterns that children can imitate in their own writing through cumulative patterns, as in *I Know an Old Lady Who Swallowed a Fly* (Hoberman & Westcott, 2004); repetitive language, as in *Are You My Mother?* (Eastman, 1960); familiar sequences, as in *The Very Hungry Caterpillar* (Carle, 1969); or catchphrases, as in *Horton Hatches the Egg* (Dr. Seuss, 1940).

Children need to share their writing with an audience. When they know they will be sharing their work, they have a purpose for writing. A child can be selected as Author of the Day to share something that he or she has written (Graves & Hansen, 1983). More than one child can be Author of the Day. Those children who shared their writings in a particular week should display them on a bulletin board in the writing center, along with photographs of themselves. When sharing work, the child can sit in a chair marked "Author's Chair." Children in the audience should be encouraged to comment about their friends' work with such statements as "I like what you wrote" or "I fell and cut my knee once, too." At first the children may not comment readily, so the teacher needs to model comments for the audience, whose young members will soon emulate the behavior.

Publishing Children's Writing

Children's work should be published. "Why publish?" almost answers the question "Why write?" "Writing is a public act, meant to be shared with many audiences" (Graves, 1983, p. 54). When children know their work will be published, they write for a defined purpose. When work is to be published, it becomes special; it needs to be done carefully. Children can publish their work in many ways. The most popular is to bind writings into books, which are placed in the literacy center and featured for others to read. Other means of publishing include creating felt-board stories or roll movies, telling stories to classmates, role-playing what has been written, or presenting the story in a puppet show.

Making books is an important activity for children to participate in throughout the school year. Books can be made by one child, a small group, or the entire class. They can be made simply by stapling a few pieces of paper together or with laminated pages bound with a bookbinding machine. A class book should be made about every topic studied. Books can be modeled after pieces of children's literature, such as a new episode for *Curious George* (Rey, 1941). Books can be about holidays or current events. For some books, the teacher may take dictation and write on the child's page; for others, she or he might use the computer to type in the child's text; and other books may have only children's writing on the pages. Books can be of all sizes and shapes. When the book is for the class, the teacher can photocopy one for everyone to take home. Class books are also put into the class literacy center. Children enjoy reading books that they make for themselves and books that are made by the entire class. They enjoy reading the pages they contributed and the pages contributed by their peers. Be sure that children sign their names on their pages in the book so that others can identify whose work they are looking at.

Handwriting

Writing requires dexterity. Some time should be spent teaching preschoolers proper letter formation. We also need to encourage children to use puzzles and sewing cards that strengthen their fine motor coordination. Other materials that help with writing and identifying letters were mentioned earlier, including magnetic letters, letter forms to be traced and copied, and white board slates to practice writing letters, words, and sentences. The letters of the alphabet (see Figure 8.7) should be displayed at eye level for children, and the teacher can model the correct formation of upper- and lowercase manuscript.

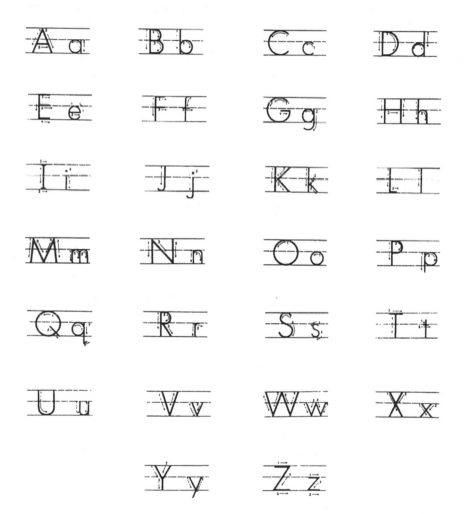

FIGURE 8.7. The alphabet. From Lesley Mandel Morrow, *Literacy Development in the Early Years: Helping Children Read and Write,* 5th ed. Published by Allyn and Bacon, Boston, MA. Copyright © 2005 by Pearson Education. Reprinted by permission of the publisher.

Legibility should be the main goal for handwriting. Learning about spaces between words is important so that words will not run into each other. There are only a few lines and shapes to learn when writing manuscript: a vertical line; a horizontal line; diagonal lines; a half circle with the opening on the left, right, top, or bottom; and a full circle (see Figure 8.8).

The straight lines in manuscript are called *sticks*. All lines are written from the top to the bottom. All circles and half circles are written from the top to the bottom. The letters *h, m, n, r,* and *u* begin with the stick and are written without lifting the pencil off the page. The *h* is made by starting at the top of the stick, descending to the line, and ascending halfway up the stick to make the half circle with the opening on the bottom. The letters *b, d, g, p,* and *q* are made by drawing a circle first and then attaching the stick.

Teach children about putting spaces between letters and words. A good rule is that one finger space will help to separate words. Children can and will develop their own handwriting style, but they need to learn that whatever their style, neat handwriting is a form of courtesy for those who will be reading what they write.

Initial writing will be on unlined paper. When a child develops dexterity, he or she can begin to use lined paper.

ASSESSMENT OF CHILDREN'S WRITING DEVELOPMENT AND THE WRITING ENVIRONMENT

As in other areas of literacy, assessment of a child's writing should take place throughout the school year. That way, the teacher can determine a child's level of development, monitor progress, and plan programs accordingly. Teachers also need to assess the classroom writing environment. The checklist in Figure 8.9 provides the teacher with information about the language the child uses, the concepts included in the writing, the purpose for writing, and some writing mechanics. The assessment helps to determine appropriate instruction and practice that a child needs in order to progress in writing development.

FIGURE 8.8. Shapes of alphabet letters. From Lesley Mandel Morrow, *Literacy Development in the Early Years: Helping Children Read and Write,* 5th ed. Published by Allyn and Bacon, Boston, MA. Copyright © 2005 by Pearson Education. Reprinted by permission of the publisher.

Name _____ Date _____

	Always	Sometimes	Never	Comments
Explores with writing materials				
Dictates stories, sentences, or words he or she wants written down				
Copies letters and words				
Independently attempts writing to convey meaning, regardless of writing level				
Can write his or her name				
Collaborates with others in writing experience				
Writes for functional purposes				

Check (✓) the level or levels at which the child is writing

	Always	Sometimes	Never	Comments
____ uses drawing for writing and drawing				
____ differentiates between writing and drawing				
____ uses scribble writing for writing				
____ uses letterlike forms for writing				
____ uses learned letters in random fashion for writing				
____ uses invented spelling for writing				
____ writes conventionally with conventional spelling				

<u>Mechanics for Writing</u>

	Always	Sometimes	Never	Comments
Forms uppercase letters legibly				
Forms lowercase letters legibly				
Writes from left to right				
Leaves spaces between words				

(continued)

FIGURE 8.9. Writing skills checklist. From Lesley Mandel Morrow, *Literacy Development in the Early Years: Helping Children Read and Write*, 5th ed. Published by Allyn and Bacon, Boston, MA. Copyright © 2005 by Pearson Education. Reprinted by permission of the publisher.

The Classroom Writing Environment	Yes	No
Space provided for a writing center		
Tables and chairs included in center		
Writing posters and bulletin boards for children to display their writing themselves		
Writing utensils (pens, pencils, crayons, Magic Markers, colored pencils, etc.)		
Computer		
Writing materials (many varieties of paper in all sizes, booklets, pads)		
A message board or private message area for children to leave messages for the teacher and other members of the class		
A place to store Very Own Words		
Folders for children to place samples of their writing		
Materials to make books		

FIGURE 8.9. *(continued)*

Teachers should maintain a portfolio of materials related to a child's writing development, such as observation notes as the child writes, samples of the child's writing over a period of time, notes from conferences with the child, notes from conferences with the child's parents, and completed checklists. The portfolio should include the best of the child's work and samples showing need for improvement as well. The portfolio can be used during parent conferences and can accompany a child to his or her next teacher. For preschoolers, an even simpler form of self-evaluation can be used. The children can evaluate with a friend or the teacher whether their work is "wow," "good," or "okay." The teacher says "wow" with a very enthusiastic voice; "good" is much more toned down; and "okay" is said in a more neutral tone. When they evaluate, they discuss why the particular word was used. The evaluation is based on their ability, as well. When teacher and child evaluate together, the teacher should see whether the child took time with his or her illustrations. Was the writing to the best of his or her ability? All of these suggestions support the purpose of assessment to (1) enhance the teacher's understanding of children's writing ability, (2) aid in program planning, and (3) help children and parents understand a child's progress and the processes involved to help gain more competence in writing.

REFERENCES

Bromley, K. (2007). Best practices in teaching writing. In L. B. Gambrell, L. M. Morrow, & M. Pressley (Eds.), *Best practices in literacy instruction* (3rd ed., pp. 243–263). New York: Guilford Press.

Calkins, L. M. (1986). *The art of teaching and writing.* Exeter, NH: Heinemann.

Dyson, A. H. (1993). *Social worlds of children learning to write in an urban primary school.* New York: Teachers College Press.

Edwards, S. A., Maloy, R. W., & Verock-O'Loughlin, R. (2003). *Ways of writing with young kids: Teaching creativity and conventions unconventionally.* Boston: Allyn & Bacon.

Fletcher, R., & Portalupi, J. (2001). *Writing workshop: The essential guide.* Portsmouth, NH: Heinemann.

Graves, D. (1994). *A fresh look at writing.* Portsmouth, NH: Heinemann.

Graves, D., & Hansen, J. (1983). The author's chair. *Language Arts, 60,* 176–183.

Graves, D. H. (1983). *Writing: Teachers and children at work.* Exeter, NH: Heinemann.

Gundlach, R., McLane, J., Scott, F., & McNamee, G. (1985). The social foundations of early writing development. In M. Farr (Ed.), *Advances in writing research*: Vol. 1. *Children's early writing development* (pp. 1–58). Norwood, NJ: Ablex.

Gunning, T. G. (2003). *Creating literacy instruction for all children* (4th ed.). Boston: Allyn & Bacon.

Halliday, M. A. K. (1975). *Learning how to mean: Exploration in the development of language.* London: Arnold.

Hansen, J. (1987). *When writers read.* Portsmouth, NH: Heinemann.

Martinez, M., & Teale, W. (1987). The ins and outs of a kindergarten writing program. *Reading Teacher, 40,* 444–451.

McCarrier, A., Pinnell, G. S., & Fountas, I. C. (2000). *Interactive writing: How language & literacy come together, K–2.* Portsmouth, NH: Heinemann.

Newman, J. (1984). *The craft of children's writing.* Exeter, NH: Heinemann.

Ritchie, S., James-Szanton, J., & Howes, C. (2003). Emergent literacy practices in early childhood classrooms. In C. Howes (Eds.), *Teaching 4- to 8-year-olds* (pp. 71–92). Baltimore: Brookes.

Spandel, V. (2001). *Creating writers through six-trait writing assessment and instruction.* New York: Longman.

Sulzby, E. (1985). Children's emergent reading of favorite storybooks. *Reading Research Quarterly, 20,* 458–481.

Taylor, D. (1983). *Family literacy.* Exeter, NH: Heinemann.

Temple, C., Nathan, R., Burris, N., & Temple, F. (1988). *The beginnings of writing.* Boston: Allyn & Bacon.

Tompkins, G. E. (2000). *Teaching writing: Balancing process and programs* (3rd ed.). Upper Saddle River, NJ: Prentice Hall.

Tompkins, G. E. (2003). *Literacy for the 21st century: Teaching reading and writing in prekindergarten through grade 4.* Upper Saddle River, NJ: Pearson/Merrill Prentice Hall.

Vukelich, C., Evans, C., & Alberson, B. (2003). Organizing expository texts: A look at the possibilities. In D. M. Barone & L. M. Morrow (Eds.), *Literacy and young children: Research-based practices* (pp. 261–290). New York: Guilford Press.

Vygotsky, L. S. (1978). *Mind in society: The development of psychological processes.* Cambridge, MA: Harvard University Press.

CHILDREN'S LITERATURE

Bemelmans, L. (1939). *Madeline.* New York: Viking.

Carle, E. (1969). *The very hungry caterpillar.* New York: Philomel.

Dr. Seuss. (1940). *Horton hatches the egg.* New York: Random House.

Eastman, P. D. (1960). *Are you my mother?* New York: Random House.

Hoberman, M. A., & Westcott, N. B. (2004). *I know an old lady who swallowed a fly.* New York: Little, Brown.

Johnson, C. (1955). *Harold and the purple crayon.* New York: Harper & Row.

Keats, E. (1962). *The snowy day.* New York: Viking.

Lionni, L. (1963). *Swimmy.* New York: Pantheon.

Rey, H. (1941). *Curious George.* Boston: Houghton Mifflin.

Viorst, J. (1972). *Alexander and the terrible, horrible, no good, very bad day.* New York: Atheneum.

AFTERWORD

Rich literacy environments for young children are created by exemplary teachers. These are teachers who have a passion to help children learn. These individuals must have the appropriate education and certification to become teachers. The preschool years are the most important years for learning, and yet many preschool teachers do not have college degrees with early childhood certifications. In addition to the appropriate training, teachers must have a plan to continue their professional development for as long as they teach. Preschool teachers should:

1. Set goals each year to improve their teaching.
2. Do small studies to determine how well they have accomplished their goals.
3. Go to professional conferences.
4. Join professional organizations and attend their meetings.
5. Read professional journals.
6. Continue to read professional books.
7. Help to plan professional development programs in their schools that include:
   a. Themes or topics to work on for the school year.
   b. Books to read about the topics.
   c. Study groups to discuss what has been read and put into practice.
   d. Discussing success experiences and situations they need help with.
   e. Coaches to help with professional development by providing resources and modeling strategies in the classroom.

f. Inviting experts for motivating presentations and following up with in-school discussions and implementation.

g. Having school personnel present workshops on topics of interest or on the theme of the year.

h. Having and making materials, or taking workshop days to create materials, for their classrooms.

i. Visiting colleagues' classrooms so that teachers can learn from each other.

j. Visiting preschools outside of one's own district or center that are known to be exemplary.

k. Administrative support.

l. Making changes slowly.

m. Working in collaboration with peers.

n. Incorporating about 100 hours of professional development, or 3 hours a week, into the school year. Research has shown that this is the only way to be sure that the program will be effective.

A strong professional development program is more important than the curriculum. It has the potential to create exemplary teachers who, in turn, create exemplary programs for their children.

Successful professional development programs for preschool should include input from teachers and strong administrative support. Researchers have identified the following requirements for effective professional development and for change to occur:

➤ Teachers need to be reflective practitioners who engage in a continuous process of questioning, planning, trying out, and evaluating their own and their students' learning.

➤ Teachers need to work toward establishing a professional community in which they rely on the collective expertise and mutual support of colleagues to inform their day-to-day judgments.

➤ Teachers need opportunities to learn about research-based strategies and pedagogy.

Professional development programs that utilize these requirements have (1) reading coaches who help teachers with new strategies for teaching and (2) teacher study groups that provide opportunities for teachers to engage in reading about new ideas, reflective planning, and evaluation. A goal for professional development is to create a collaborative community in the school. Participating in study groups and having coaches as a source of information offers the opportunity to learn about research-based practice. Preschool teachers need these opportunities to continue to grow and become expert teachers (Sparks, 1997; Sweeney, 2003; Taylor, Pressley, & Pearson, 2002; Walpole & McKenna, 2004).

REFERENCES

Sparks, D. (1997). A new vision for staff development. *Principal, 77*, 20–22.

Sweeney, D. (2003). *Learning along the way: Professional development by and for teachers*. Portland, ME: Stenhouse.

Taylor, B. M., Pressley, M., & Pearson, P. D. (2002). Research supported characteristics of teachers and schools that promote reading achievement. In B. M. Taylor & P. D. Pearson (Eds.), *Teaching reading: Effective schools, accomplished teachers* (pp. 361–374). Mahwah, NJ: Erlbaum.

Walpole, S., & McKenna, M. (2004). *The literacy coach's handbook: A guide to research-based practice*. New York: Guilford Press.

GLOSSARY

Lisa Fassi and Paula Batsiyan

Auditory discrimination—ability to hear, identify, and differentiate among various sounds, including familiar and similar sounds, rhyming words, and letter sounds.

Balanced approach to literacy instruction—choosing the theory or theories and strategies that match the learning styles of the students. Includes the use of constructivism, or open-ended instruction, and/or explicit learning strategies.

Behaviorist approach—learning theory centered around imitation through positive reinforcement, by which adults provide a model and children learn by doing what is being modeled. Little creativity involved; objective is learning a skill.

Big Books—books that are large in size (18" × 24") so that children can see the print while the teacher reads the book; teachers can point to print and young children can follow it easily.

Blend—ability to hear, isolate, recognize, and pronounce a series of isolated speech sounds together as a word, for example, the sounds of /c/, /a/, and /t/ blending together into *cat*.

Buddy reading—placement of a younger child with an older child to work as a pair in storybook reading.

Choral reading—teachers and students reading in synchronization or chanting a memorized piece together to reinforce pacing and expression.

Chunk—groups of letters within a word that are taught as whole patterns, including word families, also referred to as *phonograms,* such as *an, at, in.*

Comprehension—process by which reader constructs and interprets meaning about a text based on his or her prior knowledge and/or experience.

Constructivist theory—theory that children construct knowledge through a hands-on, active process by problem solving, guessing, and approximating.

Cultural diversity—the various backgrounds, languages, customs, and environments that make up the larger society or, in this case, the classroom.

Decoding—ability to identify words in text by using letter–sound and contextual analysis.

Digraph—two consonants that together make one new sound unlike the sound of either individual letter (e.g., /th/ or /ch/); or two vowels that together make one sound that could be either the sound of one of the vowels or a new sound (e.g., /oo/, /ou/).

Directed listening and thinking activity (DLTA) and **directed reading and thinking activity (DRTA)**—programs that provide activities and strategies utilized by teacher and student to retrieve information through prequestioning, discussion, setting a purpose for reading a story, and postreading discussion.

Early intervention—programs for children who may have special needs or who are at risk for potential problems in literacy development in early childhood; created around developmentally appropriate instruction.

Echo reading—teacher reads a line of text and the child repeats or reads the same sentence; provides a model and support for reading.

Emergent literacy—phrase coined by Marie Clay to refer to a child's early unconventional attempts at reading, writing, and listening, such as scribble writing and pretend reading.

English language learners—children whose first language is not English and who are at varying levels from little to no English.

Experience chart—large chart, probably 42" × 36", made of lined paper. Teacher writes on chart about topics of interest to children; chart is dictated by children and could be a word list, a series of facts about a topic, or a story.

Explicit instruction—approach that focuses on teacher-directed instruction in which teacher models specific steps needed to perform the task.

Family literacy—ways in which family members incorporate and initiate literacy in the daily living environment of a child. Also parent involvement in school, such as helping with homework, attending school events, etc.

Fluency—ability to decode words automatically, with appropriate pace and expression to demonstrate understanding of text.

Graphemes—letters of the alphabet or combinations of letters.

Integrated language arts—teaching of reading, writing, listening, speaking, and viewing skills in a coordinated fashion, rather than separately, to create literate individuals.

Interdisciplinary literacy instruction—integration of literacy instruction into content-area subjects.

Invented spelling—unconventional spelling of words by emergent readers; for example, *the kat haz a mos* instead of *The cat has a mouse.*

Journals—usually notebooks in which children write about particular topics of interest to them. Pages are dated; children dictate to teachers, draw pictures, write words, use scribble writing or invented spelling or other ways of symbolizing their thoughts.

K–W–L—graphic organizing strategy used to enhance comprehension; charts used to list what children Know about a topic before reading or listening, what they Want to know, and what they Learned after reading or listening.

Learning centers—spaces in classrooms that house materials for independent practice of skills taught; activities can be stored in specified areas by topic, in boxes, on shelves, etc.

Literacy center—area in classroom specified for literacy materials, such as books of multiple levels and genres; writing area with many types of paper and writing utensils; and manipulative word-study materials such as letters of the alphabet, rhyme manipulatives, etc.

Morning message—daily message written by the teacher about current topics of interest to children; can be written in advance or with the children. Teacher uses the message for skill development by pointing out alphabet letters or rhymes or leaving out letters in words for children to fill in.

Paired reading—strategy in which children work together based on ability to read; more capable readers act as tutors while reading with less fluent students.

Partner reading—strategy in which peers read together simultaneously. Partners can be of same or different achievement level; one reads or tells one page, the other reads or tells next page.

Phonemes—sounds made by individual letters and combinations of letters.

Phonemic awareness—knowing that words are made up of individual sounds and hearing the sounds in words.

Phonological awareness—ability to hear sounds in words, to substitute one sound for another to create a new word, to blend and segment words, to rhyme, and to hear how many sounds are in a word by counting the syllables.

Reading readiness—skills deemed as prerequisite in learning to read, including auditory discrimination, visual discrimination, and motor skills.

Repeated reading—reading same story often, each time to reinforce another skill.

Rich literacy environment—environments in which materials and teaching encourage and support literacy instruction.

Scaffolding—strategy in which teachers provide children with modeling and support to help them acquire a skill.

Shared book experiences—whole-class or small-group reading instruction through literature selections; Big Books often used so that children can see print and pictures and can listen to and participate in actual book readings.

Small-group instruction/guided reading—small groups, based on reading achievement levels, in which explicit reading instruction targets literacy needs.

Standards—achievement goals set by state or federal governments or professional organizations that identify what students should know at every age or grade level.

Story retellings—activity to enhance and assess comprehension of a story; can be used to emphasize or assess many different skills, such as sequence, inclusions of elements of story structure, use of expression, etc.

Story structure—elements of a well-constructed story. Structure of narrative story includes setting, theme, plot episodes, and resolution; structure of informational story includes sequence, description, cause and effect, problem, and solution.

Syntax—structure of language or rules that govern how words work together in phrases, clauses, and sentences.

Thematic unit—topic, such as the study of plants, using science to teach about that topic in art, music, social studies, math, reading, writing, listening, speaking, and play.

T-unit—an independent clause with all dependent clauses attached that is helpful in measuring a child's language complexity.

Very Own Words—collection of words on 5" × 8" cards stored in an index box or on a loose-leaf ring; words selected by individual children as being important to them to read, trace, copy, or use in a story.

Visual discrimination—ability to note similarities and differences between objects visually, including ability to recognize colors, shapes, and letters.

Word-study skills—knowledge about print including use of phonics, context, and syntax to decipher unknown words; development of sight vocabulary; use of word configuration and structural analysis.

Word wall—classroom display in which the alphabet is put across the wall and words that are important to the class are placed under the letter they begin with; preschool words include names of children in class, theme words discussed, etc.

Writing mechanics—skills related to writing, such as spelling, handwriting, punctuation, and spacing.

Zone of proximal development—period of time, based on Vygotsky's theory, when a child has been guided by an adult and no longer needs a great deal of help; adult retreats and allows child to work on his or her own to practice what was learned.

INTEGRATED LANGUAGE ARTS THEMATIC UNIT
Good Nutrition?

Harriet Worobey

This integrated language arts unit illustrates the importance of implementing thematic units across content areas. Thematic units should be based on the children's interests and incorporated in content areas when appropriate. What we present here is a mini-unit, with samples of activities that can be done in the different content areas. A unit in preschool would have many more activities than are presented here

HOW DO I START A THEMATIC UNIT?

One of the most important things to do when starting a thematic unit is ask the students what their interests are. Try to come to a consensus among about three choices that they would like to study. Once you have decided on a topic as a class, tell the children's families what you are studying. You may need volunteers; get as much help as possible before you start the unit.

WHAT DO I WRITE TO THE FAMILIES?

March 10, 2008

Dear Parents:

Over the course of the next few weeks, your child will be participating in a thematic unit on nutrition titled *Good Nutrition?* This unit will include the study of various food groups, healthy foods, and the importance of taking care of one's body through healthy eating habits.

As with all thematic units, your child will be exploring nutrition through various subject areas, such as: mathematics, language arts, science, listening, and dramatic play. To keep you updated on the class's activities, we will write weekly newsletters that share all of the hands-on, active learning experiences we engage in.

To help your child get started in our thematic unit, please begin to talk to your child about nutrition. You may even want to point out various foods in the house and during your trips to the grocery store. In fact, we will be creating our very own grocery store here at school. It would be a big help if you could send in various empty containers and boxes to add to our store.

We may need volunteers during our nutrition unit, from March 10th to the 29th. If you are available to volunteer your time, please fill out the form below. If you have any additional questions or would like to contribute ideas, please contact me. If you or someone at home is knowledgeable in this area, please consider joining us in our classroom.

Sincerely,

Ms. Harriet Worobey

Please fill in the following form and return it to school with your child.

I am available to volunteer on March _____.

I am happy to do whatever you need help with _____.

I would like (fill in how you would like to help; for example: to make a recipe from Mexico that we eat a lot and is very healthy to share with the children).

_____

_____

Child's name: _____

Parent's name: _____

Parent's signature: _____

WHAT DO I RESEARCH PRIOR TO STARTING THE THEMATIC UNIT?

Prior to starting your thematic unit, it is imperative to collect a variety of literature, both fiction and nonfiction, in your classroom library corner. This provides the classroom with a rich source of information about the theme. You are not expected to know everything about the topic of your unit, but you must make the classroom a resource of information that can answer questions that you cannot. Following are some titles that you may add to your library corner:

Berenstain, S., & Berenstain, J. (1985). *Too much junk food.* New York: Random House.

Blonder, E. (1994). *Noisy breakfast.* New York: Scholastic.

Brown, L. K. (1995). *The vegetable show.* New York: Little, Brown.

Brown, M. (1995). *D.W. the picky eater.* New York: Little, Brown.

Carle, E. (1990). *Pancakes, pancakes.* New York: Scholastic.

Ehlert, L. (1987). *Growing vegetable soup.* New York: Harcourt Brace Jovanovich.

Ehlert, L. (1989). *Eating the alphabet: Fruits and vegetables from A to Z.* New York: Scholastic.

Engel, D. (1991). *Gino badino.* New York: Morrow Junior Books.

Falwell, C. (1993). *Feast for 10.* New York: Scholastic.

Fischer, J. (2002). *Welcome to our vegetable farm.* Zenda, WI: Pyramid.

Fowler, A. (1999). *The wheat we eat.* New York: Children's Press.

Freudberg, J., & Geiss, I. (1980). *Vegetable soup.* Racine, WI: Western.

Freymann, S., & Elffers, J. (2003). *Baby food.* New York: Scholastic.

Freymann, S., & Elffers, J. (2005). *Food for thought.* New York: Scholastic.

Fulton, D. X. (1998). *Nutra fruit heroes to the rescue.* Poway, CA: Toy Box Creations.

Geisel, T. S. [Dr. Seuss]. (1960). *Green eggs and ham.* New York: Random House.

Gordon, S. (2002). *You are what you eat.* New York: Children's Press.

Gretz, S. (1999). *Rabbit food.* Cambridge, MA: Candlewick Press.

Hausherr, R. (1994). *What food is this?* New York: Scholastic.

Hutta, E. (2000). *Count and save with blue.* New York: Viacom International.

Jeunesse, G., & de Bourgoing, P. (1989). *Fruit: A first discovery book.* New York: Scholastic.

Kent, J. (1975). *The egg book.* New York: Macmillan.

Komoda, B. (1978). *Simon's soup.* New York: Parents' Magazine Press.

Krauss, R. (1945). *The carrot seed.* New York: Harper Collins.

Lawlor, T., & Kociemba, B. (1996). *Vegetable friends.* Poway, CA: Toy Box Creations.

Leedy, L. (1994). *The edible pyramid: Good eating every day.* New York: Holiday House.

Lombardo, M. (2000). *The OrganWise Guys: I think I forgot something!* Duluth, GA: Wellness, Inc.

London, J. (2001). *Froggy eats out.* New York: Scholastic.

Maccarone, G. (1995). *The lunch box surprise.* New York: Scholastic.

Morris, A. (1989). *Bread, bread, bread.* New York: Scholastic.

O'Keefe, S. H. (1989). *One hungry monster: A counting book in rhyme.* New York: Scholastic.

Reader's Digest. (2003). *Eat your dinner, please: A pop-up book.* Pleasantville, NY: Reader's Digest Children's Books.

Sharmat, G. (1980). *Gregory the terrible eater.* New York: Scholastic.
Snyder, I. (2003). *Beans to chocolate: How things are made.* New York: Scholastic.
Snyder, I. (2003). *Milk to ice cream: How things are made.* New York: Scholastic.
Snyder, I. (2003). *Tomatoes to ketchup: How things are made.* New York: Scholastic.
Wells, R. (1997). *Bunny cakes.* New York: DIAL Books for Young Readers.

WHAT ARE SOME QUESTIONS I MIGHT RESEARCH?

Prior to starting the research project, think about some questions the children may ask. Here is a sample list of questions:

1. What is good nutrition?
2. Why do we have to eat?
3. How much do I need to eat?
4. Why is breakfast an important meal?
5. What food is in a healthy breakfast?
6. What food is in a healthy lunch?
7. What food is in a healthy dinner?

CREATING THE CLASSROOM ENVIRONMENT DESIRED

So that children can explore the unit chosen, the teacher may need to add to and/or change the current environment. These new materials should be introduced to the students so that they are utilized properly. The following chart details items that can be added to the classroom to prepare the students for the nutrition unit.

Center	Added objects/activities
Writing Center	Food-related stickers, index cards, food stencils, paper with various food borders and shapes
Literacy Center	Fiction and nonfiction books, posters, and pictures about nutrition
Computer Center	Software programs, including: • Millie Meter's Nutrition Adventure • DW, the Picky Eater • Max's Magical Delivery: Fit for Kids
Science Center	Seeds, accompanying worksheets, glue, magnifying glasses
Play	Food puzzles, food board games, classifying food cards
Dramatic Play	*Our Class Grocery Store*, various food boxes, cans, etc., picnic basket, and containers from home *Different multicultural restaurants* (Italian, Japanese, Chinese, etc.)

Art	Apples, plastic knife (with adult supervision), pasta (various shapes, sizes, and colors), glue, and plenty of paper
Cooking Center	Ingredients pertinent to a recipe of choice
Listening Center	Songs: • "Apples and Bananas" • "The Fruit Song" • "Squeeze the Oranges"

BEGINNING, *GOOD NUTRITION?*

Introductory Lesson

| Objective | Help children to use their prior knowledge and begin thinking about learning new things about nutrition. |
| Activities | • Morning message: Introduce the thematic unit to students by writing a message on the board or chart paper. The following is a message you could read to the children. You may use pictures in your message to help illustrate the meaning of what is written. Morning messages help to introduce new words.

Here is a sample message:

Dear Children,
Today we will be talking about eating good foods. We call this *Good Nutrition?* Let's see what you know about good nutrition and what you want to know.
• K–W–L chart: On chart paper, divide the paper into three columns titled K, W, and L. In the first column, record what the students *Know* about nutrition by asking them to name some good foods to eat. In the second column, record what the children *Want* to know about good foods to eat. These are the questions you will explore.
• Read the story *Food for Thought* by Freymann and Elffers.
• At the end of the story, complete the last column on the chart to find out what the children *Learned* about good nutrition as a result of hearing the story that they hadn't known before. |

Math Activities

| Objectives | Children will demonstrate one-to-one correspondence through literature.
Children will learn concepts about books, concepts about print. |
| Activity | • Children will create a 10-page number book. The teacher has made the books and numbered the pages 1 to 10. On each page the child is to copy the number and select healthy-food stickers for each page. For example, one apple sticker for page 1, two peach stickers for page 2, and so on. |

Science: Including Oral Language Comprehension, Math, and Art

Objectives	Children will classify fruits and vegetables. Children will develop oral language and comprehension.
Activities	• Teacher will bring in fruits and vegetables for children to distinguish between. Teacher will discuss with students what makes up a fruit and a vegetable. Discussion about trees, vines, and seeds will take place to clarify differences. • The characteristics of particular fruits and vegetables will be discussed, such as color, taste, texture, shape, and smell.
Objectives	Children will identify and match seeds to the fruit they grow into; to develop math skills, art skills, and comprehension.
Activity	• Teacher glues seeds to one index card and a picture of the fruit with its name on another. Children match the seeds to the fruit.

Writing: Including Art, Dramatic Play, and Knowledge about Books and Print

Objectives	Children will record foods they eat daily and compare them with recommendations for excellent daily diets. Children will sequence, predict, use oral language, and write and learn concepts about print.
Activity	• Children will keep a journal by recording their daily eating habits and by responding to a series of fill-in-the-blank sentences. Children may respond with pictorial representations, by dictating to teachers, and so forth. Children will share responses. *For breakfast, I ate* _____ *Today at lunch, I ate* _____ *For dinner, I will eat* _____
Objective	Children create menus, and in doing so, develop math and art skills, use environmental print, learn concepts about print, and develop oral language, dramatic play, and concepts about books.
Activity	• Children use magazines and newspapers to illustrate a menu that is categorized into breakfast, lunch, and dinner foods. Children will practice ordering foods in dramatic play, playing the roles of waitress or waiter, manager, patron, cook, and cashier.

Social Studies: Including Language Arts and Music

Objectives	Children will learn about foods from different countries.
	Children will develop oral language, comprehension, reading and writing, and art skills.
Activity	Using the food pictures and illustrations provided by students and their families, children will share traditional and customary foods unique to their cultures.
Objectives	Children will share food related to their cultures.
	Children will develop oral language and concepts about print.
Activity	• Teacher will send home a note to parents.

Dear Parents,

During our food festival please bring a small portion of food from your cultural background. Please list what you will bring: _____.

At the festival the families and children will share food. |

CHILDREN'S LITERATURE

Lisa Fassi and Paula Aguruso

CARDBOARD CONCEPT BOOKS

Brown, M. (1997). *Say the magic word.* New York: Random House.

DK Board Books. (2002). *Things that go.* New York: DK.

Elgard, R. (1998). *Jack, it's playtime/bathtime/bedtime/Happy Birthday.* New York: Kingfisher.

Lamut, S. (1997). *1 2 peek a boo.* New York: Grosset & Dunlap.

Tracy, T. (1999). *Show me!* New York: HarperCollins.

CLOTH BOOKS

McPartland, S. (2002). *Peekaboo, I love you.* Chicago: Learning Curve International.

Pienkowski, J. (1995). *Friends.* New York: Little Simon.

Tong, W. (1996). *Zoo faces/Farm faces.* Santa Monica, CA: Piggy Toes Press.

Tucker, S. (1994). *Toot toot/Quack quack.* New York: Little Simon.

Tucker, S. (1997). *Yum yum.* New York: Little Simon.

PLASTIC BOOKS

Aigner-Clark, L. (2003). *Baby Einstein: Water, water everywhere.* New York: Hyperion Books.

Barkan, J. (1998). *Splish! Splash!* New York: Random House.
Crossley, D. (2003). *Bunnies on the farm.* New York: Backpack Books.
London, J. (2001). *Froggy takes a bath.* New York: Grosset & Dunlap.
Man-Kong, M. (1999). *Theodore's splash.* New York: Random House.

TOUCH AND FEEL

Boynton, S. (1998). *Dinosaur's binkit.* New York: Little Simon.
Kunhardt, D. (1984). *Pat the bunny/cat/puppy.* New York: Golden Books.
Milne, A. A., & Shephard, E. H. (1998). *Pooh's touch and feel visit.* New York: Dutton Children's Books.
Pledger, M. (2000). *In the ocean.* San Diego, CA: Silver Dolphin Books.
Saltzberg, B. (2000). *Animal kisses.* San Diego, CA: Harcourt.
Watt, F., & Wells, R. (2002). *That's not my dinosaur. . . .* Tulsa, OK: EDC.

CONCEPT BOOKS

Davis, K. (2001). *Soft shapes: One and off.* Norwalk, CT: Innovative KIDS.
Hoban, T. (1998). *More, fewer, less.* New York: Greenwillow Books.
Miller, M. (1998). *Big and little.* New York: Greenwillow Books.
Murphy, C. (1998). *Black cat white cat: A book of opposites.* New York: Little Simon.

ALPHABET BOOKS

Andrae, G. (2003). *K is for kissing a cool kangaroo.* New York: Scholastic.
Diaz, J., & Gerth, M. (2003). *My first jumbo book of letters.* New York: Scholastic.
Fujiwaka, G. (2002). *A to Z picture book.* New York: Backpack Books.
Golding, K. (1998). *Alphababies.* New York: DK.
Mazollo, J. (2000). *I spy little letters.* New York: Scholastic.

NUMBER BOOKS

Beaton, C. (2000). *One moose, twenty mice.* Cambridge, MA: Barefoot Books.
Ehlert, L. (2001). *Fish eyes: A book you can count on.* San Diego, CA: Harcourt Brace.
Falconer, I. (2002). *Olivia counts.* New York: Atheneum.
Gerth, M. (2000). *Ten little ladybugs.* Santa Monica, CA: Piggy Toes Press.
Strickland, P. (1997). *Ten terrible dinosaurs.* New York: Dutton Children's Books.

NURSERY RHYMES

Douglas, V. (2002). *Mother Goose rhymes.* Boston: McGraw-Hill.

Fujiwaka, G. (2002). *Mother Goose.* New York: Backpack Books.

Opie, I. (Ed.). (2002). *The very best of Mother Goose.* Cambridge, MA: Candlewick Press.

Rader, L. (1993). *Mother Hubbard's cupboard: A Mother Goose surprise book.* New York: Tambourine Books.

Scarry, R. (1992). *Richard Scarry's Mother Goose and rhymes and nursery tales.* New York: Golden Books.

A SAMPLING OF INFORMATIONAL BOOKS

Cobb, A. (1996). *Wheels.* New York: Random House.

Dussling, J. (1996). *Stars.* New York: Grosset & Dunlap.

Glaser, L. (1992). *Wonderful worms.* Riverside, NJ: Millbrook Press.

Hewitt, S. (1999). *The five senses.* Danbury, CT: Children's Press.

Hoban, T. (1983). *I read signs.* New York: HarperCollins.

Hurd, E. T. (1990). *Starfish.* New York: HarperCollins.

Klingel, C., & Noyed, R. B. (2001). *Pigs.* Chanhassen, MI: The Child's World.

Klingel, C., & Noyed, R. B. (2001). *Pumpkins.* Chanhassen, MI: The Child's World.

Montanari, D. (2001). *Children around the world.* Tonawanda, NY: Kids Can Press.

Rockwell, A. (2001). *Bugs are insects.* New York: HarperCollins.

A SAMPLING OF ALL-TIME FAVORITE NARRATIVE PICTURE STORYBOOKS

Bemelmans, L. (1939). *Madeline.* New York: Viking.

Berenstain, S., & Berenstain, J. (1966). *The bear's picnic.* New York: Random House.

Brown, M. W. (1957). *Goodnight moon.* New York: Harper & Row.

Carle, E. (1969). *The very hungry caterpillar.* New York: Philomel.

dePaola, T. (1975). *Stregna Nona: An old tale.* Englewood Cliffs, NJ: Prentice Hall.

Dr. Seuss. (1940). *Horton hatches the egg.* New York: Random House.

Eastman, P. D. (1960). *Are you my mother?* New York: Random House.

Galdone, P. (1975). *The little red hen.* New York: Scholastic.

Hoban, R. (1969). *Best friends for Frances.* New York: Harper & Row.

Johnson, C. (1955). *Harold and the purple crayon.* New York: Harper.

Keats, E. J. (1962). *The snowy day.* New York: Viking.

Kraus, R. (1971). *Leo the late bloomer.* New York: Windmill.

Lionni, L. (1973). *Swimmy.* New York: Random House.

Lobel, A. (1972). *Frog and toad together.* New York: Harper & Row.

Mayer, M. (1974). *One monster after another.* Racine, WI: Western.

Potter, B. (1902). *The tale of Peter Rabbit.* New York: Scholastic.

Rey, H. A. (1952). *Curious George rides a bike*. Boston: Houghton Mifflin.

Sendak, M. (1963). *Where the wild things are*. New York: Harper & Row.

Shaw, C. (1947). *It looked like spilled milk*. New York: HarperCollins.

Slobodkina, E. (1947). *Caps for sale*. Reading, MA: Addison-Wesley.

Steig, W. (1969). *Sylvester and the magic pebble*. New York: Simon & Schuster.

Viorst, J. (1972). *Alexander and the terrible, horrible, no good, very bad day*. New York: Atheneum.

Waber, B. (1975). *Ira sleeps over*. Boston: Houghton Mifflin.

CHILDREN'S LITERATURE FOR THEMES

Animals

Battaglia, A. (2005). *Animal sounds*. New York: Random House Children's Books.

Brown, M. W. (1994). *Big red barn*. New York: Harper Collins Children's Books.

Dyer, J., & Dyer, J. (1998). *Animal crackers: Nursery rhymes*. Boston: Little, Brown.

Martin, B. (1996). *Brown bear, brown bear, what do you see?* New York: Henry Holt.

Rosen, M. (1997). *We're going on a bear hunt*. New York: Simon & Schuster.

Sami. (2005). *Baby animals: Flip a face*. New York: Handprint Books.

Community Helpers

Ahlberg, J., & Ahlberg, A. (2001). *The jolly postman*. New York: Little, Brown.

Golden Books. (2002). *Seven little postmen*. New York: Golden Books.

Guthrie, W. (1994). *Mail myself to you*. Glenview, IL: Scott, Foresman.

Keats, E. J. (1968). *A letter to Amy*. New York: Penguin Young Readers.

Leibman, D. (2001). *I want to be a doctor*. Richmond Hill, Ontario, Canada: Firefly Books.

Leibman, D. (2001). *I want to be a firefighter*. Richmond Hill, Ontario, Canada: Firefly Books.

Leibman, D. (2001). *I want to be a nurse*. Richmond Hill, Ontario, Canada: Firefly Books.

Leibman, D. (2001). *I want to be a police officer*. Richmond Hill, Ontario, Canada: Firefly Books.

Leibman, D. (2001). *I want to be a teacher*. Richmond Hill, Ontario, Canada: Firefly Books.

Leibman, D. (2001). *I want to be a vet*. Richmond Hill, Ontario, Canada: Firefly Books.

Rockwell, A. (2000). *Career day*. New York: HarperCollins.

Insects

Bentley, D. (2004). *Buzz-buzz, busy bees*. New York: Simon & Schuster.

Carle, E. (1989). *Very busy spider*. New York: Penguin Young Readers.

Carle, E. (1994). *Very hungry caterpillar*. New York: Penguin Young Readers.

Carter, D. A. (2006). *How many bugs in a box?* New York: Simon & Schuster.

Hood, S. (2003). *Caterpillar spring, butterfly summer*. Pleasantville, NY: Reader's Digest Children's Publishing.

Sports

Brug, S. G. (2003). *Soccer beat.* New York: Simon & Schuster.

Gibbons, G. (2000). *My football book.* New York: HarperCollins.

Hallinan, P. K. (2003). *Let's play as a team.* Nashville, TN: Ideals Publications.

Punter, J. (2002). *Franklin's big hockey game.* New York: Scholastic.

Smith, C. R. (2006). *Let's play baseball!* Cambridge, MA: Candlewick Press.

Transportation

Brown, M. W. (2001). *Two little trains.* New York: HarperCollins.

Christelow, E. (2004). *Five little monkeys wash the car.* Boston: Houghton Mifflin.

Lewis, K. (2002). *My truck is stuck!* New York: Hyperion.

Maccarone, G. (1995). *Cars! Cars! Cars!* New York: Scholastic.

Mandel, P. *Planes at the airport.* New York: Cartwheel Books.

Mayo, M. (2002). *Dig, dig, digging.* New York: Holt.

Miranda, A. (2000). *Vroom, chugga, vroom-vroom: A number identification book.* New York: Turtle Books.

Mitton, T. (2005). *Busy boats.* Boston: Kingfisher.

Mitton, T. (2005). *Amazing airplanes.* Boston: Kingfisher.

Mitton, T. (2005). *Tough trucks.* Boston: Kingfisher.

Shaw, N. (1997). *Sheep in a jeep.* Boston: Houghton Mifflin.

Sturges, P. (2001). *I love trains!* New York: HarperCollins.

Widdowson, K. (2003). *Beep beep.* New York: Scholastic.

MAGAZINES FOR PRESCHOOLERS

Paula Batsiyan

Baby Bug (ages 6 months–2 years)
Carus Publishing
Cricket Magazine Group
315 Fifth Street
Peru, IL 61354
1-800-821-0115
www.cricketmag.com

Disney and Me (ages 2–6 years)
Disney.go.com

Humpty Dumpty's Magazine (ages 4–6 years)
Children's Better Health Institute
1100 Waterway Boulevard
Indianapolis, IN 46202
1-317-634-1100
www.cbhi.org

Ladybug (ages 2–6 years)
Carus Publishing
Cricket Magazine Group
315 Fifth Street
Peru, IL 61354
1-800-821-0115
www.cricketmag.com

Preschool Playroom (ages 2–5 years)
www.preschoolplayroom.com

Turtle (ages 2–5 years)
Children's Better Health Institute
1100 Waterway Boulevard
Indianapolis, IN 46202
1-317-634-1100
www.cbhi.org

Wild Animal Baby (ages 12 months–
3 years)
National Wildlife Federation
11100 Wildlife Center Drive
Reston, VA 20190
1-800-822-9919
www.nwf.org

Your Big Backyard (ages 3–5 years)
National Wildlife Federation
11100 Wildlife Center Drive
Reston, VA 20190
1-800-822-9919
www.nwf.org

PROFESSIONAL ASSOCIATIONS, RELATED PUBLICATIONS, AND WEBSITES DEALING WITH EARLY LITERACY

Kelli Dunston

PROFESSIONAL ASSOCIATIONS AND RELATED JOURNALS

American Library Association (ALA)
50 East Huron Street
Chicago, IL 60611
www.ala.org

American Montessori Society, Inc. (AMS)
281 Park Avenue South, 6th Floor
New York, NY 10010
www.amshq.org

Association for Childhood Education International (ACEI)
17904 Georgia Avenue, Suite 215
Olney, MD 20832
www.acei.org
Journals: *Childhood Education; Journal of Research in Childhood Education*

Child Welfare League of America, Inc. (CWLA)
440 First Street NW, 3rd Floor
Washington, DC 20001
www.cwla.org
Journal: *Child Welfare*

Children's Bureau
Office of Child Development
U.S. Department of Health, Education and Welfare
Washington, DC 20201
www.acf.hhs.gov/programs/cb
Journal: *Children Today*

Family Education Network
20 Park Plaza, 12th Floor
Boston, MA 02116
www.familyeducation.com

High/Scope Educational Research Foundation
600 North River Street
Ypsilanti, MI 48198-2898
www.highscope.org
Publications, videos, research, professional development

International Reading Association (IRA)
800 Barksdale Road
PO Box 8139
Newark, DE 19711
www.reading.org
Journals: *The Reading Teacher; Reading Research Quarterly;* brochures, pamphlets, and monographs

National Association for the Education of Young Children (NAEYC)
1509 16th Street NW
Washington, DC 20036
www.naeyc.org
Journals: *Young Children; Early Childhood Research Quarterly; Early Years Are Learning;* pamphlets and monographs

National Center for Family Literacy
325 West Main Street, Suite 300
Louisville, KY 40202-4237
www.famlit.org
Newsletter: *Momentum*

National Center for Learning Disabilities
Get Ready to Read
381 Park Avenue South, Suite 1401
New York, NY 10016
www.getreadytoread.org
Newsletter: *GRTR News*

National Child Care Information Center
243 Church Street NW, 2nd Floor
Vienna, VA 22180
www.nccic.org

National Council of Teachers of English (NCTE)
1111 Kenyon Road
Urbana, IL 61801
www.ncte.org
Journal: *Language Arts*

National Education Association
1201 16th Street NW
Washington, DC 20036
www.nea.org
Journal: *NEA Today*; magazine: *Tomorrow's Teachers*

National Even Start Association
2225 Camino del Rio South, Suite A
San Diego, CA 92108
www.evenstart.org
Journal: *Family Literacy Forum*

National Head Start Association
1651 Prince Street
Alexandria, VA 22314
www.nhsa.org
magazine: *Children and Families Magazine*

National Institute for Early Education Research (NIEER)
120 Albany Street, Suite 500
New Brunswick, NJ 08901
nieer.org
Newsletter: *Preschool Matters*; pamphlets, brochures

National Reading Conference (NRC)
11 East Hubbard Street
Chicago, IL 60603
www.nrconline.org
Journal: *Journal of Literacy Research*

National Institute on Early Childhood Development and Education
www.ed.gov/offices/OERI/ECI

Parents' Action for Children
1875 Connecticut Avenue NW, Suite 650
Washington, DC 20009
www.parentsaction.org
Newsletter: *Parents' Action News*; video, booklets

Pre-K Now
1150 18th Street NW, Suite 975
Washington, DC 20036
www.preknow.org

Reach Out and Read National Center
29 Mystic Avenue
Somerville, MA 02145
www.reachoutandread.org

Reading Is Fundamental
1825 Connecticut Avenue NW
Washington, DC 20009
www.rif.org
Newsletter: *Read All About It*

Scholastic, Inc.
555 Broadway
New York, NY 10012
www.scholastic.com
Publications: *Early Childhood Today*; *Instructor*

Society for Research in Child Development (SRCD)
5750 Ellis Avenue
Chicago, IL 60637
www.srcd.org
Journal: *Child Development*

Starting at 3: Securing Access to Preschool Education
Education Law Center
60 Park Place, Suite 300
Newark, NJ 07102
www.startingat3.org

Zero to Three: National Center for Infants, Toddlers and Families
2000 M Street NW, Suite 200
Washington, DC 20036
www.zerotothree.org
Journal: *Zero to Three*

WEBSITES

ABC Home Preschool
www.abchomepreschool.com

Everything Preschool—Early Childhood Education Made Easy
www.everythingpreschool.com

Gayle's Preschool Rainbow—Activity Central
www.preschoolrainbow.org

Preschool Activity Children's Videos: The Preschool Power Series
www.preschoolpower.com

Preschool Education: Discover the Fun in Learning
www.preschooleducation.com

Preschool Education/Preschool Printables
www.preschoolprintables.com

Preschool Express
www.preschoolexpress.com

Teachers First
www.teachersfirst.com

The Perpetual Preschool
www.perpetualpreschool.com

INDEX

Page numbers followed by an *f* or *t* indicate figures or tables.